THE CONSTITUTIC

This volume provides a contextual account of Pakistan's co... It aims to describe the formal structure of government in reference to origins that are traced to the administrative centralization and legal innovations of colonial rule. It also situates the tide of Muslim nationalism that gave rise to the nation of Pakistan within a terrain of nascent constitutionalism and its associated promises of representation.

The post-colonial history of the Pakistani state is charted by reference to succeeding constitutions and the distribution of powers between the major branches of government that they augured. Where conventional histories often suggest that constitutionalism in Pakistan is to be solely understood by reference to a cycle of abidance and rupture, and in the oscillation between military and civilian rule, this volume also accounts for the many points of continuity between regime types. The contours of a broader constitutionalism come to light in the ways in which state power is wielded at different periods and in the range of contests—economic, political and cultural—through which some of this power is sought to be dispersed. Chapters on Rights, Federalism and Islam detail the contextual features of some of these contests and the normative, legal parameters through which they are provisionally settled.

Pictorial Narrative

Pakistan

Pakistan's modernity is at the heart of the composition. The constitutional and judicial evolution of the state are embodied in the iconic Supreme Court in Islamabad. '1947' is etched onto its fabric, commemorating Pakistan's Independence. Underneath the significant date, Muhammad Ali Jinnah—the Founder of Pakistan, is gazing out, in close proximity to Muhammad Iqbal, the Spiritual Father of Pakistan. He was the poet who conceived the idea of Pakistan as a nation. Framed towards the right, Benazir Bhutto appears as the first woman to be elected to lead a Muslim state and the only one to be elected twice.

As echoes of empire and colonialism, the Mughal and British are represented in two architectural features which appear in deconstructed form: the Wazir Khan Mosque (top left) and (immediate below) the facade of the General Post Office, both situated in Lahore.

The battling figures in the foreground represent the genesis of Pakistan, an episode associated with the chaos and violence of partition. The towering peak of K2 occupies the apex of the composition, while the PAC JF-17 Thunder fighter jet (developed by the Pakistan Aeronautical Complex) soars in the sky as an emblem Pakistan's military power. Rising above this, the white Crescent Moon and Star, on green background denotes Islam and Pakistan's national flag. A solitary cricket ball celebrates the national sport which also bonds national unity.

Putachad
Artist

Constitutional Systems of the World
General Editors: Benjamin L Berger, Rosalind Dixon, Andrew Harding, Peter Leyland and Heinz Klug

In the era of globalisation, issues of constitutional law and good governance are being seen increasingly as vital issues in all types of society. Since the end of the Cold War, there have been dramatic developments in democratic and legal reform, and post-conflict societies are also in the throes of reconstructing their governance systems. Even societies already firmly based on constitutional governance and the rule of law have undergone constitutional change and experimentation with new forms of governance; and their constitutional systems are increasingly subjected to comparative analysis and transplantation. Constitutional texts for practically every country in the world are now easily available on the internet. However, texts which enable one to understand the true context, purposes, interpretation and incidents of a constitutional system are much harder to locate, and are often extremely detailed and descriptive. This series seeks to provide scholars and students with accessible introductions to the constitutional systems of the world, supplying both a road map for the novice and, at the same time, a deeper understanding of the key historical, political and legal events which have shaped the constitutional landscape of each country. Each book in this series deals with a single country, or a group of countries with a common constitutional history, and each author is an expert in their field.

Published volumes

The Constitution of the United Kingdom; The Constitution of the United States; The Constitution of Vietnam; The Constitution of South Africa; The Constitution of Japan; The Constitution of Germany; The Constitution of Finland; The Constitution of Australia; The Constitution of the Republic of Austria; The Constitution of the Russian Federation; The Constitutional System of Thailand; The Constitution of Malaysia; The Constitution of China; The Constitution of Indonesia; The Constitution of France; The Constitution of Spain; The Constitution of Mexico; The Constitution of Israel; The Constitutional Systems of the Commonwealth Caribbean; The Constitution of Canada; The Constitution of Singapore; The Constitution of Belgium; The Constitution of Taiwan; The Constitution of Romania; The Constitutional Systems of the Independent Central Asian States; The Constitution of India

Link to series website
www.bloomsburyprofessional.com/uk/series/constitutional-systems-of-the-world

The Constitution of Pakistan

A Contextual Analysis

Sadaf Aziz

OXFORD AND PORTLAND, OREGON
2018

Hart Publishing
An imprint of Bloomsbury Publishing Plc

Hart Publishing Ltd
Kemp House
Chawley Park
Cumnor Hill
Oxford OX2 9PH
UK

Bloomsbury Publishing Plc
50 Bedford Square
London
WC1B 3DP
UK

www.hartpub.co.uk
www.bloomsbury.com

Published in North America (US and Canada) by
Hart Publishing
c/o International Specialized Book Services
920 NE 58th Avenue, Suite 300
Portland, OR 97213-3786
USA

www.isbs.com

First published 2018

British Library Cataloguing-in-Publication Data
A catalogue record for this book is available from the British Library.

ISBN: PB: 978-1-84946-586-1
ePDF: 978-1-50991-913-0
ePub: 978-1-50991-912-3

Library of Congress Cataloging-in-Publication Data

Names: Aziz, Sadaf, author.

Title: The constitution of Pakistan : a contextual analysis / Sadaf Aziz.

Description: Oxford ; Portland, Oregon : Hart Publishing, an imprint of Bloomsbury Publishing Plc, 2018. | Series: Constitutional systems of the world | Includes bibliographical references and index.

Identifiers: LCCN 2017040705 (print) | LCCN 2017041082 (ebook) | ISBN 9781509919123 (Epub) | ISBN 9781849465861 (pbk. : alk. paper)

Subjects: LCSH: Constitutional history—Pakistan.

Classification: LCC KPL1760 (ebook) | LCC KPL1760 .A99 2017 (print) | DDC 342.549102/9—dc23

LC record available at https://lccn.loc.gov/2017040705

Typeset by Compuscript Ltd, Shannon
Printed and bound in Great Britain by CPI Group (UK) Ltd, Croydon CR0 4YY

To find out more about our authors and books visit www.hartpublishing.co.uk. Here you will find extracts, author information, details of forthcoming events and the option to sign up for our newsletters.

Preface

The contrast between India's record of fidelity and Pakistan's less steadfast relationship to constitutionalism is oftentimes the basis problematising Pakistan's very existence. By citing the pre-1947 unity of the two, the possibility of seeking explanation from that point onwards seems logical, and Islamic theocracy and military authoritarianism are somehow aligned and presented as existing within the demand for a homeland for the subcontinent's Muslims. In other instances failure is traced to the period of Muslim rule in India as indication of a culture of despotism amongst Muslims. Through invocation of both flimsy historical premises, there is a convergence in arguing that the record of frequent coup d'états and constitutional abrogation in Pakistan reflects an original sin, that of Pakistani statehood.

In line with this inescapable narrative, the little scholarly attention that has been directed at constitutional law in Pakistan deals primarily with the elaboration of an emergency jurisprudence. A number of cases spanning the decades of Pakistan's existence in which the judiciary has conferred legitimacy upon coup d'états and forged novel doctrine, legal bridges, to sustain a broader legality across regime changes are associated with such a jurisprudence. There is no denying that this record is awe inspiring for its inventiveness and the ease by which legal and political domains are collapsed, so that the attention it has received is not altogether surprising. However, these cases around coup d'états and emergencies cannot be the stand-in for understanding a broader legality in Pakistan.

These cases are not read here together as either exceptional or emblematic of judicial complicity or capitulation. Rather, situated in relation to developments in broader institutional fields and struggles, they are simply indicative of the centrifugal tendencies that have long been associated with the Pakistani state. To existing scholarship on Pakistani constitutional legality, then, this book perhaps only adds the limited innovation of reading many strands of jurisprudence together, so that the centrality of executive powers is the pivot for relating emergency jurisprudence and a broader constitutionalism.

Not only by acts of constitutional abrogation but more consequentially because of the constitutional amendments that follow in train, there is no simple line to divide emergency and a broader constitutional jurisprudence. In the landscape of Pakistani constitutionalism, emergencies are not simply time bound and coincident with martial law, but also must refer to the selective application of constitutional protections to diverse populations within Pakistan. At times this is because of the operations of a plural legality and at others, because of territorial exemptions written into the Constitution itself.

Constitutionalism in Pakistan, as elsewhere, must necessarily be understood historically, materially and at the interstices of always competing ideological structures. Thus, a deeper historicity is offered in the first two chapters, to organise the framework for understanding more thoroughly the interpretations and elaboration of the 1973 Constitution, which forms the bulk of what is studied in the remainder of the book. While there is no single relation of determination or causality that can be suggested here between the formal apparatus of law and constitutionalism and the material organisation of power and resources within Pakistan, it is important nonetheless to be more precise about the manner in which diverse domains have been organised in relation to each other.

As a historical starting point, important for understanding contemporary constitutionalism in Pakistan are the violent acts of territorial conquest, the offer or denial of state patronage, and the relative priority conferred upon regions and populations within a colonial political economy. Unequal relations established under colonial rule have continually impacted on the regimes of management through which the central government has sought to effect rule. Even in the waning decades of British colonial rule in India, the imperative of maintaining heavy administrative control was only nominally eroded by the demand for representative government. In the ferment of this time, with competing ideologies propelling the call for self-rule, the advantages conferred by the British on certain groups and within them upon manageable elites, allowed these groups to reinscribe such advantage into early state-making.

The continuities are expressed in the post-colonial Pakistani state in multiple ways. The second chapter identifies three predominant features that have had everlasting impact on the shape and abidance of formal constitutionalism in Pakistan. These include the marginalisation of regionalist demands, a propensity for over-heavy administrative centralisation, and the shifting place of Islam as normative guidance for the nation. The distributions engendered by these have influenced the shape of three successive constitutions, in 1956, 1962 and 1973. The tendency to see independence from colonial rule as marking a definitive break, and the act of framing a constitutional accord as the means of determining the line between legitimate and illegitimate exercises of power alone, is already somewhat disproved in accounting for the continuities between them and what existed prior to independence. For dominant classes in the state, the achievement of independence was significant for ameliorating their position of disadvantage against the colonisers, but for the larger populace this transition was ultimately inconsequential for addressing the deeper structuration of power in the state.

While there is a clear debt and selective borrowing of some of the schematic elements that percolate through the critical literature on Pakistani state power in this volume, there is also an attempt to subtly undo the extreme determinism of accounts that see an absolute immovability of power in spite of constitutional adjudication. The centering of a formal, normative apparatus, the Constitution and law, certainly shifts the focus of analysis so that change, conflict, crisis are all shown as mediated within the bounds of higher level norms and their institutional expressions. The institutions themselves are studied formally as well as by reference to their competitive interplay with one another. Thus, the judiciary, the executive and parliament are described in this tussle. However, the identification of the fields of contest between them is suggestive of an inheritance of control and domination, oligarchic centralisation, core-periphery relations and the search for ideological unitariness or hegemony.

If not always central to organising conflict amongst national elites or between them and the spokespersons of regional interest or a statist Islamism, the constitutional structure and the broader apparatus of legality is always nonetheless at play. At times, alongside an understanding of specific provisions and their elaboration through judicial review, extensive descriptions of such phenomenon are presented in parallel to illustrate the slippages and omissions.

As already partly described above, the first two chapters of this book chart the incipient assembly and early organisation of the Pakistani state. The history in these first two chapters is intended to acquaint the reader with particular strands of context entwined in the inheritance of a particular legalism and system of government. To a greater extent than is the case in some of the other volumes of this series, the remainder of this book foregrounds major features of the 1973 Constitution, its multiple alterations and the jurisprudence generated. If the Constitution is a mechanism of control and containment, it has already encoded a dispensation towards the conflicts investigated here and its further abrogations, mutations and revisions are invariably sites where these conflicts are opened up again.

The chapters are comprehensive rather than concise and a further set of contextual features are investigated that reflect both changes in the social sphere as well as those reflected in official policy. Chapters 3 to 5 investigate the institutions of a trichotomous governmental order and their transformations to present. Three additional chapters discuss the shape of federalism, rights guarantees and the place of Islam as given in this Constitution.

Chapter 3 presents a summation of the rules that govern the legislature, but, importantly seeks to expose the myriad ways in which the political sphere has been reshaped by successive regimes. Chapter 4 elaborates those features of the Constitution that allow for heavy executive centralisation, including emergency powers and the presidential powers to dissolve assemblies and enact legislation through Ordinances. It also traces the history of executive consolidation through military and civilian regimes and some recent movement by the higher judiciary to introduce principles of accountability into executive functioning. Chapter 5 focuses on the role of the judiciary as constitutional arbiter. By highlighting the principle of jurisdiction as conferred by the Constitution and law as the central motif of this chapter, a controversial history that includes both a wilful abidance of limitations on judicial review as well as more recent attempts to expand the powers of review is illustrated.

That the 1973 Constitution did not successfully accommodate regional and ethnic concerns through the federal formula it elaborated is made apparent by the passage of the Eighteenth Amendment to the Constitution in 2010. This package of constitution reform was intended to devolve greater powers to the provinces and Chapter 6 investigates the division of powers between federating units and the centre both prior to and after 2010. It also illustrates some instances of continuing conflict within the federation and the formal and informal aspects of federalism that intersect the grievances over representation and resources driving these conflicts. Chapter 7 provides an overview of the fundamental rights that are accorded under the 1973 Constitution and the primary interpretive doctrines that are employed in their adjudication. Two detailed cases studies of the evolving jurisprudence of particular fundamental rights are undertaken; the first of protection against sex-based discrimination and the second pertaining to constitutional safeguards accorded to persons preventatively detained by the state. The final chapter focuses on the alterations made in order to impart a more Islamic character to the country's legal system. Most of these changes can be dated to Zia-ul-Haq's reign. These include the elevation of the Objectives Resolution to the status of a justiciable instrument of the Constitution, the establishment of a parallel Shariat court system and the enactment of various Islamic laws. The developments that follow these constitutional incorporations and the particular impact upon religious minorities and women are charted in this chapter.

Acknowledgements

The most remarkable thing to me about this book is that I was, somehow, asked to write it. For that I have to thank Andrew Harding, who nurtured the belief that I could in fact complete such a vast project. To him and Rosalind Dixon who generously read repeat drafts and offered nudges and suggestions along the way, many thanks. Maria Skrzypiec read and edited the whole draft; John Hort and Anne Flegel at Hart Publishing guaranteed a smooth production process; and Ali Ahmad helpfully offered guidance on a few chapters.

In the completion of this project, no labours were more indispensable than those provided by Anoshay Malik and Umair Ahmad Kundi. At different moments, they made themselves and their diligence and support seamlessly available. I've also been lucky to have a pool of former students who I have called upon for help—Madiha, Aisha, Summaiya, Shmyla, Ali J, Maimana, Ghazanfar, Umer G, Sana and others who were undoubtedly shortchanged in these exchanges. They have nonetheless maintained the bonds of loyalty and friendship and I am grateful.

The longer intellectual debts I owe are to old and new teachers of mine. Radhika Desai may not see herself in this book, but the patterns of her thought stay with me always. Sundhya Pahuja and her whole family have provided immeasurable support in ways that belie my utter neglect in this period of that which I owe her. Shaun McVeigh rightly noted that ideas have travelled between projects and I gratefully acknowledge that his and Sundhya's contributions were instrumental to that transfer.

In Lahore, an amazing array of friends and colleagues from Lums have offered me so much: Sikander Shah and Moeen Cheema's infectious enthusiasm for legal teaching; Sarah Suhail and Asad Farooqs compassionate dedication to people and causes. May you live a long and beautiful life Sarah. Spenta Kakalia and Amber Riaz have always kept their doors open to me. Azeem and Sara, Kamal and Humeira have extended their friendship and fed me throughout with further work and life possibilities. Imran Sb, Khalid Sb and Shahnawaz are a welcome presence when I return to my office home.

In the time I spent in Islamabad, I have been extended the favour of being able to occupy space in the chambers of Barrister Shehzad

Akbar and Barrister Kamran Sheikh. Aasim Sajjad Akhtar has also been a great help in many ways.

The writing of this book overlapped with the early years of my daughter Rosa's life and I thank her for tipping the balance away from order and in favour of irrepressible love. For joining in her care and in the sustenance of our lives in this period I would, as the cliché goes, have to thank a small village. Irum, Saba, Bashir, Irfan and Zaman have, however, been instrumental to keeping our various households running in these last few years. The circle of friends who've helped in so many ways include Saima S, Huma, Bani, Arshi, Sahr, Saima K, Claire and a great many others. Adding further abundance, my brother Saqib, his wife Sahar and their beautiful daughters Ayla and Sophia have thankfully been close in these years.

To my parents, Arman and Tabassum, I dedicate this book. For their self-sacrificing love and the prayers that they say for me daily, no gratitude can be enough. I won't ever do justice to the opportunities they have provided but can only be glad that I have the breadth of their wisdom and the depth of their care as my sacred sites of sanctuary in the world.

Contents

Preface ... v
Acknowledgements ... xi
Table of Cases ... xvii
Table of Legislation ... xxiii

1. NASCENT STATEHOOD ... 1
I. Pre-Colonial India ... 2
II. Company Rule ... 4
III. Regional Expansion ... 6
IV. British Raj and Colonial Difference ... 8
V. Constitutional End-Games ... 18
VI. Partition ... 22
Further Reading ... 25

2. STATE BUILDING AND CONSTITUTION MAKING ... 27
I. Centralisation of Power ... 28
II. Regionalism ... 35
III. Islam ... 39
IV. The 1956 Constitution ... 43
V. Ayub and the 1962 Constitution ... 46
VI. Yahya/Bangladesh ... 51
VII. The 1973 Constitution ... 53
Further Reading ... 57

3. REPRESENTATIVE GOVERNMENT ... 59
I. Parliamentary Structure ... 61
II. Parties and Politicians ... 68
III. Electoral System ... 82
IV. Parliamentary Democracy/Parties, Class, Etc ... 89
Further Reading ... 92

4. EXECUTIVE GOVERNMENT ... 93
I. Exceptional Powers ... 95

II. A Militarised Executive 100
III. Courts as Referees—Article 58(2)(b), President v PM 106
IV. A Prime Ministerial Executive 109
V. Taming the Executive 113
VI. Presidential Ordinances 118
Further Reading 120

5. THE JUDICIARY 121
I. History and Structure of the Post-Independence Judiciary 122
II. Military Loyalty 128
III. The 1990s Judiciary 133
IV. Chief Justice Iftikhar Chaudhry and Extensive Review 136
V. The Lawyers' Movement and Judicialisation of Politics 138
VI. Basic Structure 142
VII. Judicial Independence 145
Further Reading 149

6. FEDERALISM 151
I. Political Structure of Federalism 152
II. Exceptions to the Federal Formula 154
III. Federal/Provincial Powers 157
IV. Emergency 165
V. Ethnic Conflict and the Federal Formula 167
VI. Local Government 180
Further Reading 182

7. RIGHTS: EQUALITY AND LIBERTY 183
I. Rights and Review until 1973 184
II. The Structure of Fundamental Rights in the 1973 Constitution 187
III. Gender Equality and Equality Law 192
IV. Preventive Detention 199
Further Reading 213

8. ISLAM 215
I. Islam and State 216
II. Zia and Islamisation 220

III. Blasphemy 240
IV. Musharraf Reform and After 242
Further Reading 248

CONCLUSION 249

Index 251

Table of Cases

Abdul Aziz v Province of West Pakistan PLD [1958] SC (Pak) 499 185
Abdul Mujeeb Pirzada v Federation of Islamic Republic of Pakistan PLD [1990] Karachi 9 67
Abdul Rasheed (Dr) v Government of Balochistan PLD [2014] Quetta 186 175
Abdul Rauf v Chief Commissioner, Islamabad PLD [2006] Lahore 111 207
Abdul Waheed v Asma Jehangir PLD [1997] Lahore 301 230
Abdur Rehman Mubashir v Ameer Ali Shah PLD [1978] Lahore 113 237
Afroze Ehsan Haq v Government of Pakistan PLD [1995] Karachi 56 61
Ahmad Tariq Rahim v Pakistan PLD [1992] SC 646 .... 107, 108
Ahmadyar v Sartaj Aziz MLD [1999] Lahore 3341 64
Air League of PIAC Employees v Federation of Pakistan SCMR [2011] SC 1254 .... 162, 163
Aitchison College v Muhammad Zubair PLD [2002] SC 326 197
Akbar Gul Khan v Government of Pakistan CLC [1995] Lahore 1189 97
Akbar Khan and Faiz Ahmad Faiz v Crown PLD [1954] FC 87 69
Al Jehad Trust v Federation of Pakistan SCMR [1999] SC 1379 156
Al Jehad Trust v Federation of Pakistan PLD [1996] SC 324 .... 128, 146, 147
Alleged Corruption in Rental Power Plants SCMR [2012] SC 773 115
Arshad Ali Khan v Government of the Punjab SCMR [1994] SC 1532 208
Asma Jilani v Government of the Punjab PLD [1972] SC 139 .... 47, 51, 54, 55, 114, 224
Ata Ulla v State PLD [2000] Lahore 364 .... 239, 244
Attiya Bibi Khan v Federation of Pakistan through Secretary of Education SCMR [2001] SC 1161 .... 102, 175
Aurangzeb Shah Burki v Province of Punjab PLD [2011] Lahore 198 153
Bakhtawar v State PCrLJ [1976] Lahore 393 204
Balochistan Law and Order case. *See* President, Balochistan High Court Bar Association v Federation of Pakistan SCMR [2012] SC 1958 .... 179, 180
Balochistan Missing Persons case. *See* Human Rights case no 29388-K of 2013, PLD [2014] SC 305 .... 172, 211
Bank of Oman case. *See* Bank of Oman Ltd v East Trading Co Ltd PLD [1987] Karachi 404 225
Bazal Ahmad Ayyubi v West Pakistan Province PLD [1957] (WP) Lahore 388 185
Begum Shireen Bahar Cheema v Federation of Pakistan PLD [1993] Lahore 822 61
Benazir Bhutto v Federation of Pakistan PLD [1988] SC 416 .... 71, 80, 133
Chairman PIA Corp v Sherin Dokhth SCMR [1996] SC 1520 198
Chaudhry Ata Elahi v Parveen Zohra PLD [1958] SC 298 192

Chaudhry Muhammad Siddique v Government of Pakistan PLD [2005] SC 1 ... 160
Chief Justice of Pakistan Iftikhar Muhammad Chaudhry v President of Pakistan PLD [2010] SC 61 ... 138
Criminal Miscellaneous Application No 189 of 2006 SCMR [2006] SC 1805 ... 137
Darshan Masih v State PLD [1990] SC 513 ... 133
Darwesh M Arbey v Federation of Pakistan PLD [1980] Lahore 206 ... 96
Deep Chand v State of UP AIR [1959] SC 648 ... 159
Ehsanul Haque v Federation of Pakistan PLD [1976] Lahore 501 ... 194
Elahi Cotton Mills v Federation of Pakistan PLD [1997] SC 582 ... 159, 160
Engineer Iqbal Zafar Jhagra v Federation of Pakistan [2009] SCMR 1399 ... 116
Engineer Iqbal Zafar Jhagra and Senator Rukhsana Zuberi v Federation of Pakistan PTD [2014] SC 243 ... 116
Engro Fertilizers Ltd v Islamic Republic of Pakistan and Federation of Pakistan PLD [2012] Sindh 50 ... 178
FB Ali v State PLD [1975] SC 506 ... 55, 102, 187
Federation of Pakistan v Dr Mubashir Hassan PLD [2012] SC 106 ... 120
Federation of Pakistan v Gul Hassan Khan PLD [1989] SC 633 ... 232
Federation of Pakistan v Hazoor Bakhsh PLD [1983] FSC 255 ... 223
Federation of Pakistan v Malik Muhammad Miskeen PLD [1995] SC AJ&K 1 ... 156
Federation of Pakistan v Maulvi Tamizuddin Khan PLD [1955] FC 240 ... 32
Federation of Pakistan v Muhammad Saifullah Khan PLD [1989] SC 166 ... 107
Federation of Pakistan v Munir Hussain Bhatti PLD [2011] SC 752 ... 148
Federation of Pakistan v Sindh High Court Bar Association PLD [2012] SC 1067 ... 148
Foundation for Fundamental Rights v Federation of Pakistan PLD [2013] Peshawar 94 ... 155
Gadoon Textile Mills v WAPDA SCMR [1997] SC 641 ... 154
Ghulam Ahmad v Punjab Province PLD [1976] Lahore 773 ... 205
Ghulam Rasool v Government of Pakistan PLD [2015] SC 6 ... 118
Government of Balochistan v Azizullah Memon PLD [1993] SC 341 ... 135
Government of Punjab v Naila Begum PLD [1987] Lahore 336 ... 195
Government of West Pakistan v Begum Agha: Abdulkarim Shorish Kashmiri PLD [1969] SC 14 ... 187
Haji Lal Muhammad v Federation of Pakistan PLD [2014] Peshawar 199 ... 91
Hakim Khan v Government of Pakistan PLD [1992] SC 595 ... 226
Hashwani Hotels Ltd, Karachi v Government of the Punjab PLD [1981] Lahore 211 ... 157
Hazoor Bakhsh v Federation of Pakistan PLD [1981] FSC 145 ... 222, 223
High Court Bar Association, Bahawalpur v Federation of Pakistan PLD [2015] Lahore 317 ... 148
Huma Saad v Chairman, Joint Admission Committee, Medical/ Dental Colleges, KPK, Peshawar CLC [2012] Peshawar 891 ... 175

Humaira Mehmood v State PLD [1999] Lahore 494 231
Human Rights Case No 13-L of 2006 SCMR [2006] SC 1769 137
Human Rights Case No 3062 of 2006 SCMR [2006] SC 1780 137
Human Rights Cases No. 2668 of 2006, 1111 of 2007 and 15283-G of 2010 PLD [2010] SC 759—Action Taken on news clipping regarding fast food outlet in F-9 Park, Islamabad. 181
Humera Satwat Yusuf v Government of the Punjab PLD [1971] Lahore 641 193
Iffat Razi v Government of Punjab PLD [2002] Lahore 194 207
Imran Khan v Chief Election Commissioner PLD [2013] SC 120 85
Imrana Tiwana v Province of Punjab PLD [2015] Lahore 522 181
Irshad H Khan v Parveen Ijaz PLD [1987] Karachi 466 225
Islamic Republic of Pakistan v Abdul Wali Khan PLD [1976] SC 57 .... 71, 170
Jamat-i-Islami Pakistan v Federation of Pakistan PLD [2000] SC 111 135
Jehan Mina v State PLD [1983] FSC 183 229
Jibendra Kishore Achharyya Chowdhury v Province of East Pakistan PLD [1957] SC 9 .... 185, 187
Justice Hasnat Ahmed Khan v Federation of Pakistan PLD [2011] SC 680 147
Karachi Law and Order case of 2011. *See* Watan Party v Federation of Pakistan PLD [2011] SC 997 .... 74, 86, 179
KESC v NIRC PLD [2014] Sindh 553 .... 157, 162
Khawaja Muhammad Asif v Federation of Pakistan SCMR [2013] SC 1205 117
Khurshid Ahmad v Government of Punjab PLD [1992] Lahore 1 238
Lahore Development Authority v Imrana Tiwana SCMR [2015] SC 1739 181
M Ghafoor v Government of NWFP PLD [1974] Peshawar 28 204
MA Khuhro v Federation of Pakistan PLD [1950] Sindh 49 76
Mahmood Khan Achakzai v Federation of Pakistan PLD [1997] SC 426 .... 108, 109
Major (Retd) Tipu Sultan v Shahzad Hassan SCMR [2004] SC 1215 102
Malik Ghulam Jilani, Inayatullah and Nazir Ahmad Chaudhari v Government of West Pakistan PLD [1967] SC 373 .... 201, 202
Malik Muhammad Miskeen v Government of Pakistan PLD [1993] Azad J&K 1 156
Malik Taj Mohammad v Bibi Jano SCMR [1992] SC 1431 123
Malik Umar Aslam v Sumair Malik SCMR [2014] SC 45 80
Manzoor Ahmed Wattoo v Federation of Pakistan PLD [1997] Lahore 38 166
Manzoor Elahi v Federation of Pakistan PLD [1975] SC 66 .... 100, 135, 170
Masal Khan v District Magistrate, Peshawar PLD [1997] Peshawar 148 .... 207, 208
Mehram Ali v Federation of Pakistan PLD [1998] SC 1445 .... 134, 135
Memogate Case. *See* Watan Party v Federation of Pakistan PLD [2012] SC 292 140
Mir Javaid Al v Government of Sindh MLD [1988] Karachi 879 208
Mohammad Aslam Khaki (Dr) v Senior Superintendent of Police (Operation) Rawalpindi PLD [2013] SC 188 199
Mohammad Azhar Siddiqi v Federation of Pakistan PLD [2012] SC 774 81
Mohtarma Benazir Bhutto v President of Pakistan PLD [1998] SC 388 .... 107, 145

Moulvi Tamizuddin Khan v Federation of Pakistan PLD [1955] Sindh 96 32
Muhammad Asghar Khan v Mirza Aslam Baig PLD [2013] SC 1 88
Muhammad Ismail Qureshi v Pakistan PLD [1991] FSC 10 241
Muhammad Kamran v Federation of Pakistan CLC [2014] Lahore 1549...............91
Muhammad Khan Junejo v Federation of Pakistan SCMR [2013] SC 1328...........80
Muhammad Nasir Mahmood v Federation of Pakistan PLD [2009] SC 107.........80
Muhammad Siddiq Khan v District Magistrate PLD [1992] Lahore 140............ 208
Mulazim Hussain Shah v Province of Punjab PLD [2006] Lahore 108.............. 208
Mumtaz Ali Bhutto v Deputy Law Administration Sector I Karachi PLD [1979] Karachi 307 205
Mumtaz Qadri v State PLD [2016] SC 17.. 247
Munir Hussain Bhatti v Federation of Pakistan PLD [2011] SC 407.................... 148
Mussarat Uzma Usmani v Government of Punjab PLD [1987] Lahore 178 194
Naseem Firdous v Punjab Small Industries Corp PLD [1995] Lahore 584.......197, 198
Navid Malik v President of Pakistan SCMR [1998] SC 1917 68
Nawaz Sharif v President of Pakistan PLD [1993] SC 473........................72, 80, 107
Nazar Elahi v Government of Punjab CLC [2013] Lahore 1457.......................... 197
Nek Amal v Political Agent, Malakand PLD [1975] Peshawar 67 205
Niaz Ahmad (Dr) v DCO PLD [2014] Lahore 516 207
Niaz Ahmed Khan v Province of Sindh PLD [1977] Karachi 604.........................96
Noor Daraz Khan v Federation of Pakistan PLD [2016] Peshawar 114............. 161
Nusrat Bhutto v Chief of Army Staff PLD [1977] SC 657 .... 34, 129, 130, 133, 205, 206
NWFP v Muhammad Irshad PLD [1995] SC 281...136, 155
Pakistan International Airlines Corp v Samina Masood PLD [2005] SC 831 198
Pakistan Lawyers Forum v Federation of Pakistan PLD [2004] Lahore 130...105, 106
Pakistan Muslim League (Q) v Chief Executive of Islamic Republic of Pakistan PLD [2002] SC 994..79, 80
Pakistan Telecommunication Co Ltd v Member NIRC SCMR [2014] SC 535.... 160
Prem Kevalram Shahani v Government of Pakistan PLD [1989] Karachi 123 62
Province of Sindh v MQM PLD [2014] SC 531...86, 87
Qazalbash Waqf v Chief Land Commissioner PLD [1990] SC 99....... 191, 226, 227
Qazi Hussain Ahmed v General Pervez Musharraf PLD [2002] SC 853............. 105
Qazi Hussain Ahmad v Secretary to Government of NWFP YLR [2003] Peshawar 330... 207
Quetta Textile Mills Ltd v Province of Sindh PLD [2005] Karachi 55.........159, 160
Rafique Ahmad Sheikh v Crown PLD [1951] Lahore 17....................................... 201
Raja Rab Nawaz v Federation of Pakistan SCMR [2014] SC 101......................... 182
Reference No 2 of 2005 by the President of Pakistan PLD [2005] SC 873 244
Reko Diq case. *See* Maulana Abdul Haq Baloch v Government of Balochistan PLD [2013] SC 641 .... 116, 117, 178
Rohaifa v Federation of Pakistan PLD [2014] SC 174 211
Rustam Ali v Martial Law Administrator Zone 'C' PLD [1978] Karachi 736...... 205

Sabir Shah v Federation of Pakistan PLD [1994] SC 738 166
Safia Bibi v State PLD [1985] FSC 120 230
Saiyyid Abula'la Maudoodi v Government of West Pakistan PLD [1964] SC 673 .... 70, 186, 187, 201
Sajida Bibi v In charge Chouki No 2 Police Station Sadar Sahiwal PLD [1997] Lahore 666 231
Sardar Farooq Ahmed Khan Leghari v Federation of Pakistan PLD [1999] SC 57 .... 98, 99
Sarwari Bibi v Arshad Ali Khan YLR [2007] Lahore 702 .... 197, 198
Shahid Orakzai v President of Pakistan SCMR [1999] SC 1598 99
Shamas Din v Deputy Martial Law Administrator Lahore PLD [1979] Lahore 74 208
Shamas Textile Mills Ltd v Province of Punjab SCMR [1999] SC 1477 160
Sharaf Faridi v Federation of Islamic Republic of Pakistan PLD [1989] Karachi 404 128
Shaukat Ali Mian v Federation of Pakistan CLC [1999] Lahore 607 100
Shazia Batool v Government of Balochistan SCMR [2007] SC 410 175
Shehla Zia v WAPDA PLD [1994] SC 693 134
Sheikh Liaquat Hussain v Federation of Pakistan PLD [1999] SC 504 .... 97, 100, 134
Shirin Munir v Government of Punjab PLD [1990] SC 295 .... 133, 195, 196
Sindh High Court Bar Association v Federation of Pakistan PLD [2009] SC 879 .... 114, 120, 144
Sobho Gyanchandani v Crown PLD [1952] FC 29 69
State v Abdul Ghaffar Khan PLD [1957] (WP) Lahore 142 .... 170, 202
State v Dosso PLD [1958] SC 533 .... 46, 47, 186, 187, 201, 217, 224
State v Zia-ur-Rehman PLD [1973] SC 49 224
State of Assam v Horizon Union AIR [1967] SC 442 159
Steel Mills Privatisation case. *See* Watan Party v Federation of Pakistan PLD [2006] SC 697 115
Sui Northern Gas Pipelines Ltd Lahore v Government of the Punjab PLC (CS) [2001] Lahore 383 160
Suo Motu Case No 10 of 2009 SCMR [2010] SC 885 -Complaint regarding establishment of Makro Habib store on playground 181
Suo Motu Case No 4 of 2010, PLD [2012] SC 553—Contempt Proceedings against Prime Minister Syed Yousaf Raza Gillani 140
Syed Ali Nawaz Gardezi v Lt Col Muhammad Yusuf PLD [1963] SC 51 193
Syed Jalal Mehmood Shah v Federation of Pakistan PLD [1999] SC 395 .... 98, 165
Syed Zafar Ali Shah v General Parvez Musarraf PLD [2000] SC 869 104
Syeda Sadia v Bahauddin Zakariya University YLR [2011] Lahore 2867 196
Talal Haleem v Principal Bolan Medical College, Quetta PLD [2015] Quetta 97 196
Tamizzuddin Ahmed v Government East Pakistan PLD [1964] Dacca 795 70
Tika Ramji v State of Uttar Pradesh AIR [1956] SC 676 159

Twenty-first Amendment case, District Bar Association Rawalpindi v Federation of Pakistan PLD [2015] SC 401 144
University of Dacca v Zakir Hussain PLD [1965] SC 90 197
Usif Patel v Crown PLD [1955] FC 387 33
Wajihuddin Ahmed v Chief Election Commissioner PLD [2008] SC 13 106
Water and Power Development Authority v Mian Muhammad Riaz PLD [1995] Lahore 56 159
Workers Party Pakistan v Federation of Pakistan PLD [2012] SC 68 182
Wukula Mahazv Baraiv Tahafaz Dastoor v Federation of Pakistan PLD [1998] SC 1263 112
Yaqoob Ali v Presiding Officer, Summary Military Court, Karachi PLD [1985] Karachi 243 131
Zafar Ali Shah v General Pervez Musharraf PLD [2000] SC 869 .... 34, 143, 242
Zaheeruddin v State SCMR [1993] SC 1718 238
Zaverbhai Amaidas v State of Bombay AIR [1954] SC 752 159
Zia-ur-Rehman v State PLD [1972] Lahore 382 224

Table of Legislation

Abolition of Privy Council Act 1950 ... 123
Action in Aid of Civil Power Regulation 2011 ... 211, 212
Anarchic and Revolutionary Crimes Act 1919 ... 200
Anti-Terrorism Act 1997 ... 73, 135, 207
  Sch III ... 207
Army Act of 1952 ... 144
Azad Jammu and Kashmir Interim Constitution Act 1974 ... 156
  Art 21 ... 156
Balochistan States Union 1952 ... 37
Basic Democracies Order 1959 ... 48
Bonded Labour System (Abolition) Rules 1995 ... 133
Charter of Democracy ... 139
Code of Criminal Procedure 1898 ... 199
  s 491 ... 201
Conduct of General Elections Order 2002 ... 61, 62, 79
Constitution 1956 ... 28, 34, 43–46, 48, 62, 123, 184–86, 188, 190, 192, 201, 203, 218
  Art 4 ... 184
  Art 5 ... 192
    (1) ... 192
  Art 18 ... 191
  Art 198 ... 46
Constitution 1962 ... 28, 46–51, 62, 123, 124, 186, 190, 193, 201, 216
  Art 2 ... 192
  Art 6 ... 192
  Art 30 ... 48
  Art 50 ... 48
  Art 66 ... 48
  Art 92 ... 48
  Art 98 ... 48
  Third Schedule ... 49
  First Amendment 1963 ... 48, 186
  Second Amendment 1964 ... 48
Constitution 1973
  Preamble ... 187, 188
  Pt II ... 188
    Ch I ... 188

Ch II ... 188
Art 2A ... 223, 225, 239
Art 2B ... 112
Art 4 ... 99, 100
Art 6 ... 114
Art 8 ... 189, 233
(1) ... 188, 189
(2) ... 188, 189
(3) ... 225
Arts 8–28 ... 188
Art 9 ... 100, 134, 189, 199, 230
Art 9A ... 96
Art 10 ... 100, 189, 204–06, 212
(4) ... 207
Art 10A ... 189
Art 11 ... 191
Art 12 ... 189
Art 13 ... 189
Art 14 ... 189
(2) ... 190
Art 15 ... 99
Arts 15–19 ... 190
Art 16 ... 99
Art 17 ... 72, 73, 76, 99, 162
(1) ... 70
(2) ... 70, 72, 73
(4) ... 73
Art 18 ... 99
Art 19 ... 99, 208
Art 20 ... 190, 237, 239, 247
(1) ... 238
Art 22 ... 190, 195–97
Art 23 ... 191
Art 24 ... 99, 191
Art 25 ... 87, 100, 102, 192, 195–97, 199
(2) ... 193, 195, 196
(3) ... 193, 194
Art 27 ... 174, 190, 197
(2) ... 198
Art 28 ... 218
Arts 29–40 ... 188
Art 34 ... 190
Art 35 ... 230
Art 36 ... 190

Art 37 ... 190
Art 38 ... 190
Art 47 ... 103
Art 48 ... 103, 119
Art 50 ... 61
Art 51 ... 61
(2) ... 84
(5) ... 86
Art 58(2)(b) ... 94, 103–09, 111, 146
Art 62 ... 62, 77, 78, 80, 81
(2) ... 79
Art 63 ... 62, 77, 78, 80, 81
(1)(g) ... 78, 81
(k) ... 78
(2) ... 77, 81
Art 63A ... 111
Arts 70–83 ... 65
Art 71 ... 66
Art 88 ... 65
Art 89 ... 118
Art 90 ... 63, 103, 105, 117
Art 91 ... 63
Art 92(3) ... 64
(6) ... 64
Art 95 ... 64
Art 96A ... 110
Art 97 ... 164
Art 128 ... 153
Art 129 ... 153
Art 137 ... 164
Art 140A ... 180–82
Art 141 ... 157
Art 142 ... 158, 161
(b) ... 154, 161
(c) ... 161
Art 143 ... 159–61
Art 144 ... 162
Art 148 ... 164
(c) ... 164
Art 149 ... 164
(b) ... 164
(c) ... 164
Art 158 ... 177
Art 160 ... 175

Art 161 ... 177
Art 172 ... 178
Art 175 ... 124, 126, 128, 146
(2) ... 124, 126
(3) ... 127
Arts 175–209 ... 124
Art 175A ... 147, 148
Art 180 ... 127
Art 184 ... 125, 189
(3) ... 81, 125, 133, 140, 189
Art 185 ... 125
Art 189 ... 126
Art 196 ... 127
Art 198 ... 125
Art 199 ... 96, 125, 129, 130, 155, 189, 207, 231
Art 200(4) ... 127
Art 202 ... 124
Art 203 ... 124
Art 203B ... 221
Art 203C ... 222
Art 212A ... 129
Arts 213–21 ... 82
Art 218 ... 83
Art 227 ... 244
Art 228 ... 218
Art 232 ... 97, 99, 111, 165
(2) ... 99
Art 233 ... 99, 204, 236
(1) ... 99
Art 234 ... 164, 165, 167
Art 235 ... 97
Art 236 ... 98
(b) ... 98
(2) ... 99
Art 237 ... 114
Art 238 ... 114
Art 239 ... 126
(3) ... 179
Art 242 ... 95
(3) ... 95
Art 245 ... 89, 95–97, 100, 110
(3) ... 96, 97
(b) ... 114

Art 246 ... 154
Art 247 ... 154, 155
(5) ... 136
(7) ... 135
Art 260(3) ... 62
Art 264 ... 119
Art 270A ... 120
Art 270AA ... 120
Art 270AAA ... 114
Sch I ... 189, 225, 233
Sch IV ... 158, 161
Sch VII ... 233
First Amendment Act 1974 ... 70, 76, 127
Second Amendment Act1974 ... 219, 220, 237
Second Amendment Order 1979 ... 129
Third Amendment Act 1975 ... 204
Fourth Amendment Act 1975 ... 62, 127, 204
Fifth Amendment Act 1976 ... 127, 204
Seventh Amendment Act 1977 ... 96, 110
Eighth Amendment Act 1985 ... 56, 64, 67, 103, 104, 109, 131, 145, 153, 206
Thirteenth Amendment Act 1997 ... 56, 111, 153
Fourteenth Amendment Act 1997 ... 111
Fifteenth Amendment Act 1998 ... 112
Seventeenth Amendment Act 2003 ... 73, 105, 109, 136, 153
Eighteenth Amendment Act 2010 ... 60, 63, 65, 76, 80, 89–91, 109, 128, 144, 147, 152–54, 158, 160, 161, 163, 166, 174, 176–78, 180, 181, 199, 233
Nineteenth Amendment Act 2011 ... 148
Twentieth Amendment Act 2012 ... 91
Twenty-First Amendment Act 2015 ... 83, 144
Twenty-Second Amendment Act 2016 ... 83, 87, 91
Contract Act 1872 ... 9
s 88 ... 9
Criminal Law Amendment Act 2004 ... 232
Code of Criminal Procedure 1898 ... 232
Dastoor-ul-Amal Diwani State Kalat 1952 ... 123
Defence of India Act 1915 ... 200
Defence of India Act 1939 ... 200
Defence of Pakistan Ordinance 1965 ... 202
Delimitation of Constituencies Act 1974
s 9 ... 87
Local Government Ordinances 2001 ... 180

Electoral Bodies Disqualification Order 1959 (EBDO) 70, 77
Electoral Rolls Act 1974 84
Enforcement of Shariah Ordinance 1988 225
Enforcement of Shariah Act 1991
  s 8 225
Environmental Protection Act 1997 134
Pakistan Essential Services Maintenance Act 1952 69
Frontier Crimes Regulation 1901 (FCR) 13, 37, 135, 156
Gilgit-Baltistan (Empowerment and Self-Governance) Order 2009 157
  Art 22 157
  Art 23 157
Government of India Act 1858 .... 8, 9
Government of India Act 1909 15
Government of India Act 1919 15
Government of India Act 1935 .... 17, 31–33, 35, 44, 45, 76, 97, 123, 151, 158
High Courts Act 1861 8
High Courts (Appointment of Acting Chief Justice) Order, 1977 (President's (Post Proclamation) Order (2 of 1977) 129
High Treason Punishment Act 1973 114
Hudood Ordinances 223, 227–34, 241, 244
Indian Independence Act 1947 .... 24, 32, 33
Indian Councils Act 1861 9
Indian Councils Act 1892 12
Indian Penal Code 1860 9
  s 295 240
Industrial Relations Act 2008 163
Industrial Relations Act 2012 .... 162, 163
Karachi Agreement 1949 30
Lahore Resolution 1940 19
Law of Evidence (Qanoon E Shahadat) 1984 .... 228, 229
  Art 17 229
  Art 151(4) 229
Laws Continuance in Force Order 1958 47
Laws Continuance in Force Order 1977 (LCFO) 126–28
Legal Framework Order 1970 51
Legal Framework Order 2002 (Chief Executive Order No 24) 62, 73
Maintenance of Public Order Ordinance 1960 207
Martial Law Order No 12 of 1977 (Preventive Detention) 205
Muslim Family Law Ordinance 1961 (MFLO) 50, 193, 216, 225
Mutual Defence Assistance Treaty 1954 46
National Accountability Ordinance 1999 .... 79, 161
National Judicial Policy 2009 137

National Reconciliation Ordinance (NRO) 2007 140
Objectives Resolution 1949 .... 40, 41, 122, 128, 187, 215, 218, 221, 223–27, 239
Ordinance XLI 1978 71
Pakistan Armed Forces (Acting in Aid of Civil Power) Ordinance 1998 ..... 134, 135
Pakistan Penal Code (PPC) 1860 .... 227, 232, 238
  s 53 135
  s 295B 240
  s 295C 240, 241
  s 298B 238
  s 298C 238–40
  s 311 232
Police Act 1861 8
Political Parties Act 1962 (PPA 1962) 70–73, 186
Political Parties Order 2002 (PPO 2002) 72–74, 76, 155
  s 3 73
President to Hold another Office Act 2004 105
Presidential Order No 11 of 1961 123
Presidential Order No 1 of 1980 130
Presidential Order No 24 of 1984 127
Presidential Order No. 20 of 1985 119
Presidential Succession Order 2001 105
Press and Publications Ordinance 1963 49
Prohibition and Punishment Ordinance XX 1984 .... 237, 240
Protection against Harassment of Women at the Workplace Act 2010 199
Protection of Pakistan Act 2014 (PPA) 211, 212
  s 6 212
Provisional Constitutional Order 1981 130
Provisional Constitutional Order 1999 (PCO) 104, 136
Provisional Constitutional Order 2007 138
Public and Representative Offices (Disqualification) Act 1949 (PRODA) 76
Public Safety Ordinance 1949 200
Punjab Laws Act 1872 9
Representation of the People Act 1975 83
Revival of the Constitution of 1973 Order of 1985 .... 63, 67, 71, 77, 103, 110, 131, 133, 206, 223, 225
Security of Pakistan Act 1952 .... 77, 200, 207
Special Areas (Restoration of Jurisdiction) Order 1961 123
West Pakistan Civil Courts Ordinance 1962 123
Women's Protection Act 2006 (Protection of Women (Criminal Law Amendment) Act 2006) 230
Zakat and Ushr Ordinance 1980 236
Zina Ordinance 228, 229

International

Convention on the Elimination of all Forms of Discrimination against Women ... 231
UN Resolution No 47 1958 ... 30

United States

Bill of Rights ... 44

1

Nascent Statehood

Pre-colonial India – Company Rule and Administration – British Raj – Government of India Acts – Indian National Congress – Muslim League – Muslim Nationalism – Partition

ON 14 AUGUST 1947, Pakistan emerged as a sovereign nation-state through the division of territories and the migration of populations across borders drawn to divide what was previously British India. This chapter in large part presents a pre-history of the creation of the Pakistani state, with attention to the ways in which forces aligned towards the achievement of independent statehood but also to shape important contextual features for the further development of constitutionalism in the new state.

Here we follow a more or less linear path in looking at the emergent state-like apparatus of Mughal India, through the divided sovereignty that was exercised under the British East India Company (1601–1858) and at the period of direct British colonial rule in India (1858–1947). A final long part of the chapter deals with the development of Muslim nationalism from within a broader anti-colonial nationalism; a sentiment and then movement in which a certain populace came to imagine Pakistan as their rightful homeland. Eventually finding a voice through Mohammad Ali Jinnah, the sentiment gained concrete expression in rounds of constitutional negotiations in which he at first represented the demands for 'sufficient' representation of Muslim minorities in India. Failing to reach a satisfactory accommodation he thereafter dedicated his efforts towards the recognition of a distinct nation for Muslims of the subcontinent. In this set of movements, advances and compromises, some of the potent reasons for the compromised position of Pakistani constitutionalism become more clear.

I. PRE-COLONIAL INDIA

With the necessary caveat that 'any historical interpretation of the spread of Islam in the subcontinent needs to be attentive to regional specificities in the domains of economy and culture as well as the great variety of Muslims that came to populate the subcontinent',[1] it is nonetheless possible to locate the beginnings of a consolidated Indo-Islamic culture and mode of statecraft in the Delhi Sultanate of the twelfth century. The Sultanate, as a general rule, upheld the supremacy of Sharia while affording broad exemptions for non-Muslim subjects, who were 'allowed to retain their customary and religious laws'.[2] The Sultanate was also notable for its own internal syncretism, consisting by turns of rulers drawn from the Persianate aristocracy and 'slaves' of Turkic origin.

The succession of the Delhi sultans ended in a pivotal battle with Zaheeruddin Babar in 1526, establishing thereafter the foundations of Mughal rule. It was Babar's grandson, Akbar, who ensured the Mughals' greatest geographic expansion through a set of military conquests extending to territory that was almost equal to that governed later by the British and now comprising the independent states of Pakistan, India and Bangladesh. They also oversaw trade that made India a major node not just in the commerce of goods towards Europe but also in a vast Indian Ocean trading zone that included the other major Muslim empires of the time, the Ottomans and Safavids.

Contrary to the myths of inherent degeneracy that gained circulation to describe Mughal decline, it is important to recognise that as a governmental entity it had some of the features thought consonant with the more evolved and benevolent of the European states. It possessed a rationally-organised administrative structure, a formal and independent justice system and also a mode of managing a religiously plural population that, at least at higher levels of a class-divided system, was quite inclusive.

In fact, the administrative structure of Mughal rule allowed in many ways for the incorporation of alternate poles of authority than the

[1] A Jalal and S Bose, *Modern South Asia: History, Culture, Political Economy* (Oxford, Psychology Press, 2004) 12.

[2] ibid.

Emperor alone.[3] As a system of rule oriented to securing smooth functioning through changes at the top, a permanent administrative structure comprising several intermediary and interdependent functionaries was also introduced throughout the Mughal domain. High patronage positions were regularly granted in large numbers to members of the Hindu and minority Shia communities.[4]

While certain forms of law were administered that had their derivation from Sharia-based principles, in particular the criminal law, the administration of civic life was left to be done through plural and religiously-founded practice. Imperial edicts lent uniformity to the system, although it is also agreed that the Mughal Empire did not display the legislative centralisation that would enable its classification as a state.[5]

Over much of the eighteenth century the Mughal Empire was repeatedly assailed by local contenders to power, making apparent certain tensions and an inability ultimately to manage the sub-continent's disparate populace through a given complex of power.[6] In these sites of tension, Europeans found opportunity to benefit by lending military might to those who would award them economic concessions in exchange for the titular right to rule. In such a manner, the East India Company was a great beneficiary, having extended its domain through the creation of tribute-paying potentates, systems of rule that were inherently unstable and would result within years in the Company's direct annexation of further parts of the subcontinent. By 1764, the Company had been granted the right to collect land revenue in Bengal by the Mughal Emperor.

Altogether, the displacement of Mughal rule was staged over a long period. In fact, the Mughal Emperor would be retained on a salary by the Company officials until being finally and formally dethroned by the British Crown in 1858.

[3] C Singh, 'Centre and Periphery in the Mughal State: The Case of Seventeenth-Century Panjab' (1988) 22 *Modern Asian Studies* 299, 303.

[4] IA Khan, 'Tracing Sources of Principles of Mughal Governance: A Critique of Recent Historiography' (2009) 37 *Social Scientist* 45.

[5] A Ali, 'Towards an Interpretation of the Mughal Empire' (1978) 1 *Journal of the Royal Asiatic Society of Great Britain and Ireland* 48.

[6] J Wilson, 'Early Colonial India Beyond Empire' (2007) 50 *The Historical Journal* 951.

II. COMPANY RULE

Famously, the East India Company itself was founded on the first monopoly charter granted as royal prerogative by Queen Elizabeth I in 1600. Over the next two and a half centuries, the initial mercantile nature of the Company's activities in India transformed through grants to collect land revenue, in the creation of fortifications for the protection of its physical assets and in the warfare and plunder it executed towards such ends. It thereby also expanded its sphere of governmental activity by turns claiming legitimacy to do so as well as endeavouring to disguise the sovereign authority it exercised when at other times that proved more convenient.[7] All the while, the Company in India was repeatedly subject to the questioning of its exclusive rights relating to its activities, a concern mediated at times by the desire to exact loans and tax revenue by the British Parliament when settler colonies in North America grew more restive and other European powers attempted to establish competing outposts in the subcontinent.[8]

Successive Kings' Charters were the mechanism for enabling the Company to implant zones of governmental activity in three administrative zones, termed Presidencies. These were Madras, Calcutta and Bombay. The early charters recognised a governor responsible for laying out the law in the form of company regulations through each of these Presidencies. Jurisdictionally, the Presidencies were further divided into presidency towns and the *mofussil*. The *mofussil* was considered to be the administrative hinterland, constituted of village communities and agrarian social relations. Where king's courts and company courts administered a mostly uniform law in presidency towns, the systems of law in the *mofussil* were more locally varied, consisting of an admixture of 'Hindu and Muslim personal law, Islamic criminal law, and Company Regulations'.[9]

[7] E Stokes, *The English Utilitarians and India* (New Delhi, Oxford University Press, 1990).

[8] M Mukherjee, *India in the Shadow of Empire: A Legal and Political History 1774–1950* (New Delhi, Oxford University Press, 2010).

[9] E Kolsky, 'Codification of Colonial Difference: Criminal Procedure of British India' (2005) 23 *Law and History Review* 641.

Instances of native rebellion as well as company indebtedness attracted a keen public eye to the Company's workings back in Britain, and led Parliament to pass Acts to regulate the Company itself. In 1774 this resulted in the establishment of the office of a Governor-General, of a Supreme Court at Bengal and the establishment of a council of governmental appointees to advise the Governor-General. The first Governor-General, Warren Hastings, established the apparatus for a permanent civil service as well as a standing army that would be inclusive of large numbers of Indians. Hastings himself would be later impeached and tried in Parliament on the charges of corruption, bribery, high crime and misdemeanours.[10]

Land was the primary basis of wealth in this early colonial configuration, and land revenue management tended to dictate systems of rule across the Presidencies.[11] The last of the Kings' Charters to the Company was issued in 1833 and it radically altered the legislative and administrative landscape. An all-India Legislative Council was created, with general and wide powers of law-making, which supplanted the independent legislative powers of the three Presidencies. Additionally, the town and *mofussil* distinction was abolished. These and other alterations gave rise to questioning of the form and administration of law for all of British India. To this end, successive law reform commissions made up of prominent British lawyers tried to arrive at a system of laws that would accommodate British interests as well as streamline systems of justice.

The proceedings of the law reform commissions show a recurrent grappling with the question of codification and with issues of making and enforcing uniform laws between local and English subjects in the subcontinent. Codification itself seemed to imply the equalisation of laws for all, even though it had its grander claims built into a structure of enlightened and benevolent governance. The Company acted in limited ways upon the counsel of the more reform-minded of its advisors. It prohibited the Hindu practice of widow immolation or *sati* in 1829,

[10] M Mukherjee, 'Justice, War, and the Imperium: India and Britain in Edmund Burke's Prosecutorial Speeches in the Impeachment Trial of Warren Hastings' (2005) 23 *Law and History Review* 589, 602.

[11] DA Washbrook, 'Law, State and Agrarian Society in Colonial India' (1981) 15 *Modern Asian Studies* 649, 650.

and in 1832 it stopped the application of 'Mohammadan criminal law' as a rule to all persons.[12]

As a predominantly commercial entity, the Company ultimately did not venture too far in the direction of social reformism, but rather sought certainty of rule in territories within its possession. To this end, extensive anthropological studies were undertaken to understand the essential character of segments of the population, and their relative usefulness, or threat, to colonial administration was clearly outlined. This resulted in the designation of specific clans and families as being local rulers and thus assigned *zamindari/jagirdari* (land-owner, revenue collector) status. Also, other groups, often spuriously on the basis of their nomadic or non-sedentary modes of organisation, were classed as criminal tribes and placed under surveillance, with their movements restricted and confined.[13]

Religious communities were assumed to be internally coherent in their desire to 'rigidly and ritualistically follow their own law in all matters of social custom, religious duty, and commercial transaction'.[14] In reality, however, it required great effort to forge this coherence. The mode of doing so tended in the direction of codifying religiously mandated law so as to render it applicable through a hierarchical court system that relied upon precedential reasoning. What ensued was the selective compilation of religious sources in order to forge both Anglo-Hindu and Anglo-Mohammadan law.[15]

III. REGIONAL EXPANSION

The regions of India that would later become Pakistan were mostly the last to be joined into Company rule. The logic behind the Company's conquest of Sindh, Punjab, and the areas now known as Khyber Pakhtunkhwa[16] and Balochistan was an attempt to secure the

[12] VD Kulshreshtha, *Landmarks in Indian Legal History and Constitutional History* (Lucknow, Eastern Book, 1968).

[13] R Singha, *A Despotism of Law: Crime and Justice in Early Colonial India* (Delhi, Oxford University Press, 1998).

[14] SA Kugle, 'Framed, Blamed and Renamed: The Recasting of Islamic Jurisprudence in Colonial South Asia' (2001) 35 *Modern Asian Studies* 257, 270.

[15] ibid.

[16] Known as the North-West Frontier Province from 1947–2010.

'natural borders' of the subcontinent all the way to Kabul and beyond. Embroiled in the imperial Great Game against Russia, the British feared for all their holdings in India, thanks to the Russian advance into vast areas of Central Asia.[17] In quick succession Balochistan in 1839, Sindh in 1843 and Punjab in 1849 were conquered. The British faced crippling defeat in their further advances towards current day Afghanistan in several campaigns.

The territories acquired were administered in ways that both reflected the relative violence of conquest as well as British notions about the temperament of each region's populace. Balochistan had become integral to British interests when British cavalry were forced to cross its territory on route to what became the first Afghan War.[18] They entered into a treaty with Khan of Kalat, who ruled over much of current day Balochistan, and continued to pay him tribute for the next century. Dismayed that the Khan was unable to secure them safe passage through what was in fact a tribal confederacy, the British engaged in palace intrigue rather than incorporate Balochistan into their larger bureaucratic and administrative enterprise.[19] The territory of Sindh was annexed to the Bombay presidency but left, in the manner of a *mofussil*, to be managed in customary fashion. Land was allowed to be held in perpetuity by existing landholders and tribal chiefs in exchange for revenue extraction.

The conquest of the Punjab began with an attempt to exert influence on the child regent and successor to the long-standing Emperor Ranjt Singh.[20] Competing regional claims on power enabled the British to enter the fray and to annex a region seen as pivotal to their security concerns. While sporadic resistance against British rule continued early on, there was also a quick amelioration of dissent owing to British willingness to win the loyalty of the populace of this relatively wealthy region, including by way of channelling investment into the building of canal networks to aid agricultural production.

[17] NS Sarila, *The Shadow of the Great Game: The Untold Story of India's Partition* (New Delhi, HarperCollins, 2006).

[18] JH Syed, 'The British Advent in Balochistan' (2007) 28 *Pakistan Journal of History and Culture* 53, 58.

[19] M Axmann, *Back to the Future: The Khanate of Kalat and the Genesis of Baluch Nationalism, 1915–1955* (Karachi, Oxford University Press, 2012).

[20] I Talbot, *Punjab and the Raj: 1849–1947* (New Delhi, Manohar, 1988).

In 1849 the British also annexed what was described as the North-West Frontier and brought it within the administrative sway of the Punjab province. Revenue extraction happened through an array of systems that transformed the local tribal structure in the subsequent decades. This region, north of the Indus River, had been paying tribute both to Sikh and Kabul Kingdoms and the Company faced continuing resistance to its assertion of sovereign control here.

IV. BRITISH RAJ AND COLONIAL DIFFERENCE

A set of uprisings against Company power, albeit across a limited geographic expanse in North West India, would lead to the eventual assumption of direct British governmental rule in India and the end of the Company's administration in 1857. The British Parliament's hesitant attempts to control Company activity in India gave way to a wholesale alteration of the governmental structure thereafter. By transferring sovereign control to the Queen in Parliament, and extending the status of subjecthood to all Indians, the transitions in the structure of government seemed at least marginally responsive to Indian discontent with British rule to date. The Government of India Act 1858 effectively established that no extension of existing territory would be undertaken, no interference in religious matters would be made, no distinctions of caste or creed would be maintained in admission to service, ancient rights and customs of India would be respected and the 'administration of the Government would be for the benefit of all the subjects'.[21]

While these high-sounding salutary principles would be flouted time and again over the next 89 years, an altogether new system of governance was engineered. The 1858 Act contained formulae for a federal division of powers between existing and newer provinces, for the division between executive and legislative powers as well as adapting and reforming a civil service that had been established under Company rule. In quick succession a set of Acts to establish a uniform system for a higher judiciary,[22] a uniform policing apparatus[23] and others conducive to homogeneity of the governance function would also be passed.

[21] Kulshreshtha, *Landmarks in Indian Legal History* 346.
[22] High Courts Act of 1861.
[23] Police Act 1861.

Perhaps the most noteworthy thing about the 1858 Act was that it provided for a single and identifiable locus of sovereign authority. However, below the Queen, proclaimed Empress of India in 1877, there would be some elbowing for space between the Secretary of State for India, the Indian Legislative Council and the Governor-General as the institutions at the apex of the governmental order.[24] It was a tricky balance between dispersed and concentrated nodes of power. The Secretary of State was often referred to as the 'great white Mughal' on account of the vast expanse of discretionary authority he exercised. The 1858 Act had also granted wide-ranging powers to the Governor-General and made it compulsory to secure his assent for every enactment passed by the Legislative Council. The rather anomalous feature of executive ordinances was also first introduced under the 1858 Act, empowering the Governor-General to unilaterally proclaim law for all of British India.[25] Shortly after, by way of the Indian Councils Act 1861, the office of the Governor-General came to be associated with a council that allowed for the inclusion, by appointment, of Indians.

The codified laws that had been suggested by law commissions in previous decades were resurrected in the early years of transition, and codes of civil and criminal procedure were enacted in 1858 and 1860. The Indian Penal Code was also passed into law, thus ensuring a mixed civil and common law system for the subcontinent.[26]

The rationalisation and systematisation of the law that was undertaken did not preclude official recognition of customary practices. Through enactments such as the Punjab Laws Act and Contract Act of 1872, valid custom was to be the basis of making awards in cases touching upon property transfer, succession, inheritance, and the like.[27] In the realm of personal law, which continued to be governed through religious codes, a strong preference had been shown for the testimony of a certain class of religious scholars and in the case of customary laws, the status of putative religious elders was sanctified.[28]

[24] D Williams, 'The Council of India and the Relationship between the Home and Supreme Governments, 1858–1870' (1966) 81 *The English Historical Review* 56.

[25] See text in Chapter 4, section VI.

[26] Kolsky, 'Codification of Colonial Difference' 641.

[27] Contract Act 1872, s 88 (repealed).

[28] This reflected a propensity to find a clergy where neither of the major religious traditions of the subcontinent had an equivalent to the clerics of the Christian tradition.

The idea that the 1857 Rebellion had been fostered by discontent at the disruptions to 'traditional' life had gained currency, and colonial policy-makers would play a dual game of incorporation and deference to tradition to maintain their control.[29] In the recruitment and appointment of Indians into the various services, a further dualism was expressed: the doors of the judicial branch would be opened wide, while the covenanted civil services would be retained as exclusively British for some time. What this also revealed was the unspoken acceptance that the actual work of governing was being done at the sub-provincial, district level by someone akin to a mini-monarch. This was the district magistrate/collector in whom was vested the powers of magistracy, administrator, revenue collector and others.[30]

These and many other features of colonial rule in India displayed to its subjects the operations of a fundamental rule of colonial difference. Just below the platitudinous benevolence of colonial government, the operation of assumptions about the civilisational and racial superiority of the colonisers particularly impacted those groups in India who had fostered hopes of being incorporated into governance. Thus, at first moderate and then increasingly more radical sets of demands and challenges to colonial rule were framed against the operations of the rule of difference.

A. The Uneven Spread of Nationalist Thought

When, after 1858, there was an incremental incorporation of Indians into state services, a cadre of young men, educated in the manners of Englishmen, were mainly recruited from the centres of old Company rule. These were mostly Hindu members of an ascendant middle class who had been influenced by liberal ideologies to the extent that they would both try to forge a national culture and to demand representative government.[31] This class came to be highly distrusted by British

[29] CA Bayly, *Empire and Information: Intelligence Gathering and Social Communication in India, 1780–1870* (Cambridge, Cambridge University Press, 2000).

[30] T Metcalf, *The Aftermath of Revolt India 1857–70* (Princeton, Princeton University Press, 1964) 281.

[31] M Tudor, *The Promise of Power: The Origins of Democracy in India and Autocracy in Pakistan* (Cambridge, Cambridge University Press, 2013).

officials, who directed their attentions to renewing allegiances with what remained of a high landholding elite.

In 1885 the Indian National Congress (INC) was formed in Calcutta to raise what have been termed 'moderate nationalist demands' against the colonial government. These included the call for elected councils, 'holding the civil service examination in India as well as England, separating the judicial and executive functions' as well as decreasing the financial burden placed on India through the salt tax and home charges.[32] The notion of the continuing uneven nature of the relationship of the colonial government with its subjects would lead in the future to a more heightened anti-imperialism.[33]

From within the seams of this middle class disaffection a group consciousness amongst Muslims was also generated, one which worked in many ways with the categories of colonial knowledge production. As has been noted, the British introduced a 'framework of interpretation over India's past' that divided it into 'Hindu, Muslim and British periods' and 'they tabulated its peoples under religious headings.'[34] In the latter part of the nineteenth century the British also preoccupied themselves with the relative strength of communities and publicly affirmed the perception that Muslims were falling behind on a variety of measures.[35] In turn, such a notion of decline became a preoccupation for those populations who had perhaps lost the most from the slow dissipation of Mughal power.

The Muslims of the Central and United Provinces, where the rebellion of 1857 had played out, had initially been frozen out of governmental patronage. By 1886 Muslim communities in these regions had organised under the banner of the Aligarh movement to counsel Muslims to adopt western and scientific education. The founders at Aligarh and their adherents remained true to a view of remaining fundamentally apolitical but thereafter there was a marked generational transition towards greater political participation.

[32] H Khan, *Constitutional and Political History of Pakistan* (Karachi, Oxford University Press, 2001).

[33] CA Bayly, *Rulers, Townsmen, and Bazaars: North Indian Society in the Age of British Expansion* (Cambridge, Cambridge University Press, 1983).

[34] F Robinson, 'The British Empire and Muslim Identity in South Asia' (1998) 8 *Transactions of the Royal Historical Society* 271.

[35] PR Brass, 'Muslim Separatism in United Provinces: Social Context and Political Strategy before Partition' (1970) 5 *Economic and Political Weekly* 167, 171.

In 1892 the Indian Councils Act was passed as a response to the call for greater representation of Indians in government. Under this reform, elections were held for representatives, and amongst those contesting it was predominantly Hindu professionals who were the victors, many with Congress affiliations.

This sets the context somewhat for understanding how early anti-colonial nationalists had internalised the notion of majority rule, partly through the protocols of assembly voting. This then 'logically extended this idea of majority predominance to the larger political arena'.[36] While the INC came to be known as the party that represented Hindu–Muslim unity and a programme of official secularism, its membership was considered to be predominantly Hindu. Muslim aristocrats and landlords in the United and Central Provinces would thereafter propound the cause of separate electorates to forestall the powers of a majority Hindu populace and were in some ways offered official patronage as a counter to the reformism being demanded by the INC.

This form of early Muslim nationalism had little immediate traction in the other regions that would become part of Pakistan. Vast differences in modes of governance impacted heavily on receptivity to both secular and Muslim nationalist thought; where Muslims were in a majority, such anxieties were in any case not so great and these included all the regions that ultimately formed Pakistan.

The British policy of working with existing forces in Punjab after it became a province in 1849 ensured a broad-based loyalty and generally harmonious relations between religious communities. Colonial anthropology had determined that the populations of Punjab and the North-West Frontier were 'martial races' and fit for enlisting in the imperial army. In fact, the British relied upon Punjab as the 'source for over half the recruits to their entire Indian army'[37] and this provided a wage-based subsidy to an untold number of families. Additionally, efforts to intensify agricultural production in the Punjab were complemented by

[36] S Guha, 'The Politics of Identity and Enumeration in India c. 1600–1990' (2003) 45 *Comparative Studies in Society and History* 148.

[37] I Ali, 'Malign Growth Agricultural Colonization and the Roots of Backwardness in the Punjab' (1987) 114 *Past & Present* 110; see also I Talbot, *Punjab and the Raj: 1849–1947* (New York, Riverdale Company Publications, 1988).

statutes to safeguard against a pure monetisation of the land market, so that agrarian elites were more secure.[38]

In Sindh, a policy of non-interference by the British in the customary patterns of landholding created somewhat conducive conditions for inter-communal harmony at the elite level. A variety of organisations, both India-wide and more local, sought to organise and represent the large body of peasantry in the province, mostly along non-communal lines. Ultimately however, the disparity in representation by a middle class is what would dictate a move towards an alignment with the goals of Muslim nationalism in the province.[39]

In the North-West Frontier, the border with what would also later emerge as Afghanistan was not settled until the Durand Line was drawn in 1893.[40] For British administrative purposes the region of the Frontier was itself sub-divided into settled areas and what were termed the tribal agencies, most of which constitute the Federally Administered Tribal Areas (FATA) in present day Pakistan.[41] The Frontier Crimes Regulation of 1901 (FCR) was promulgated as the highest law in the tribal areas. The FCR established the office of Political Agent as intermediary between the central government and the local populace and such administration was unchecked by any higher law. In the appointment of Political Agents, distinctions were drawn between tribes considered loyal and the rest, who were termed 'restive, combative'. It was a system of indirect rule but one in which the British retained the right to enforce loyalty, even by means of aerial bombardment when the subject population showed signs of rebellion. While such resistance was often self-consciously aimed at overthrowing foreign rule, the British preferred to see it as an expression of traditions of warfare amongst the Pashtun and therefore not politically motivated.[42]

[38] I Ali, *The Punjab Under Imperialism, 1885–1947* (Princeton, Princeton University Press, 2014).

[39] AK Jones, *Politics in Sindh, 1907–1940: Muslim Identity and the Demand for Pakistan* (Karachi, Oxford University Press, 2002).

[40] SMM Qureshi, 'Pakhtunistan: The Frontier Dispute between Afghanistan and Pakistan' (1966) 39 *Pacific Affairs* 99.

[41] H Abbas, 'Militancy in Pakistan's Borderlands: Implications for the Nation and for the Afghan Policy' (2010) *The Century Foundation* 1, 8.

[42] M Banerjee, *The Pathan Unarmed: Opposition & Memory in the North West Frontier* (New Delhi, Oxford University Press, 2000).

Hindu domination was not perceived as a threat and therefore political forces were far more syncretic in their merger of nationalist goals and religious identity.[43]

The instability in Kalat/Balochistan was addressed by its promotion to the status of province of British India in 1877. This was only a fraction of the territory of current day Balochistan, much of the rest continued to exist as a princely state, but one which was subject to far greater political interference from the British than others. The Prince, or Khan of Kalat shared space in a system of divided sovereignty between himself and other tribal sardars under ultimate 'British supremacy'. Interestingly the ready presence of heavy troops stationed in a custom-built cantonment in Quetta lent a very garrison-like quality to the British presence in Balochistan, a colonial legacy that carries on.[44] In the lead-up to 1947, there was a percolation of some leftist thought in these areas so that organised political activity was aimed as much at displacing sardars as at their colonial masters.[45]

B. Intensified Nationalism

In Bengal, the heartland of middle-class nationalist sentiment in the early years of the twentieth century, the British fanned the flames of hostility between Muslims and Hindus by contriving the partition of the province in 1905. Muslims residing in the eastern parts 'were easily persuaded that they had much to gain from the new arrangement': the creation of a Muslim majority province.[46]

Although quickly reversed, the announcement of the partition resulted in wide-scale communal riots and a continuing mutual disaffection amongst communities. The protest movements initiated in West Bengal quickly shifted the focus of their rhetoric from the fact of partition to a direct struggle against British rule at large.

[43] See text in Chapter 1 at section V.

[44] *Balochis of Pakistan: On the Margins of History* (The Foreign Policy Centre, 2006) 1.

[45] Himayatullah Yaqubi, 'Leftist Politics in British India: A Case Study of the Muslim Majority Provinces' (2013) 34 *Pakistan Journal of History and Culture* 63.

[46] P Heehs, 'Bengali Religious Nationalism and Communalism' (1997) 1 *International Journal of Hindu Studies* 117.

The truth of an existing Indian polity was aligned in some articulations to its missing vernacular essence. Organisations such as the *Swadeshi* movement also elaborated a thoroughgoing critique of the political economy of imperialism and simultaneously distanced themselves from the Anglicised middle classes, who were perceived as having always aided the British.[47]

Sporadic violence against the colonial government and a festering fear of more insurrectionary activity pushed the government towards accommodation on the demand for responsible government. The principle of direct elections to the provincial and imperial councils recommended by the 1909 Morley-Minto reports were incorporated in the Government of India Act of the same year. The 1909 reforms also introduced the innovation of separate seats and electorates for Muslims.

The concession of group representation for Muslims was also an attempt to moderate the temper of this new political sphere. The demand had arisen primarily from an alliance of important Muslim landholders who had founded the Muslim League in 1906. The British saw them as capable of being appeased by the retention of customary rights that they had long exercised, and therefore not threatening to British control over the subcontinent. Although courted by the League, Mohammad Ali Jinnah, the renowned constitutional lawyer from Bombay, was not initially a member, even though he had first won public office through the system of separate electorates.

Through the First World War, relations between the colonial government and nationalists in India grew increasingly fraught. Alongside repressive legislation criminalising dissent,[48] the Government of India Act of 1919 broadened the franchise as well as the numbers of representatives to be elected. The Act also devolved greater powers to the provinces, but in doing so inaugurated the principle of dyarchy as an organisational tool for separating powers between the legislative and executive branch. Matters to do with revenue, finance, police and administration were reserved for nominated members of the legislature

[47] A Sartori, 'The Categorical Logic of a Colonial Nationalism: Swadeshi Bengal, 1904–1908' (2003) 23 *Comparative Studies of South Asia, Africa and the Middle East* 271.

[48] See text in Chapter 7 at section IV.

who were solely responsible to the Governor-General. Elected members of these provincial assemblies could legislate upon other matters of public works and welfare.[49] This was unsatisfactory for Indians broadly and agitational politics would gain ground in the coming years as Mohandas Gandhi assumed a more central role within the Congress party and in many ways helped to create mass support for the nationalist cause.

The year 1920 is interesting in bringing to the fore the contradictions that lay latent behind what may now seem like a teleological and certain realisation of distinct nations. The *Khilafat* movement was a wide-scale protest waged against the removal of the Ottoman Emperor, who had assumed the notional rank of *Khalifa* or 'ruler' over the global Muslim community. A campaign of civil disobedience or non-cooperation ensued, under the joint leadership of Gandhi and several distinguished members of the Indian *Ulema* (Islamic clerics).[50]

Continuing in his role of being to this point a proponent of a single civic identity for Indians across religious divides, Jinnah resigned from the INC in protest against the party's support of the Khilafat movement. He objected to the tactic of non-cooperation with the elected councils of the time and broadly considered the movement dangerous for exciting the 'irrational' religious sentiments of the masses. Jinnah would distance himself from nationalist politics and Congress at a time when 'the breach between Indian politicians began to widen' in the late 1920s, and return to the fray in 1934 as a spokesperson for the Muslim cause after his services were sought by a constellation of forces within the League.[51]

Voted life-long leader of the Muslim League, Jinnah rejoined the field of constitutional negotiations between nationalist groups and the colonial government at a point when the issues at stake had been defined in a triangular fashion. Jinnah became from that point forward the voice of a Muslim minority seeking 'sufficient' representation at the centre of a federal state. Congress differed radically insofar as it now affirmed

[49] H Khan, *Constitutional and Political History*.

[50] V Nasr, *Mawdudi and the Making of Islamic Revivalism* (New York, Oxford University Press, 1996).

[51] M Hasan, 'The Muslim Mass Contact Campaign: An Attempt at Political Mobilisation' (1986) 21 *Economic and Political Weekly* 2273.

an absolute preference for a unified electorate but shared demands for the abolition of diarchy and for a strong federal government with the League. It additionally was looking for guarantees for self-government or at least formal dominion status for India. The British at this time were playing upon the disaffection between Congress and a Jinnah-led Muslim League, and their own interests were ultimately reflected in the nature of the 1935 Government of India Act.

The 1935 Act, in addition to defining the basis of provincial autonomy, had also granted a third of total representation to Muslims at the centre of this federal structure. Friends and collaborators, like the Unionist Party in Punjab, were awarded and somewhat content with greater autonomy in the provinces.[52] Control at the top was maintained by barring Indian representatives at the centre from legislating on some vital budgetary matters, foreign relations and defence so that extensive powers remained with the Imperial Viceroy.

In the elections held after the 1935 Act came into being, Congress achieved unprecedented success at the polls in Muslim majority and minority provinces. Separate electorates had not in fact established a ready-made constituency for the Muslim League. Instead, vigorous mass-contact campaigns with Muslims and the support of the *Ulema* as well as Islamist parties had ensured these Congress victories.[53]

C. Muslim Pluralism

It is important at this point to understand that even as the League eventually sought the mandate to speak in one voice for the Muslims of the subcontinent, the field was muddied not only by the proliferation of political positions but also by faith-based groups that did not offer a determinate stance on the relationship between religion and state. For instance, the two dominant schools within south Asian Sunni Islam, Deoband[54] and Bareilvi expressed radically different stances towards

[52] A Jalal, *The Sole Spokesman: Jinnah, the Muslim League and the Demand for Pakistan*, Reprint edn (Cambridge, Cambridge University Press, 1994) 15.

[53] ibid.

[54] See, generally, Sana Haroon, 'The Rise of Deobandi Islam in the North-West Frontier Province and its implications in Colonial India and Pakistan 1914–1996' (2008) 18 *Journal of the Royal Asiatic Society* 47.

the nationalist and partition movements. The Bareilvis maintained an apolitical stance vis-à-vis the Congress-led rise of nationalist politics until close to Partition. The Deobandis on the other hand allied themselves with the Congress and counselled active participation for their adherents.

The antipathy of the Deobandis to the Muslim League and the Pakistani demand stemmed from a deep adhesion to the notion that they, as *Ulema*, would correctly guide members of the Muslim community. The idea that seemingly secular politicians such as Jinnah were seeking to represent the community in political terms challenged their priority in being able to 'interpret religious law and guide Muslim public opinion' through a 'uniform religious ideology'.[55]

An additional number of Muslim groups were actively engaged in 'staking out political positions', including but not limited to the '*Khaksars, Momins, Ahrar* and *Khudai Khidmatgar*'.[56] Amongst these, the *Khudai Khidmatgar* (Servants of God) would have a continuing place of importance in the post-independence state of Pakistan. In contrast to the rampant stereotyping of the Pakhtun as fierce, as atavistic and as bound to Islamic orthodoxy, the most potent political force to rise in the Frontier in the lead-up to Partition was dedicated to non-violence, and framed its political programme in an Islamic idiom. The Khudai Khidmatgars would enter into alliance with the Congress from the start and their leader, Abdul Ghaffar Khan, be known throughout India as Frontier Gandhi.[57]

V. CONSTITUTIONAL END-GAMES

For historians of South Asia, particularly those with a formal, legalistic bent, the real meat of partition history is located in the years that Jinnah was articulating the demands of a Muslim community. What happened in the years between 1938 and 1947 was a rapid succession

[55] See T Metcalf, *The Aftermath of Revolt India 1857–70* (Princeton, Princeton University Press, 1964) 445.

[56] B Metcalf, 'The Madrasa at Deoband: A Model for Religious Education in Modern India' (1978) 12 *Modern Asian Studies* 111.

[57] See, generally, Banerjee, *The Pathan Unarmed.*

of constitutionalist conferences and talks between great leaders of the time. These important years are interpreted in quite variant ways by historians of Partition. The famous Lahore Resolution, passed by the Muslim League in 1940, has become the hinge upon which a revisionist perspective builds its case for arguing that the creation of Pakistan reflects a failure to achieve the less extreme but ultimately unrealisable goal of a federation with equal representation between Muslims and Hindus.[58] An orthodox view is that the Lahore Resolution is the initial articulation of a demand for an independent Pakistan.

The Lahore Resolution propounded the idea that Muslims form a distinct nation, emanating from a distinct civilisation and that the issue of their being lumped into a territory as a numerical minority must be dealt with on the principle of self-determination. In addition, it called for the marking out of territory in which Muslims formed a contiguous majority, particularly in the North West and South East. The former of course contained the provinces of North-West Frontier, Sindh, Balochistan and Punjab, and the latter, the territory now called Bangladesh. This notion of providing faith-denominated populations the cover of political sovereignty introduced the idea of splitting provinces on the same lines.

Whether for the goal of equal representation or for a separate nation, the League was able to build mass support after announcing the Lahore Resolution. This support was unequally distributed around the subcontinent. While the League was a pan-Indian organisation, its outward extensions were quite loosely integrated into the strong centre controlled by Jinnah. The tension was at times opportune, as in the case of Bengal, or challenging, as in the case of Punjab.

The Muslim majority province of Bengal became a representative field for the many tensions that inhered in the definitions of Muslim statehood. The first umbrella for Muslim party politics was provided by a peasant and tenant party that formed a coalition government with the Muslim League after 1935.[59] The League itself was considerably more radical here than elsewhere, as it was forced to compete in a field

[58] A Roy, 'The High Politics of India's Partition: The Revisionist Perspective' (1990) 24 *Modern Asian Studies* 385.

[59] The *Krisha Projak* Party, see n 1, 143–145.

where socio-economic interests were foregrounded.[60] While Jinnah's tendency was to periodically rein in the populism of the local league's redistributionary sloganeering, the League's strength here reflected its inclusionary agenda, which was not readily given such centrality elsewhere.[61]

In Punjab, Jinnah was competing and oftentimes collaborating with the Punjab Unionists, who ruled that provincial assembly unbrokenly from 1937 to 1947. The Unionists sought a place at the constitutional table mainly to advocate for greater provincial autonomy. They were averse to too forceful a declaration about Muslim unity, given that their ability to control the Punjab dictated alliances with non-Muslim minorities in the province. While Unionists relied on Jinnah's services as a representative of Muslim interests at the centre, they were also quick to abandon him when he traded in aspects of provincial autonomy in favour of the minority Muslim demand for stronger central government with a parity of representation between Muslims and Hindus. In the lead-up to 1946, the Muslim League under Jinnah sought Unionist support in part by abandoning aspects of a progressive socio-economic agenda.

As the League consolidated its political programme on the ideological grounds of Muslim nationalism, global changes were auguring well for the broader demands of self-governance. The brewing of tensions in Europe and Great Britain's involvement in the Second World War were of considerable importance. Jinnah promised the Viceroy his ardent support in rallying Muslim recruits for the Imperial army, whereas Congress lost much ground during wartime as the Quit India Movement initiated by Gandhi in 1942 resulted in high-handed suppression and much of the party's high command languished in jail until 1945. In the intervening years, a succession of proposals for limited dominion government and self-rule were presented by the British, laying on the table, for the first time, the possibility of secession for Muslim majority areas from a common union at the elapse of a decade.[62]

[60] See, generally, A Hashim, *Let Us Go to War* (Dhaka, 1945); A Hashim, *The Creed of Islam* (Dhaka, Umar Bros, 1950).

[61] I Talbot, 'Planning for Pakistan, the Planning Committee of the All-India Muslim League' (1994) 28 *Modern Asian Studies* 875, 881.

[62] Simon Cripps Plan 1942.

It was against the swirling currents of alternate proposals, and with the failure of another constitutional conference in 1945 that the hard-ball stance of the Muslim League gained expression. In December of that year, elections were held and Jinnah campaigned hard for League victories. It was in these elections that the League, in its disorganised local units, sought and secured support by drawing on the allegiance of the faithful for the defence of Islam. While there was a wide-ranging syncretism to the Islam that its candidates could be seen to be professing, there was nonetheless a simple binary presented that a vote against the League was a vote to live in *Kufristan*.[63] This marked a stark departure from previous campaigns in which the issue of Muslim representation was tied to the material rather than moral uplift of the community. On a limited franchise then, the League took over power in Sindh, Bengal and for all intents and purposes, it seemed as though Congress had conceded the Muslim vote long ago.[64]

While Congress and League were still at war over what would be the dispensations post-independence, some of the widening political participation throughout the polity was expressing itself in a menacing way. The elite politics of the time had long recognised the spectre of violence that existed in its shadow. While the origins of communalist sentiment can be traced to the existence of violence and separateness that pre-existed even colonial rule here, there is no disagreement about the fact that the introduction of representative government as well as party politics hurried the articulation of the notion of distinct communities and nations. Young men were enlisting in militias and there was a general increase in communal animosity all around. The last year of British rule in India saw the outbreak of communal violence in large pockets of eastern Bengal and in numerous districts of Punjab.

When the final round of British-mediated peace talks proposed the Cabinet Mission plan, a semblance of what Jinnah could have hoped for, 'an adjustment of votes and of territorial division which would give a Hindu–Muslim balance', seemed possible.[65] Congress, although

[63] *Kufristan* is not a proper noun but is meant to denote 'land of the unbelieving'.

[64] See, generally, Y Khan, *The Great Partition: The Making of India and Pakistan* (New Haven, Yale University Press, 2007) 37; see also I Ahmed, 'The 1947 Partition of India: A Paradigm for Pathological Politics in India and Pakistan' (2002) 3 *Asian Ethnicity* 9.

[65] AG Noorani, 'The Partition of India' (2002) 18(26) *Frontline*.

initially also supportive under the Presidency of Maulana Azad, turned its back on the possibility of a weak federal centre and the grouping of provinces into broad zones where a greater degree of power would be vested. In response to this failure, Jinnah called for a day of direct action in which Muslims would, in his view, protest peacefully for a recognition of their rights. What happened instead when many thousands gathered in Calcutta to hear the speech of the Bengal Leaguer, Nazimuddin, was the fomenting of hatred and the start of a spiral of violence that would spread to neighbouring Assam from Bengal and leave over 4,000 dead in the course of a few days.[66] This would be only a mild precursor of the violence that was to ensue when the largest human migration in history would take place across a newly-drawn border.

VI. PARTITION

Whereas the British had earlier indicated 1948 as the date of their departure from India, their plans were accelerated in the aftermath of the Conservative Party's defeat at the polls and the coming to power of a Labour Government under Clement Attlee in Britain. Given the domestic issues of wartime debt and reconstruction, the government made haste in the manner of its execution.

The last imperial Viceroy was dispatched by London to Delhi and on 3 June 1947, he announced an early deadline of 15 August for British withdrawal. Although the Muslim League rejected the notion of their partition, Congress and the British sought assembly votes on whether the provinces of Bengal and Punjab would be divided. Both the assemblies returned a vote favouring such a division. What remained thereafter was for the Viceroy to announce an award on the territorial division of the subcontinent. To do this he established the Boundary Commission, headed by the British lawyer, Cyril Radcliffe.

Much of the official justification that would attend the creation of law and order states after Partition was furnished by the disorder of Partition. People faced aggravated uncertainty when confronted with a territorial division that was the product of a secret act by a man who

[66] A Mitra, 'The Great Calcutta Killings of 1946: What Went before and After' (1990) 25 *Economic and Political Weekly* 273.

knew nothing of the topography of the regions that he would divide. The need for a policing apparatus to monitor population flows was anticipated, but at the same time the high command of the Muslim League and Congress were imploring their own constituencies to stay where they were and were later to admit that there was no 'policy with regard to exchange of population'.[67] Given the uncertainty about the location of the new border until the last minute 'people in the divided provinces of Punjab and Bengal did not know until the fact whether their village was part of Pakistan or India'.[68]

It is accepted that more than 15 million people became migrants and refugees and probably close to two million people lost their lives in the violence that ensued from these disorders. However, as Aisha Jalal states about Partition, it is 'is neither beginning nor end, partition continues to influence how the peoples and states of postcolonial South Asia envisage their past, present and future.'[69] Importantly, two regions that continue to have a somewhat peripheral role within the Pakistani nation often turn to their inauspicious inclusion in the new federation to locate their marginality.

The elections of 1946 had returned a Congress Ministry in the Frontier province under the leadership of Khan Abdul Jabbar Khan. Brother of Abdul Ghaffar Khan, the two together had requested inclusion of the option to declare an independent '*Pakhtunistan*' when residents of the province were asked to vote on the question of whether to join India or Pakistan. Of the total voting population, only 55% went to the ballot but amongst them an overwhelming majority chose Pakistan. For the tribal regions of the province, the terms of accession were set with tribal elders and no attempt was made to gauge the popular will in these areas.

Ahmad Yar Khan, the 'last' Khan of Kalat, in the lead-up to Partition lent some moral support to the Muslim League and to the promise of Muslim nationhood. A close friend of Jinnah's, he signed a stand-by agreement shortly after Partition to decide at a later date the terms, if

[67] VFY Zamindar, *The Long Partition and the Making of Modern South Asia: Refugees, Boundaries, Histories* (New York, Columbia University Press, 2007).

[68] S Toor, *The State of Islam: Culture and Cold War Politics in Pakistan* (London, Pluto Press, 2011) 15.

[69] A Jalal, *The Pity of Partition: Manto's life, Times, and Work across the India-Pakistan Divide* (Princeton, Princeton University Press, 2013) 4.

there were to be any, for complete accession to Pakistan. While Jinnah established a council to ensure some representation for the Baloch in the management of their affairs, considerable pressure was simultaneously being exerted upon the Khan of Kalat to accede unconditionally at this time.[70] Then, cutting through such complications unilaterally, the Governor-General invoked the 'Extra-Provincial Jurisdiction Order' of April 1949 to establish central control in large pockets of Balochistan.[71]

The other territorial acquisitions of Pakistan included a number of princely states that were called upon to accede to either Pakistan or India by the terms of the Indian Independence Act 1947. Those that joined Pakistan included Swat, Dir, Hyderabad, Lasbela, and others. The Muslim League did not campaign hard in any of these, relying upon geography and the fact that there were Muslim leaders in all as sufficient indication that they would choose Pakistan. However, a combination of British inducement as well as Congress pressure brought even a number of Muslim princes and their majority Muslim populations into the Indian Union. These included Bhopal, Hyderabad Deccan and also, in what remains one of the most explosive unsettled territorial disputes in the world today, Kashmir.

When, after first signing a standby agreement with Pakistan, the Maharaja of Kashmir State then signed an instrument of accession with India, this was a highly contentious act. Kashmir state had a 78 per cent Muslim population, much of which was agitating against this possibility. The fact that the Radcliffe line had been drawn to keep certain districts in the Punjab on the Indian side, and thereby maintain a land-link for India to Kashmir led to heavy speculation that Britain was on side with the Indians to deny the wishes of the Muslim majority. As will be discussed in the next chapter, this created the conditions for a continuing territorial battle between the two states of India and Pakistan.

[70] The Khan of Kalat's brother led a rebellion against the Pakistani state that resulted in defeat in 1948.

[71] Axmann, *Back to the Future.*

FURTHER READING

P Chatterjee, *Nationalist Thought and the Colonial World: A Derivative Discourse* (London, Zed Books, 1993).

M Daechsel, *The Politics of Self-expression: The Urdu Middle-class Milieu in Mid-twentieth-century India and Pakistan* (London, Routledge, 2006).

A Jalal, *The Sole Spokesman: Jinnah, the Muslim League and the Demand for Pakistan*, Reprint edn (Cambridge, Cambridge University Press, 1994).

E Kolsky, *Colonial Justice in British India* (Cambridge, Cambridge University Press, 2011).

TR Metcalf, *Ideologies of the Raj—The New Cambridge History of India* (Cambridge, Cambridge University Press, 1997).

M Mukherjee, *India in the Shadows of Empire: A Legal and Political History 1774–1950* (New Delhi, Oxford University Press, 2010).

NS Sarila, *The Shadow of the Great Game: The Untold Story of India's Partition* (New Delhi, HarperCollins, 2009).

VF Zamindar, *The Long Partition and The Making Of Modern South Asia: Refugees, Boundaries, Histories* (New York, Columbia University Press, 2007).

2

State Building and Constitution Making

Military/Bureaucratic Oligarchy – Governor-General – East Pakistan – One Unit – Objectives Resolution – Ahmadiyya Movement – Ayub Khan – Doctrine of Revolutionary Legality – Bangladesh – Pakistan/Indian Wars – ZA Bhutto

JINNAH'S INAUGURAL SPEECH as the President of the Constituent Assembly is considered amongst his most important, one 'in which he clearly outlined the ideal and concept of Pakistan, its constitutional structure, and the hopes and aspirations of its people'.[1] Pakistan's leading commentator on constitutional law and history laments Jinnah's death almost immediately after Partition for having robbed the nation of a meditative force that would have enforced 'a due sense of proportion to moderate selfish aspirations and, above all, to convince the elite that the drawing up of a constitution presented a task which the nation must quickly undertake'.[2] He goes on nonetheless to acknowledge that the substantive preoccupations of these politicians were quite serious and included 'how power was to be divided between the centre and the provinces and between East and West Pakistan'. Also, given the rising influence of the Ulema they were forced to consider 'how far the shape of a modern state could be squared with the principles of Islam'.[3] Taken together, such factors are often referred to when explaining the loss of liberal democratic possibility for Pakistan.

[1] H Khan, *Constitutional and Political History of Pakistan* (Karachi, Oxford University Press, 2001) 49.

[2] Khan, *Constitutional and Political History* 64.

[3] ibid.

In presenting a political history of these early years, this chapter simply schematises these factors to suggest that there are three tendencies that converge in the early years of Pakistan's existence to explain its frequent and cyclical oscillations between democracy and militarism and the absence of a fuller flourishing of a progressive agenda that would afford distributive and formal justice for its citizens.

The first tendency is the empowerment of a military-bureaucratic elite, early on in the service of the executive powers of a constitutionally-guided state, but one which increasingly felt itself capable of bypassing constitutional rigidity altogether. The second is the sidelining of regional demands, which circumvented in the longer run a need to address progressive redistributive politics, perforce framed in the language of local inequity or provincialism. Lastly, the espousal of a state religion within the structure of a liberal constitutionalism thereafter marked a challenge for the coexistence of, at times, radically contrary normative orders.

In all, Pakistan has had three formal constitutions, passed in the years 1956, 1962 and 1973. This chapter provides an overview of the political context in which each was authored. The factors identified as influencing the course of early state development continued to impact the shape of constitutional and political developments in the country through to the passage of the Constitution of 1973. They continue to have resonance in the many shape-changing alterations made to the Constitution, as well as the less formal mechanics by which social goods are distributed throughout the polity.

I. CENTRALISATION OF POWER

The absence of public political culture that had preceded its evolution in the UK was cited as a reason for doubting the suitability of the parliamentary system for the newly-independent nations of South Asia. A recent commentary suggests the 'studied ambiguity' of such a system was nonetheless thought attractive to the high political elites involved in the making of these constitutions.[4] A good deal of the

[4] H Kumarasingham, 'Exporting executive accountability? Westminster legacies of executive power' (2013) 66 *Parliamentary Affairs* 579.

attraction lay in the fact that executive accountability in the form of institutionalised checks and balances, as per the American system, was absent. Thus, even where, as in India, 'long and detailed' constitutions were fashioned, inherited conventions were thought to be sufficient checks on executive power. The malleability of convention in that case enabled the office of the Prime Minister to accrue far greater powers in the mode of personalised rule than was first imagined.[5] In the case of Pakistan, horizontal power grabs by the Prime Minister from cabinet, and upward tugs at something akin to an illimitable sovereign power refortified the preeminence of executive government.

A striking rightward orientation of government from the moment of Pakistan's inception, in contrast even to elite discourse prior to Partition, was expressed in the consolidation of a law-and-order state. Entailed in such a description is a hierarchically-organised structure oriented to quelling dissent and regional challenge. Such tendencies had taken root from an earlier propensity within the Muslim League itself.[6] Jinnah's assumption of the title and powers associated with a colonial style 'Governor-General' reinforced the impression of authoritarian, centralising drift.

In a contrasting view though, Ayesha Jalal offers an appraisal of the move in line with the strategic objectives that Jinnah was safeguarding. According to Jalal, Jinnah recognised that Pakistan's interests would not be adequately represented if there was a common Governor- General for two Dominions, one of which was to be regarded as the 'successor' and the other as the 'seceder'.[7] If Pakistan was to survive its 'secession' it needed a strong central government which could impose its authority over provinces that for so long had been governed from New Delhi.[8]

[5] H Kumarasingham, 'The Indian Version of First among Equals—Executive Power during the First Decade of Independence' (2010) 44 *Modern Asian Studies* 709.

[6] S Toor, *The State of Islam: Culture and Cold War Politics in Pakistan* (London, Pluto Press, 2011).

[7] A Jalal 'Inheriting the Raj: Jinnah and the Governor-Generalship Issue' (1985) 19 *Modern Asian Studies* 29, 29.

[8] HA Rizvi, *The Military and Politics in Pakistan, 1947–1997*, 3rd edn (Lahore, Progressive Publishers, 1986).

The manifold difficulties of Partition included the loss of the larger part of the government of India's military machinery to India. In light of border disputes with India, Pakistan's sovereignty came to be viewed as dependent on its ability to develop adequate defence capacity to stave off the Indian threat. Importantly, the outstanding issue of Kashmir as contested territory provided the ideological legitimation for the army's resource capture in these early years.

When the Indian army violently suppressed the Kashmiri revolt against the Maharaja's accession to India in 1947, the commander of the Pakistan armed forces did not deploy troops directly but rather large contingents of 'tribal fighters' were organised and sent to aid Kashmiris in their struggle.[9] The idea of a spontaneous resistance from within Pakistan's territory fuelled the idea that 'Muslim' Kashmir needed liberating from 'Hindu' India. Upon a complaint by India to the UN, Resolution No 47 was passed, calling upon Pakistan to ensure the withdrawal of their fighters. More importantly, the resolution called for the 'democratic method of a free and impartial plebiscite' to allow for the exercise of self-determination by the Kashmiri people to decide their future as part of either India or Pakistan. In 1949, a cease-fire line was drawn through the state of Jammu and Kashmir.[10] The territory held by Pakistan has been known since as Azad [free] Jammu and Kashmir, and the 'liberation' of all of Kashmir thereafter became a part of the official and national credo of patriotic Pakistanis.

The early centrality of the army allowed it to assume a place alongside the bureaucracy and together they reinforced and benefited from the weaknesses of the young state's political sphere.[11] Given the limited nature of representative government even in late colonial India as well as the remoteness of the British legislature to Indian concerns, the bureaucratic apparatus, commandeered at the top by appointees to the Indian Civil Service, had been the 'steel frame' through which rule had been effected. Pakistan's share of Indian Civil Service personnel was limited, and to reconstitute its administrative services 'the government

[9] N Mangrio, 'A Historical and Political Perspective of Kashmir Issue' (2012) 7 *The Dialogue* 255.

[10] Karachi Agreement 1949, United Nations Peacemaker: <www.peacemaker.un.org/indiapakistan-karachiagreement49>; Truce Subcommittee of the UN Commission for India and Pakistan.

[11] See text in Chapter 3, section IIB.

decided to retain 355 British officers from amongst those already present in Pakistan and the services of 129 officers were obtained from England to meet the immediate shortage of officers.'[12] Within a weak political sphere, the existing apparatus of the civil bureaucracy was given great powers. For example, 'three of the four governors were British and former Indian Civil Service officers and two of these Governors presided over Cabinet meetings'.[13]

Early federalism was subservient to the imperatives of centralised control. With its wide-ranging powers, the central government could dismiss provincial governments and resort to Governor's rule at the least provocation. These were mechanisms available through the 1935 Act and resulted in the bolstering of central bureaucratic authority. The North West Frontier Province (NWFP), Sindh and Punjab Assemblies all suffered this fate early on.

At the federal centre, the Constituent Assembly comprised those representatives of the provincial Assemblies that had been elected according to the provisions of the 1935 Act in the elections of 1946. In addition to these members, who totaled 69 for a unified Pakistan on the eve of Partition, were added another 11 members, including representatives of the migrant population, the Princely States and other territories incorporated with varied legal statuses within the new country. The Constituent Assembly was to be the forum for deciding the features and form of the new constitution to govern these amalgamated territories. In addition it was to function as a legislative assembly until such a point that a government was established under a new constitution.

The Constituent Assembly fared no better in being able to withstand or fend off high executive assault than the provincial Assemblies, however. While during Liaquat Ali Khan's tenure as Prime Minister (1947–1951) greater powers were vested in his office in recognition of the principles of cabinet government, Prime Ministers after him were threatened by the expanse of powers that the Governor-General's office wielded. Khwaja Nazimuddin had succeeded to the post of

[12] KB Sayeed, 'The Political Role of Pakistani's Civil Service' (1985) 31 *Pacific Affairs* 131.

[13] ibid.

Governor-General at the time of Jinnah's death in 1948 and then traded office to assume the position of Prime Minister in 1951 when Liaquat Khan was assassinated. The Governor-General who succeeded him, Ghulam Muhammad, dismissed the Prime-Ministership of Nazimuddin in 1953, ostensibly for being unable to meet the demands of a law-and-order situation that had arisen in the Punjab.[14] However, the instigators of this dismissal were thought to be many: the military for having had its budget curtailed; the politicians of the Punjab who had been accused of having fomenting hate-based rioting in their province against the Ahmadiyya community;[15] and the cadre of West Pakistani bureaucrats who expressed dislike of the Bengali Nazimuddin's authority.

As Constitutional deliberations continued, the Assembly also tried to increase its powers through a number of laws aimed at amending the governmental formula implanted by way of the 1935 and 1947 Acts. Opposition to these democratic forces was on the rise and the Governor-General responded more forcefully next, dismissing the Constituent Assembly itself in 1954, just three days prior to the passage of what would have been the country's first Constitution. It was against this act that the first of the major string of cases dealing with the proper bounds of executive authority was launched, the *Maulvi Tamizzuddin*[16] case.

Maulvi Tamizzuddin Khan, Speaker of the dissolved Assembly, first sought relief at the Sindh High Court by filing writs against the Council of Ministers appointed by Ghulam Muhammad and requested that the act of dissolution be reversed. Importantly, writ jurisdiction had been accorded to the courts by the Assembly just prior to dissolution. The High Court assumed jurisdiction on this basis and granted a verdict that was favourable to the dismissed Constituent Assembly.[17] In contrast, at appeal in the Federal Court, the primary issue was reframed as whether such amendments were in fact law given that they had not been assented to by the Governor-General.

[14] Khwaja Nazimuddin had previously served as the Governor-General from Jinnah's death until 1951.

[15] See text at section III below.

[16] *Federation of Pakistan v Maulvi Tamizuddin Khan* PLD [1955] FC 240.

[17] *Moulvi Tamizuddin Khan v Federation of Pakistan* PLD [1955] Sindh 96.

Tamizzudin relied upon the Rules of Procedure framed by the Constituent Assembly to argue that the Governor-General's assent was not a necessary step in the creation of law.[18] A majority decision of the Federal Court declared that the Governor-General's assent was, however, a necessary feature of law under the two constitutional documents that were guiding all divisions of power within the government.[19] Thus the decision of the Sindh High Court was reversed and it was found to have had no lawful authority for the granting of relief. In choosing to ask the question of whether or not the Assembly had acted ultra vires in presuming to pass legislation without the authorisation of the Governor-General, the question of whether the Governor-General had exceeded his own authority in dissolving the Assembly was elided by the Federal Court.

In the subsequent 1955 *Usif Patel*[20] case, the Federal Court endeavoured to correct the Governor-General's ensuing misapprehension that the *Tamizzudin* verdict was in any way a licence for him to exercise unfettered legislative powers. Citing the general scheme of the 1935 Government of India Act and the 1947 Indian Independence Act, the court imposed limits on such powers. This then created the spectre that the executive government of the Governor-General was operating without legal authorisation in many fields. In the aftermath of *Usif Patel* and facing the possibilities of widespread nullification of laws, the Governor-General posed a reference to the Federal Court.[21] The Court was asked to determine whether 'there was any provision in the Constitution or any rule of law applicable to the situation' which would confer authorisation for the continuance of laws threatened with judicial nullification.

In a majority judgment, with two notable dissents, the court conjured up the doctrine of state necessity as the 'rule of law' to increase the Governor-General's legislative competence to provide for the continuance of these laws. Accepting that the combined force of the 1935 and 1947 Acts did not offer the Governor-General the kinds of discretionary authority he was seeking in law, this doctrine was forged from a

[18] Khan, *Constitutional and Political History*.

[19] N Hussain, *The Jurisprudence of Emergency: Colonialism and the Rule of Law* (Ann Arbor, University of Michigan Press, 2003).

[20] *Usif Patel v The Crown* PLD [1955] FC 387.

[21] Reference by HE The Governor General PLD [1955] FC 435.

variety of private law principles and some vague public law maxims. Altogether, the court condoned a range of executive acts which 'would otherwise be illegal' but for being undertaken 'under the stress of necessity'.

This initial invocation of the doctrine of state necessity gave impetus to its use in the service of validating military coups in Pakistan in subsequent decades, as detailed later in this book.[22] Nasser Hussain posits that the court invented the idea that an intractable political deadlock between executive and legislator could be mediated by 'rules' as a necessary step in illustrating the place of ultimate sovereign authority. The doctrine of state necessity provided thereby the principal rule that rules can be broken, bent or ignored when the state itself is in a situation of peril. It also accepted that the executive branch is most advantageously able to meet such peril. In the factual scenario of the army possessing disproportionate power and resources within the country, it is not too much of a leap for the judiciary to accept it as the ultimate decision-taker on matters of state necessity. The minor constraints on exceptionalism still in place with the doctrine of state necessity were altogether absent when the same court accepted the purely positivist notion of 'revolutionary legality' to justify the assumption of power by Pakistan's first military ruler, Ayub Khan, in 1958.

Altogether then, the movement towards executive centralisation was enacted through mechanics that enjoined the judiciary in their operations. In the *Governor-General's Reference*, the court categorically accepted that the powers of dissolution and of reconstitution of the Constituent Assembly were within the prerogative powers of the Governor-General. It thereby accepted that a second Constituent Assembly could be indirectly elected through the existing provincial Assemblies in May 1955, as mandated by an executive order of the Governor-General.[23] This would be the Assembly that ratified Pakistan's first Constitution in 1956.

[22] *Nusrat Bhutto v Chief of Army Staff* PLD [1977] SC 657; see also *Zafar Ali Shah v General Pervez Musharraf* PLD [2000] SC 869.

[23] S Naseer, 'Federalism and Constitutional Development in Pakistan' (2007), a paper presented at an international seminar on '*Constitutionalism and Diversity in Nepal*' organised by Centre for Nepal and Asian Studies, Kathmandu, Nepal, p 7.

II. REGIONALISM

The second tendency manifest early on in Pakistan's history was the organisation of resources and power to comport with the centralising imperatives of the government. Parochial interests undergirded the construction of a putatively national political sphere, insofar as Punjabis and Urdu-speaking migrants from Muslim minority states together occupied the larger share of positions in the central administrative structure and in the army. Pakhtuns also enjoyed levels of incorporation somewhat proportionate to their population, particularly through army enlistment. In combination, this power elite was able to represent itself as legitimate custodian of the national interest.

On the other hand, Bengalis, nearly 53 per cent of the total population were woefully under-represented in the central government. With Karachi declared capital of the new state and the army high command also mainly stationed in the Western wing, Bengali remoteness from power would increase with time. The first federal formula put in place to replace the structure provided under the 1935 Act was contrived specifically to denude Bengali majoritarianism at the centre. The containment of regional politics was such as to create other troublesome populations, leading the Sindhi and the Baloch also to voice demands for a greater share of political and economic power within the union.

While provincial Assemblies were in existence as per the 1935 Government of India Act at the moment of Pakistan's founding, there were rumours from the outset that there would be mergers across these administrative boundaries. Such advice was first dispensed by a special advisor to Governor-General Jinnah in 1948. Sir Archibald Rowland had recommended the merger of the western wing of Pakistan, comprising Sindh, Punjab, the NWFP and Balochistan in order to facilitate economic growth and development. While Jinnah did not immediately take to this advice, it steadily gained traction through the efforts of Punjabi politicians as well as the English language press, who saw in this proposal the additional benefit of being able to demand parity of representation between East and West.

Jinnah, for his part, used his powers of inducement with political leaders from the provinces to vest greater fiscal control at the centre by allowing it to be the sole collector of income tax revenue. Combined with the inability of provinces to raise sovereign debt on the open market, and given that the centre was generating over 90 per cent of all taxation revenue in the country, a situation of provincial dependency was clearly being created.[24] The National Finance Award was contrived in 1951 as the official mechanism to engineer a distribution between the provinces and the centre for governmental revenue and finances. As a formula, it provided that the centre retain between 50 and 60 per cent of overall revenue for its own uses, whereas the provinces were accorded a share of the remainder on the basis of their population.[25]

The earliest expression of regional disaffection was in Bengal. An initial demand was voiced for 'full regional autonomy' by the Parliamentary Party of the East Pakistani branch of the Muslim League itself.[26] The demand was directed to retaining power at the provincial level for all functions of government other than defence and foreign affairs. Early on, patterns of under-funding from the centralised revenue pool indicated to elite Bengalis how material inequality could compromise their status in the nation itself.[27]

Additionally, cultural chauvinism was expressed by the West when the Basic Principles Committee specified that Urdu would be the official language of government in Pakistan. This set off a slow-building agitation and was central to the creation of a coalition that won a resounding victory in the first East Bengal elections held in 1954. Shortly after being sworn in, the Assembly was dissolved by the Governor-General on the basis of spuriously-levelled charges of sedition against a leading member of the coalition.[28]

The primacy of Urdu for the power establishment at the centre was owed both to its close association with Mughal rule as well as to the centrality of the Urdu-speaking elite in the Partition movement, as recounted in Chapter 1.[29] Punjabis have always also been supportive of

[24] NR Khattak, Iftikhar Ahmed and Jangraiz Khan, 'Fiscal Decentralization in Pakistan' (2010) 49 *The Pakistan Development Review* 419, 436.

[25] R Broadway and A Shah, *Fiscal Federalism* (London, Cambridge University Press, 2009).

[26] RU Kokab, 'Constitution Making in Pakistan and East Bengal's demand for Provincial Autonomy (1947–58)' (2011) 12 *Pakistan Vision* 165.

[27] GW Choudhury, 'Bangladesh: Why it Happened' (1972) 48 *International Affairs (Royal Institute of International Affairs)* 242.

[28] A Shah, *The Army and Democracy* (Cambridge, Harvard University Press 2014).

[29] Referred to there as the Muslims from the United Province and Central Province.

Urdu as the unifying language at the national level, even as the coalition of interest between them and the migrants would come under considerable strain in subsequent decades.

Migrant Muslims from the United and Central Provinces of India were rendered *Muhajir* or refugee in the first census, and this 'official category of enumeration' continues to define them.[30] The greater number of *Muhajirs* settled in Sindh, primarily in urban centres and this established a fault-line between *Muhajirs* and Sindhis.[31] From an initial period of being a dominant minority in the new state, Muhajir power would recede in the coming decades as Punjabi dominance grew more marked, and events such as the relocation of the federal capital to Islamabad created barriers to their access to power.

In these early years, the central government set a pattern for the future by retaining the colonial policy of indirect rule for populations considered ungovernable. Thus, the Frontier Crimes Regulations of 1901 (FCR) was carried over for the administration of five tribal agencies within the NWFP. These areas were re-named the Federally Administered Tribal Areas (FATA). In 1952 a Balochistan States Union (BSU), not dissimilar to the treaty enforced by the British in the 1830s, was signed between the Khans of four Baloch territories, including Kalat. Each of these leaders 'was to receive an annual allowance and to be part of a council of rulers'. One interesting development in this period was that a minister in the cabinet of the BSU 'codified and compiled Baloch traditional law Riwaaj' and promulgated it as regular law, under the cover of the FCR, which was also administered here in parts of the province.[32]

Coinciding with the declaration of the BSU, huge reserves of natural gas were discovered in Balochistan in 1952 and commercial exploitation was begun. The mineral and energy resources of the province altered in many ways its relationship with the rest of the country. On the one hand, this development augured in a more intensified form the quasi-feudal *sardari* system, as resources were to be extracted in

[30] O Khalidi, 'From Torrent to Trickle: Indian Muslim Migration to Pakistan, 1947–97' (1998) 37 *Islamic Studies* 339.

[31] TP Wright, 'Center-Periphery Relations and Ethnic Conflict in Pakistan: Sindhis, Muhajirs, and Punjabis' (1991) 23 *Comparative Politics* 299, 303.

[32] M Axman, *Back to the Future: The Khanate of Kalat and the Genesis of Baluch Nationalism 1915–55* (Karachi, Oxford University Press, 2012) 267.

exchange for the payment of royalties to local *sardars*. On the other, the bureaucratic office of the Chief Commissioner was the mechanism for exercising central primacy in most policy domains. This continued to fuel discontent well into the future, amongst the customary rulers of the region as well as the broader population.[33]

Through these early years an establishment clique at the centre persisted in elaborating plans that would work to subsume regional demands in the West and prevent a majoritarian take-over by Bengalis at the centre. They endeavoured to do this through a refashioning of political units and by tinkering with the principles of proportional representation. Notably, this clique was not yet willing to ride roughshod over the aspirations for self-rule or representative government that had fueled the independence and Partition movements, in this drive to expand its own powers. Various plans to provide for parity, an equality of representation between the two wings in the central legislature, with or without the addition of other counter-majoritarian measures, were tabled.[34]

Finally, in November 1954, the One Unit scheme, a proposal to merge Sindh, Punjab, NWFP and Balochistan into a single province, was announced in the Assembly. Although ultimately an executive Act would make the plan a reality, the first Constituent Assembly debated the contours of the proposal prior to its dissolution.[35] As noted by Sadia Toor, the idea of forging a singular identity amongst the West Pakistani population borrowed heavily from the ideas that had earlier been used to unify Muslims across the subcontinent.[36] The irony in positing that geographical contiguity had bred similarities in primarily cultural terms was that such an argument was a rejoinder to the characterisation of Muslims, who shared a moral order deriving from common faith, as themselves a distinct nation. Politicians from East Pakistan, Bengal, were quick to point this out and a similar resistance

[33] See text in Chapter 6, section V.

[34] L Binder, *Religion and Politics in Pakistan* (Oakland, University of California Press, 1963) 313.

[35] M Nazir, *Federalism in Pakistan: Early Years* (Lahore: Pakistan Study Center, University of the Punjab, 2008) 159–60.

[36] S Toor, *Being Bengali: At Home and in the World* (London, Routledge, 2014); see also S Toor, *The State of Islam: Culture and Cold War Politics in Pakistan* (London, Pluto Press, 2011).

was voiced by political spokespersons of all but the Muhajir and the Punjabi in what became for some time (1955–70) the province of West Pakistan.

As will be seen in Chapter 6, the formal parameters of federalism have effaced some of these tensions through the mechanics of formal recognition. Nonetheless, both intra-group and centre-province relations in the federation continue to profoundly recreate situations of unrest and regional disequilibrium.

III. ISLAM

In discussing the role of Islam in these years, one should make some mention here of what is perhaps the most repeated quote from Jinnah's inaugural speech to the Constituent Assembly in 1947, one that gets continual replay even in contemporary political discussion in the country:

> You are free; you are free to go to your temples, you are free to go to your mosques or to any other places of worship in this state of Pakistan. You may belong to any religion or caste or creed—that has nothing to do with the business of the state … you will find that in course of time, Hindus would cease to be Hindus and Muslims would cease to be Muslims, not in the religious sense, because that is the personal faith of each individual, but in the political sense as citizens of the state.[37]

This public affirmation of a divide between a private realm of religious practice and a public 'political realm' of equal citizenship has faced endless challenge in the course of Pakistan's history. There was perhaps nothing controversial about the speech at the time that it was given; as shown in the previous chapter, Muslim nationalism in South Asia was not founded on the striving for a theocracy. The *Ulema*, with some exceptions, had taken a stand for a unified India prior to Partition.[38] The amplification of Jinnah's speech in the service of maintaining an official secularism needs to be understood in reference to changes that were perceptible even as it was being delivered.

[37] R Afzal, *Speeches and Statements of Quaid-e-Azam MA Jinnah* (Lahore, Research Society of Pakistan, 1966).

[38] Q Zaman, *The Ulama in Contemporary Islam: Custodians of Change* (Princeton, Princeton University Press, 2007) 32–37.

After Partition, while some classically trained jurists would try to establish a political foothold through elections, these parties would eventually face almost insurmountable competition from Abul-ala-Maudoodi, a towering figure whose influence extended through much of the Muslim world.[39] Maudoodi organised the Jamaat-e-Islami in 1941 in a unified India and after first counselling non-participation in political processes, his interest in seizing and reforming the state towards a holistic implantation of Islamic law came to be articulated. However, not just the Jamaat but seemingly secular politicians were also interested in using a universalist religious idiom for propounding certain factional interests.[40]

The first quasi-constitutional document that was forged and advanced in the Constituent Assembly was the Objectives Resolution in 1949. As a list of aspirational norms, much of what the Resolution enunciates is a banal recycling of features generally accepted as coterminous with liberal democracy: an independent judiciary and the vesting of fundamental rights in citizens. It furthermore avows the desirability of a federal system. What were considered controversial from the start, however, were the following clauses: 'Wherein the principles of democracy, freedom, equality, tolerance and social justice as enunciated by Islam shall be fully observed'; and 'Wherein the Muslims shall be enabled to order their lives in the individual and collective spheres in accordance with the teachings and requirements of Islam as set out in the Holy Quran and the Sunnah'.

Considerable debate raged in the Assembly over these clauses. Members from East Pakistan, many of them Hindu, were most vociferously denunciative. They remarked that the recognition of a religious principle in the constitutional structure of the country would mark a clear betrayal of promises made to the Bengalis in particular about the realisation of Pakistan as a multi-faith and secular state. Some of the members felt that the incorporation of religion was to 'cripple reason',

[39] See SVR Nasr, *Mawdudi and the Making of Islamic Revivalism* (New York, Oxford University Press, 1996).

[40] Noted in Report of the Court Inquiry 1954 (Punjab Disturbances), see M Munir, *Report of the Court of Inquiry constituted under Punjab act II of 1954 to enquire into the Punjab Disturbances of 1953* (Punjab, Government Printing Press, 1954).

curb the possibilities of dissent and set in train an inevitable trajectory towards authoritarianism in the country.[41]

Prime Minister Liaquat Ali Khan's defence of the Resolution was impassioned. He noted that the Resolution 'lays emphasis on the principles of democracy, freedom, equality, tolerance, and social justice and further defined them' by saying that these principles should be observed in the constitutions, as they have been enunciated by Islam. He further implied that these terms were generally used 'loosely' and thus Islam was used in the Resolution to give them a more exact meaning. To illustrate the precision which Islam lends, he made reference to the historical examples of the Ottoman Empire giving shelter to the persecuted Jews of Europe. Further, he averred to the idea that principles of social justice pervaded Islam insofar as 'it guarantees to men a life free from want and rich in freedoms'.[42]

It is important that the debate about the Objectives Resolution seems to square the existence of the Quran and the Sunnah with the status of textual authority so that authoritative pronouncements about Islamic law could be derived from them. Further, a faith in the compatibility between Islamic legal precepts and liberal democratic principles is overwhelmingly expressed. In an episode that would have far-reaching impact on constitutional development in the country and the place of minorities, the anti-Ahmadiyya movement that unfolded in the Punjab over the years 1952–1954 would severely test this notion.

The Ahmadi are a minority sect who consider themselves to be within the community of Muslims. The founder of the sect, Mirza Ghulam Ahmad (1835–1908) 'claimed the status of prophet but while upholding the supremacy of Prophet Mohammad'.[43] It has traditionally been an article of faith amongst Muslims that the Prophet Mohammad (pbuh)[44] is the 'seal' upon a long line of Prophets who brought divine revelation to the earth's inhabitants and founded the religion of Islam. Whilst Ahmad's declaration of Prophethood set off protests among

[41] GW Choudhury, *Documents and Speeches on the Constitution of Pakistan* (Dacca, Green Book House, 1967).

[42] ibid.

[43] S Saeed, 'Political Fields and Religious Movements: The Exclusions of the Ahmaddiya Community in Pakistan' (2012) 23 *Political Power and Social Theory* 189.

[44] Peace Be Upon Him.

the faithful even during his lifetime, a movement to uphold the finality of the Prophet Mohammad's revelation and counter what was considered the pernicious 'modernising' influence of the Ahmadi movement, gained its fuller expression in the years after Partition.[45]

A constellation of religious parties and *Ulema* sought the state's aid in declaring Ahmadis non-Muslim. This movement gave broad publicity to Maudoodi and the Jamaat-I-Islami. Against the backdrop of acute grain shortages, and with the aid of the Punjab Chief Minister, this movement steadily built up to rioting and attacks on Ahmadis.[46] This, in turn, led to the local declaration of martial law in the city of Lahore in 1953. Thereafter, an independent commission of enquiry headed up by Chief Justice Munir was set up to enquire into the matter of whether or not the state could or should make such a determination.[47] While the Committee famously declared that the state should not venture into the domain of fixing matters of private faith for public purposes, it did this in a circuitous manner. While warning against the prospect of using Islam to define state capacities as well as citizenship, it did invite much comment by its witnesses on whether or not Ahmadis are apostates or unbelievers. Records of the Committee's proceedings have had a long history, used alternately by Islamists and secularists.[48] The Ahmadiyya question would be resurrected again two decades later, shortly after the framing of the 1973 Constitution, the consequences of which are described further in Chapter 8.

This was not the only sectarian issue expressed in the early years to mark divides amongst the Muslims of Pakistan. A major cleavage that has come to be increasingly important is that between Shia and Sunni, the predominant sects in modern Islam. While there had been local sites even prior to Partition where Sunni and Shia conflicts about the bounds of correct, and often public practice of ritualised forms of worship had boiled over into conflict, there was much, particularly in the sense of

[45] AA Ahmed, 'The Paradoxes of Ahmadiyya Identity: The Legal Appropriation of Muslimness and the Construction of Ahmadiyya Difference' in Naveeda Khan (ed), *Beyond Crisis: A Critical Second Look at Pakistan* (New Delhi, Routledge, 2010).

[46] Khan, *Constitutional and Political History* 158–59.

[47] Munir, *Report of the Court of Inquiry*.

[48] N Khan, *Muslim Becoming: Aspirations and Skepticism in Pakistan* (Durham, Duke University Press 2012) 101–106. See also AU Qasmi, *The Ahmadis and the Politics of Religious Exclusion in Pakistan* (London, Anthem Press, 2014).

retaining a common antipathy towards the majority Hindu community and in denouncing colonial governance, that maintained political unity amongst them.[49] After Partition, the All Pakistan Shia Convention was formed to voice distinct demands informed by the jurisprudential and rights traditions inherent to the minority Shia community.[50]

The place of Islam within a constitutional order is one that inscribes authoritative judgment about the texts and sources of Islam. It does this in the context of considerable fracture and fragmentation on major issues even amongst the major branches of Sunni jurisprudence, not to mention Shiite law. It therefore begs the question of whether or not an Islamically-guided state should have a body of clergy as a constitutionally authorised source for such authoritative pronouncements on whether laws conform with Quran and Sunnah. The most liberal response to this dilemma was given by one of the ideologues of the Pakistan movement and the person considered the country's poet-laureate; Mohammad Iqbal foresaw this role as devolving upon a representative body of legislators alone, so that the mechanisms of democratic deliberation are held to be tantamount to the Islamic legislative deliberative practice of *Ijma* (consensus based deliberation). However, as Chapter 8 shows, the most thorough attempt to Islamise the constitutional and legal structure was undertaken during a period of dictatorial unaccountable military rule in the years 1977–1985.

IV. THE 1956 CONSTITUTION

The second Constituent Assembly delivered Pakistan's first Constitution in 1956. It enjoyed only brief historical existence as the highest law of the land. Altogether, the first Constitution could have set back some of the centralising and authoritarian tendencies of the foundling state as the Constituent Assembly was engaged in wresting power back for the political sphere against the claims of discretionary and arbitrary executive authority. The unicameral legislative assembly that was

[49] MH Hasan, 'Sectarianism in Indian Islam: The Shia-Sunni divide in the United Provinces' (1990) 27 *Indian Economic Social History Review* 209.

[50] A Rieck, 'The Struggle for Equal Rights as a Minority: Shia Communal Organizations in Pakistan 1948–1968' in R Brunner and W Ende (eds), *The Twelver Shia in Modern Times: Religious Culture and Political History* (Leiden, Brill, 2000) 275.

proposed had parity of representation between the two territorial wings of Pakistan. It was to be filled by 300 members elected by a general vote with the addition of ten women members elected solely by women in their exercise of a dual franchise.[51]

Given the broad basis of the anti-British agitations that had led to independence, it remained a fairly settled matter that the Constitution would contain a list of fundamental rights somewhat in conformity with the American Bill of Rights. Thus, the list of such enumerated rights included 'familiar liberties such as equality of status, of opportunity and before law; social, economic, and political justice; freedom of thought, expression, belief, faith, worship, and association'.[52] In addition, 'the federal government, the National Assembly, a provisional government or legislature, or any local authority'[53] were barred from making any laws repugnant to any of the fundamental rights and to the extent that any such law was repugnant, it could be held to be void.

The machinery for redressal of rights violations by citizens or affected parties was that of a refashioned superior court system. The Supreme Court had replaced the old Federal Court and a system of High Courts was established for each of the provinces. Courts were given broad powers and writ jurisdiction was constitutionally conferred. The situation was and remains thereby somewhat different from the UK, where it is stated authority that writ jurisdiction can be taken away by a mere act of parliament.[54]

The balance of powers between executive and legislature was deeply contested within the Constituent Assembly debates. This Constitution provided that representative actors would exist at the pinnacle of both branches of government. While the 1935 Act had enabled the Governor-General to appoint a cabinet and allow it to retain power subject to his pleasure, this power was whittled down for the President, so that the acts of summoning, proroguing or dissolving the National Assembly were to be undertaken 'on the advice of the cabinet'. The President was to appoint the Prime Minister 'in his discretion' from

[51] See text in Chapter 7, section III.

[52] Khan, *Constitutional and Political History* 168.

[53] ibid.

[54] AK Brohi, *Fundamental Law of Pakistan* (Lahore, Din Muhammad Press, 1958) 449.

amongst the members of the National Assembly as the person 'most likely to command the confidence of the majority of the members of the national assembly'. As with the colonial Governor-General, the President retained the right to promulgate laws, called Ordinances, a continuing power that is described further in the Executive Chapter.[55]

In terms of regional politics, federal, concurrent and provincial lists of legislative competence established initially by the 1935 Act were carried over in form.[56] The powers accorded to provinces were increased and important areas including industries and railways were apportioned to them. Residuary powers, those subjects not enumerated within the lists, were to be assumed by the provinces. However, as against the demands of members from East Pakistan, the issues involved with fiscal transfer and the like were not settled towards equal sharing between the two wings.

Already by the 1950s, strong biases in economic development had emerged which were blatantly tilted against the eastern wing. For example, state institutions in the 1950s such as PICIC (Pakistan Industrial Credit and Investment Corporation) and PIFCO (Pakistan Industrial Finance Company) concentrated on industries in West Pakistan.[57] Similarly, there was a strong anti-East bias through the provisioning of finance and loans for further institutional and infrastructural development. The flourishing industries of the West were a stark contrast to the realities of underdevelopment in the East.[58]

As counter to the above, a major accommodation to Bengali sentiment was made in the pronouncement that Urdu and Bengali would share the status of official state language. By the time of the Constitution's promulgation, political elites in the East were seeking reconciliation with the centre.[59] They welcomed guarantees for greater representation within the bureaucracy and military being offered at the time.

[55] See text in Chapter 4, section VI.

[56] See text in Chapter 6, section IIIA.

[57] AS Zaidi, 'The Political Economy of Decentralistion in Pakistan' Transversal Theme 'Decentralisation and Social Movements' (2005) 1 *Swiss National Centre of Competence in Research* 7.

[58] AV Desai, 'Case for Bangla Nationalism' (1971) 6 *Economic and Political Weekly* 1035.

[59] MA Zaman, 'Emergence of Bangladesh Its Historical Perspective' (1975) 25 *Civilisations* 272, 275–76.

Lastly, this Constitution declared that Pakistan was an Islamic nation and that within an elapse of six years existing laws would be brought into conformity with the guidance provided by the Quran and Sunnah.[60] All laws held to be repugnant to the Quran and Sunnah would also be considered to be void. However, the question of repugnancy and thus voidability was to be addressed within the National Assembly itself. There was not, at this point, a deferral to the courts for making declarations about the correct interpretation or application of what could cumulatively be understood as Shariat.

V. AYUB AND THE 1962 CONSTITUTION

The 1956 Constitution was abrogated before an election was held or a government sworn in under its provisions. A lifelong bureaucrat, Iskander Mirza, deposed the Governor-General, who was out of the country on account of illness in 1955, and then was elected President by the Assembly when the Constitution defined this role in 1956. A delay in elections led to a period of heightened political turmoil and frequent changes at the head of government. These governments faced quite straightened circumstances, dealing with food shortages, balance of payments deficits, and the continuing problems associated with the resettlement of Partition refugees. The military struck a fairly strong-footed alliance with the US by signing the Mutual Defence Assistance Treaty, whereby arms and weapons transfers were considerably speeded up. In March 1957 Iskander Mirza declared Presidential rule.

When then the Khan of Kalat declared independence for Kalat from Pakistan, President Mirza proclaimed martial law and named General Ayub Khan the Chief Martial Law Administrator. Assemblies and provincial governments were dissolved, political parties were abolished, group meetings were banned, politicians were arrested, and martial law regulations replaced the Constitution.[61] Former allies Ayub and Iskander differed on key matters and finally, with evidence that the army was backing him, Ayub took direct power by displacing Iskander.

That this takeover of power did not face widespread or popular opposition was a factor that was cited in the famous *Dosso* case, which

[60] Constitution of Pakistan 1956, Art 198.

[61] Khan, *Constitutional and Political History* 118.

effectively legitimised this coup.[62] *Dosso* also articulated the now famous revolutionary legality doctrine. Having no precedent in common law, it was a doctrine fashioned from the theoretical postulations of the Austrian jurist Hans Kelsen, who reportedly later clarified that the judgment has misrepresented his work. In *Dosso* the court accepted that an effective transfer of power had shifted the *grundnorm*, the highest norm that grounds all further positive laws including the constitution, so that a wholly new legal order was in place. Unlike the doctrine of state necessity, revolutionary legality would not be revived to legitimate extra-constitutional takeovers of power, largely due to the decision in *Asma Jilani*,[63] described below.

Having learnt from the missteps of Ghulam Mohammad in the years 1954–55, the military regime now led by President Ayub Khan issued a set of supreme commandments to exercise de facto rule, towards restoring the body politic into a governable entity. Thus, although the Constitution itself had been abrogated by Mirza, the 1958 Laws (Continuance in Force) Order was passed to ensure the functioning and legitimacy of existing law and civil institutions.

Ayub would institute wide-ranging changes to the structure of government, doing away with the democratic pretensions of early years. In fact, in his retrospective position on the matter, the defenders of democracy who suggested that Ayub's assumption of power retarded its realisation were characterised as arguing that 'we did not have a long enough rope to hang ourselves with'.[64] He located the impossibility of realising democracy in the Pakistani terrain as flowing from the fractious nature of the Pakistani political sphere, which spawned endless parties and did not allow for stable coalitions. Both this and the somewhat messianic zeal of imparting a programme of multifaceted 'reform' are the factors that allowed him to proclaim his economic and political policies as 'revolution'.

The Constitution that Ayub eventually fashioned differed in substantial ways even from the conservative recommendations offered by

[62] *State v Dosso* PLD [1958] SC 533.

[63] *Asma Jilani v Government of the Punjab* PLD [1972] SC 139.

[64] MA Khan, *Field Marshal Mohammad Ayub Khan: A Selection of Talks and Interviews, 1964–1967*, Nadia Ghani edn (Lahore, Oxford University Press, 2010) 133.

a Constitutional Commission that he himself had appointed in 1960.[65] Commission members had suggested that parliamentary government was now innately a part of the South Asian genus, given its incremental introduction through the colonial experience. As Chief Martial Law Administrator, Ayub had, by 1960, instituted the 'Basic Democracy' system. It allowed for the creation of an electoral college through local, non-party elections throughout Pakistan and they in turn gave him an overwhelming mandate to promulgate his Constitution from the office of President.[66] Thus empowered, Ayub offered up a system of government that enshrined a pyramidical structure of assemblies beginning with the creation of 80,000 constituencies across the country. The Constitution was presidential insofar as he/she would hold the power to veto any legislative action, as well as powers for the appointment of many important offices, including the Governors of provinces, the Chief Justice of the Supreme and High Courts as well as retaining emergency powers.[67] It was, in short, a Constitution that exhibited a general distaste for politics and politicians, and by extension the people they would represent. A range of formal limitations on political participation through the mechanics of disqualification of politicians and the control of political parties were operationalised in this era.[68]

The Constitution specifically barred the Supreme Court from exercising jurisdiction in any area not directly conferred by it. It limited writ jurisdiction to High Courts and severely circumscribed its availability.[69] In addition, although it provided a list of 'principles of law' that were to guide the legislature in the making of law, judicial review on the basis of such principles was specifically disallowed. These principles included freedom of speech, freedom from arbitrary arrest and a host of other human rights. Significant changes were augured in through the First and Second Amendments to this Constitution. Whereas the original Constitution had been promulgated for the Republic of Pakistan, the first amendment was an act of rechristening the country the 'Islamic

[65] KB Sayeed, 'Pakistan's Constitutional Autocracy' (1963–64) 36 *Pacific Affairs* 365.

[66] Basic Democracies Order 1959.

[67] See Constitution of Pakistan 1962, Arts 30, 50, 66 and 92.

[68] See text in Chapter 3, section IIB.

[69] See Constitution of Pakistan 1962, Art 98.

Republic of Pakistan'.[70] The second amendment allowed for principles of law to be justiciable insofar as 'laws inconsistent or in derogation' of such enumerated rights could be held to be void.

The 1962 Constitution provided for a formal distribution of powers between the centre and the provinces, but one that worked in favour of the centre. A Third Schedule provided an expansive list of areas for exclusive federal jurisdiction and included the express provision that 'where the national interest' including the goals of maintaining security, financial stability, planning and coordination and the achievement of uniformity, were at stake, the central legislature could act without being questioned over want of jurisdiction.

Importantly in this era of heavy administrative centralisation, Bengalis, Baloch and Sindhis were vastly underrepresented in the military and in the federal bureaucracy. As things would not have noticeably improved, a 1955 tabulation suggests that there were no Bengalis at the level of General or Major-General, and for ranks thereunder on average only 1–2 per cent of the total strength at the intermediary ranks of Colonel and Major. For the bureaucracy, again, no Bengali occupied the highest office of Federal Secretary and for the ranks below, including Additional and Deputy Secretary, themselves highly powerful posts within the Provincial Civil Services (PCS), they consistently remained below the 10 per cent threshold.[71] Rather than seeking to placate regionalist discontent, Ayub sought in fact to insulate the operations of government further and moved the capital from Karachi to a purpose-built capital in northern Punjab, Islamabad. This alienated Muhajirs as well and set in train a decline in their centrality within the governance structure.

The authoritarianism of the Ayub regime was exercised through such measures as the tight regulation and frequent censorship of the press.[72] He also regularly achieved denunciation from Bar Associations across the country for having made public statements disparaging their profession. However, the Assembly and after the passage of the First Amendment to the Constitution mentioned above, the courts also became the site for the ventilation of grievance and some challenges to

[70] See Report of the Constitution Commission 1962.

[71] MM Khan, 'Ruling Elite and Major Administrative Reforms: the Case of the Pakistan Civil Service' (1980) 41 *Indian Journal of Political Science* 729.

[72] Press and Publications Ordinance of 1963.

governmental authority, often through use of their writ jurisdictional powers.[73]

Popular opposition to Ayub grew and disparate, as well as at times antagonistic, agendas aligned. The Jamaat-i-Islami, which wanted to see reversals of the modernisation of personal laws through the 1961 Muslim Family Law Ordinance, shared a platform with the deeply secular National Awami Party and many others to form the Combined Opposition Party (COP).[74] In 1965 Ayub, as per the Constitution, was forced into calling a presidential election, albeit an indirect one on the basis of the electoral college of local bodies' electors. The COP lent its full support to Ayub's rival and the sister of Mohammad Ali Jinnah, Fatima Jinnah. While the results were closer in the East than in the West, it was a definitive victory for Ayub, albeit one plagued by allegations of rigging. In characteristic arrogance, Ayub would later say that Fatima Jinnah and the opposition had been 'trying to fool people into believing that their rights had been denied under the 1962 constitution'.[75]

Later in 1965 an event of considerable significance—war with India—would cleave through the existing disparities between East and West Pakistan to leave them even more remote from each other. The absence of accounting for the East's defence at the time of the war became a significant rallying cry against the central government. In addition, the deliberations of the National Assembly registered a higher level of concern being raised about the relative underdevelopment of the East's economy. The composition of this Assembly itself reflected the relative ascendance of an educated cadre vis-à-vis the diminishing power of landholders coming from the East; whereas from the West a mostly conformist landlord class with some power-sharing with a rising industrialist mercantile class offered greater support to presidential dictate. In addition to the trouble in the Eastern Wing, the long sublated ethnic tensions in the Western wing were starting to boil over. Most damagingly for Ayub, members of his own cabinet were

[73] R Braibanti, 'Public Bureaucracy and Judiciary in Pakistan' in J Khan (ed), *Evolution of Pakistan's Administrative System* (Islamabad, Pakistan Public Administration Research Centre, 1987) 38.

[74] M Rashiduzzaman, 'The National Awami Party of Pakistan: Leftist Politics in Crisis' (1970) 43 *Pacific Affairs* 394.

[75] Khan, *Field Marshal Mohammad Ayub Khan* 177.

defecting—most famously Zulfiqar Ali Bhutto, in his case to help establish the Pakistan People's Party in 1967.

VI. YAHYA/BANGLADESH

After widespread student and labour agitation against the increasingly authoritarian rule of Ayub helped to displace him from power, he was succeeded by another General, against the formula for succession established under the 1962 Constitution. General Yahya Khan placed the country under martial law in 1969 and abrogated the Constitution. He also issued a range of orders that would form the basis of a challenge to the whole edifice of martial law through the *Asma Jilani* case discussed below.

Yahya declared an intention to hold elections under the Legal Framework Order of 1970. The Order dissolved the One Unit system and decreed that the basis of the coming elections would be strict proportional representation. Sheikh Mujibur Rehman led the Awami League to a decisive win in Bengal and thereby gained the majority of seats at the Centre. He campaigned on the platform of a renewed federation centred on a list of demands, the Six Points.

The Six Points indicated that the fiscal, administrative and security apparatus should be expressly controlled through constitutional means. They also contained a proposal to limit federal powers to controlling only currency, foreign affairs and defence. Zulfiqar Bhutto, as leader of the Pakistan People's Party (PPP), which commanded the second greatest number of seats in the Assembly, declared that the Six Points in practice would lead to an effective dissolution of the federation.

It is not hard to see how, given a shared history of nearly 30 years, the growing disparities in opportunities between East and West necessitated a thoroughgoing renegotiation that would unearth the real basis of such inequality, beyond simply the focus on issues of representation alone. Mujib's demand was for a viable nation and he was bargaining for the right to rule over all of Pakistan in the negotiations that would get underway soon after the elections.

Yahya stalled on calling an Assembly. Following the failure of negotiations between Mujib and Yahya, and then between Mujib and Bhutto, 'Operation Searchlight' was launched by the military to identify recalcitrance from the Bengalis by March 1971. The violence unleashed by the Pakistani army was unremitting, so much so that this year is recalled as the 'year of chaos' amongst Bengalis who lived through the events.[76]

India had surreptitiously been supplying arms and aiding secessionist groups within East Bengal but intervened outright when such rebels were unable to match the force of the Pakistan army. It used the pretext of a large influx of Bengali refugees into its territory and made a general worldwide case for 'humanitarian invasion' for its eventual involvement, leading the Pakistanis to counter-strike in Western India.[77] It was a short-lived war and the Pakistani army laid down its arms, its commanders having their stripes cut and surrendering their badges to the Bengalis who for posterity within Pakistan would be remembered unfairly as traitors rather than as people who were seeking redress for their grievances.

The conditions for an independent Bangladesh were not propitious, 'drained of economic resources over the past decades, with little industry, with an acute shortage of trained administrators, with no army to speak of'.[78] It has thus been inferred that it was not Mujib's desire to secede altogether, much in the way that revisionists argue in reference to the Pakistan demand, as discussed in the previous chapter. Nonetheless, independence was declared by Bangladesh in March 1971, Yahya resigned on 20 December 1971 and asked Bhutto to assume the position of Chief Martial Law Administrator, which he accepted and then relinquished in favour of the office of President under a new interim Constitution the following year.

East Pakistan's succession was the second instance of mass violence that had beset a state born in the throes of turmoil and human transfer. However, even as some of the war against India was experienced in West Pakistan, the absence of direct experience of what was

[76] *Gondogoler Bochor* is the Bengali term. See N Mookherjee, 'Denunciatory practices and the constitutive role of collaboration of the Bangladesh war' in S Thiranagama and T Kelly (eds), *Traitors: Suspicion, Intimacy and the Ethics of State-Building* (Philadelphia, University of Pennsylvania Press, 2010) 62.

[77] S Ganguly, *Conflict Unending: India-Pakistan Tensions since 1947* (New York, Columbia University Press, 2013).

[78] P Oldenbury, 'A Place Insufficiently Imagined: Language, Belief, and the Pakistan Crisis of 1971' (1985) 44 *The Journal of Asian* Studies 711, 714.

happening in the East has resulted in vast denial of the army's role in perpetrating a veritable genocide there.[79] No official apology has been tendered from the Pakistani government or military to the Bangladeshi people. A judicial enquiry commissioned in 1972 submitted a report that remained classified until 2009. Although it laid blame on a range of politicians and military functionaries, it has never been made the basis for even mild rebuke of those involved.

VII. THE 1973 CONSTITUTION

The Constitution looked at in detail through the remainder of this book is the one Zulfiqar Ali Bhutto is credited with having gifted to the nation; he was the President under whose aegis it was drafted in 1973. After assuming power, Bhutto's first act was to call on the leaders of all the parliamentary parties to contribute to building a consensus about the nature of the new Constitution that would govern Pakistan. While himself a proponent of a strong presidential system, a series of compromises would lead to the promulgation of a Constitution that provided for a federal parliamentary system.

The federation was to comprise the four provinces, FATA, the Northern Areas, and Azad Jammu and Kashmir; and the formula of power sharing seemingly one that favoured devolution to a greater extent than in 1962. The Prime Minister was also designated the Chief Executive and Head of Government. He could only be removed by a vote of no-confidence of the Assembly. The President would be the Head of State, voted in by a joint session of the bicameral legislature and act only on the advice of the Prime Minister. The upper house of the legislature, the Senate, was conceived as a counter-majoritarian, regionally representative, and indirectly-elected body. The system of proportional representation that was the electoral formula for the 1971 elections was retained for the lower house, the National Assembly. Additionally, an expansive list of fundamental rights was guaranteed for citizens and, for some rights at least, other non-citizen residents of Pakistan.

[79] S Bose, *Dead Reckoning: Memories of the 1971 Bangladesh War* (London, C Hurst and Co Publishers, 2011).

Although Bhutto traded the office of President for that of Prime Minister, his record was not one of steadfast adherence to this constitutional division of powers. While he would succeed through much of his tenure to keep the army occupied and away from politics,[80] it must be noted that Bhutto's inheritance and choice in many ways was to replicate the style and substance of martial rule. The class basis of the support that the PPP had secured was quite diverse and included the ranks of the small peasantry, students and the urban working class. Nonetheless, the basis of power for the regime was in fact an insecure coalition of 'the military-bureaucratic elite, the urban bourgeoisie, the landowners and the neo-colonialist military-capital interests'[81] and its role was to mediate, through strong central governance, the competition between them. Thus, in reference to both electoral and strategic power, the choice was to adopt constitutional divisions of power and decentralise through federalism, whilst enabling the military in particular to remain strong by bolstering its budget and enforcing laws that restricted criticism of it.

Significantly, Bhutto used an emergency provision of the Constitution to whittle down the expanse of fundamental rights guarantees on the day that the Constitution was passed. Further, his regime passed a number of constitutional amendments aimed at curtailing the powers of the judiciary and undermining its independence. While Bhutto was actively engaged in seeking to insulate and expand his powers as Prime Minister, he was also establishing the conditions for his own demise. One regrettable aspect of this was the way in which he himself compromised judicial independence.[82]

In 1973 the Supreme Court had delivered a verdict on Yahya's rule which declared him a usurper to power and the doctrine of revolutionary legality inapplicable to his claims for power. The case was decided after Yahya had been ousted, but was significant nonetheless for articulating a higher morality to ground valid laws and legitimate authority. Had a strict line been drawn from this, the *Asma Jilani* case onwards, it is hard to see how the two military coups following the passage of the 1973 Constitution could have been validated so readily by the courts.

[80] I Ali, 'The Balochistan Problem' (2005) 58 *Pakistan Horizon* 41.

[81] A Ahmad, 'Editorial: Whither PPP?' (1972) 3 *Pakistan Forum* 3.

[82] See text in Chapter 5, section IB.

However, both for political expedience and in the pursuit of radical transformations through a programme of Islamic socialism, Bhutto coopted the courts into his enterprise of rule. Thus, when Bhutto took special interest in the dispensation of a case involving army personnel who had helped to dispose Yahya in an act of mutiny, allegedly to install one of Bhutto's competitors in power, the Supreme Court compliantly delivered a judgment that upended many of the principles that *Asma Jilani* had elaborated.[83] The case was an appeal by these former officers not to be tried by military tribunals, as Yahya had authored the change in law that allowed for such trial of retired officers. Whereas *Jilani* had laid out the principle that only those acts of a usurper that were conducive to the good of the populace would be condoned, in the *FB Ali* judgment it was given that neither standard of 'reason or morality' nor any 'philosophical concepts of law' would be the means of judging the validity of existing law. Rather 'positive law, that is to say, a formal pronouncement of the will of a competent law-giver' is always to be construed as valid.[84]

The tension between seeking a higher law to contain executive and legislative powers as against the maintenance of a minimalist position of according deference to procedural validity has played out repeatedly in the higher courts in the decades since the passage of the 1973 Constitution. This is discussed in subsequent chapters through a number of cases, in which the *basic structure doctrine* is employed to argue that such a higher law exists in the form of ascertainable principles that undergird the Constitution as a whole.[85] This tension was ablated during Bhutto's rule through the determinate affirmation of a minimalist position by the court, and this surely indicated to another usurper, Zia-ul-Haq, that the judiciary could be relied upon to abstain from straining itself in complicated jurisprudential exercises.

There have been two lengthy military dictatorships, which followed upon the promulgation of the 1973 Constitution, both validated by courts through the doctrine of state necessity. General Zia engineered the second coup in Pakistan's history in 1977, declared martial law and eventually ensured Bhutto's execution. Seven years of his reign (1977–1988) occurred in a state of constitutional abeyance. The 1973

83 For further discussion see text in Chapter 8, section IIB.

84 *FB Ali v The State* PLD [1975] SC 506.

85 See text in Chapter 5, section VI.

Constitution was only restored after significant alterations were made through the Eighth Amendment of 1985. The most significant change augured by this instrument was to bolster the powers of the President, to the extent that he could order the dissolution of elected Assemblies on the basis of fairly broad criteria.

It was only in such conditions that Zia could countenance the return of democracy, which during his life was controlled to the further extent of ensuring that the first electoral exercise of 1985 was held on a non-party basis. When in 1988 the first free elections were held after Zia's death, the government that was installed had Benazir Bhutto, daughter of Zulfiqar, as its Prime Minister. However, this Assembly was dissolved by President Ghulam Ishaque in 1990. Nawaz Sharif, a favourite of the establishment that included the army elite and the President was then elected in 1990 but his government too was to face the same fate, now at the elapse of three years. Bhutto and Sharif would each have one more reign in power during the 1990s but neither, again, was able to complete their constitutionally-mandated term of five years in office. Although Sharif ensured the passage of the Thirteenth Amendment to the constitution, taking away the President's powers of dissolution, the seizure of power by General Parvez Musharraf in 1999 was the means by which this Assembly and Sharif's majority government stood dissolved.[86]

By the time that General Musharraf engineered his coup in 1998, a previously authored script for military rulers engaging in such extra-constitutional acts was available for reenactment. Like Zia before him, Musharraf administered a loyalty oath upon members of the higher judiciary and promulgated a Provisional Constitutional Order. One stark difference was that he was compelled by a judicial decision to reconstitute the National Assembly within three years from the time that he assumed the office of President. Ultimately, Musharraf's reign tottered when a popular uprising framed in the idiom of rule of law set in chain a series of events that led to elections and the assumption of power by a People's Party government in 2008. This was to be the first Assembly in Pakistan's history that both served its mandated five-year term and was smoothly succeeded by another elected government.

[86] See text in Chapter 4, sections II and IV.

FURTHER READING

H Alavi, 'State and Class under Peripheral Capitalism' in H Alavi and T Shanin (eds), *Introduction to the Sociology of 'Developing Societies'* (London, Macmillan, 1982).

M Daechsel, 'Sovereignty, Governmentality and Development in Ayub's Pakistan: the Case of Korangi Township' (2011) 45 *Modern Asian Studies* 131.

SA Zaidi, *Issues in Pakistan's Economy: A Political Economy Perspective* (Karachi, Oxford University Press, 2015).

3

Representative Government

National Assembly – Senate – Voting Practices – Political Parties – Political Sphere – Elections – Disqualifications – Rigging – Militancy

THE CONSTITUTION OF 1973, as we have seen from the previous chapter, was birthed afresh to redress grievances long fostered against military and centralised rule under Ayub. This Constitution mandated parliamentary democracy based upon universal suffrage, and direct elections as the form of government. In what is now the fourth decade of this Constitution's existence, radical discontinuity imposed through recurrent military rule and executive consolidation has reshaped the structure of government anticipated by its drafters.

From this chapter onwards, a topical rather than linear account of constitutional development in Pakistan is presented. However, the haziness that attends the project of describing governmental structure, what many consider to be the core attribute of constitutionalism, requires that the identification of the major disjunctive events of these last few decades be undertaken at the outset. The first major event was the seizure of the state by General Zia in 1977, his suspension of the Constitution until 1985, when it was restored in an altered, quasi-presidential form. Zia sought legitimacy, importantly, in the promotion of Islam and thereby reshaped the political sphere, including by way of dividing the electorate on the basis of faith. In almost direct emulation, in 2002 General Musharraf resurrected the Constitution in a form similar to that earlier contrived by Zia. As opposed to Zia's Islamic reformation, Musharraf's choice of legitimating rubrics, including anti-Islamic militancy, anti-corruption and a technocratic developmentalism also impacted the realm of electoral politics. As discussed in this and the following chapter, the mimetic cycle between these military rulers was not exclusive to them but also influenced the actions of civilian politicians who either shared power with, or defiantly sought to insulate their power from, military actors.

A set of constitutional revisions enacted in 1985 went to the bone of parliamentary structure by including the President amongst the institutions of Parliament's composition. More recent alterations, importantly through the Eighteenth Amendment Act of 2010, have been oriented to increasing the independence and supremacy of the elected assemblies. However, the mere fact that the President is formally still a placeholder in Parliament indicates the ways in which the initial breach of a trichotomous order has gained base subsistence in the governmental structure. This is also discussed in greater detail in Chapter 4.

Importantly, the recurrence of military takeovers has impacted on—but not displaced—the electoral arena of representative politics. In all episodes of military rule, regimes have sought legitimation through elections and the establishment of assemblies so that the political arena has not itself been closed down for very long. Rather, the elaborate regulation of political parties and politicians has been aimed at redrawing the political terrain to bring it into alignment with central control. Resort to such mechanisms is not the exclusive preserve of military regimes, and governing parties have also engaged the apparatus of the state in seeking to curtail or bar the activities of rival politicians and parties. However, through challenges to such mechanisms of control, the judicial elaboration of foundational political rights has slowly defined a protected realm of recognition and immunities for political actors.

As a formally more autonomous political sphere takes shape, the nature of political contests is also changing. For instance, the conduct of elections is increasingly challenged and subjected to judicial review. While the drive to make elections conform to principles of fair play is an important one, it is looked at here in the context of another perceptible shift in political practice. This is the marked narrowing that has happened in terms of the class of persons who contest and win electoral office, as well as the limitations of any meaningful political programmes and choice for the poor in particular.

I. PARLIAMENTARY STRUCTURE

Article 50 of the 1973 Constitution provides that 'Parliament shall consist of the President and two houses to be known respectively as the National Assembly and the Senate'. The formula of electing representatives to the two assemblies is described below and, following that, the relative place of each assembly in the broader legislative process is detailed. Finally, the issue of presidential inclusion in the parliamentary structure, by way of an amendment to the Constitution dating to 1985, is discussed with reference to its impact on legislative processes.

A. Representation

Article 51 lays out numbers and classes of seats to be occupied through a mixed system of representation for the lower house, the National Assembly. The majority of the 272 seats in the lower house of Parliament are 'single-member territorial constituencies' where representatives are 'elected by direct and free vote in accordance with law'. These general seats have been apportioned to the provinces, Federally Administered Tribal Areas (FATA) and the federal capitals 'on the basis of population in accordance with the preceding census officially published'.

In addition to these general seats, an allocation for women's seats is made to political parties to fill in accordance with the share of general seats won in a given election. In the making of the 1973 Constitution, 20 seats in total, for a period to last 10 years, were marked as women's seats.[1] However, when elections were once again held from 1985, the provision had lapsed and there were no reserved seats for women until 2002.[2] The total number of such seats is now 60, as per the Conduct of General Elections Order of 2002, promulgated by General Musharraf.[3]

[1] See 'Legislative Quotas for Women: A Global & South Asian Overview of Types and Numbers' (2012) Aurat Foundation, available at af.org.pk/Publications/1358744372.pdf.

[2] See *Afroze Ehsan Haq v Government of Pakistan* PLD [1995] Karachi 56; see also *Begum Shireen Bahar Cheema v Federation of Pakistan* PLD [1993] Lahore 822.

[3] M Krook and Diana Z O'Brien, 'The Politics of Group Representation: Quotas for Women and Minorities Worldwide' (2010) 42 *Comparative Politics* 253. Note: a far smaller number of seats was reserved for women by Ayub and then Yahya.

Women are not barred, nor have they been in any electoral contest, from campaigning for general seats.

The other class of seats also filled on the basis of proportional representation is non-Muslim minority seats. In the previous two Constitutions, religious minorities were accorded no special or differential status in terms of political representation, although the Second Constituent Assembly did vote on dividing the electoral system for West Pakistan between Muslims and Non-Muslims after the 1956 Constitution had been passed. The Fourth Amendment to the 1973 Constitution introduced six minority seats to be filled in the same manner as women's seats. In 1985 the Zia regime increased the number of these seats to ten, but also provided that the electorate was to be split between Muslims and non-Muslims. A challenge to the Supreme Court alleging discriminatory treatment failed in 1989 and the system of apartheid-like dual electorates was in place for a total of five elections.[4] A unified electorate was restored in 2002, while the ten minority seats were retained as special representation for minorities. While Musharraf's 2002 Conduct of General Elections Order also removed the stipulation that prevented non-Muslim minorities from contesting general seats,[5] the need for candidates to declare their religion, coupled with the criteria of qualification and disqualification under Articles 62 and 63, discussed further below, reinforce the impression that only Muslims can compete for them.

In addition to the 342 representatives, inclusive of women and minorities, in the National Assembly, there are 114 members of the Senate. The Senate was established for the first time under the 1973 Constitution to reinforce the principle of inclusive federalism. The formula for its composition is that 14 general members, 4 women plus 4 members who are technocrats or *Ulema* are to be elected from each of Punjab, Sindh, Khyber Pakhtunkhwa and Balochistan. In addition, one member of a religious minority is also to be elected from each of the assemblies. Dominant political parties within the provincial

[4] *Prem Kevalram Shahani v Government of Pakistan* PLD [1989] Karachi 123. Also Art 260(3) ascribes the status of minority to Hindus, Buddhist, Sikhs, Parsis, Ahmadis and members of Scheduled Castes and this population was to jointly contest and vote for these seats.

[5] Legal Framework Order 2002.

assemblies are able to forward candidates for Senate elections. In all cases, the term of senators is six years, with half the seats being vacated and filled every three years.

In each military coup after the promulgation of the 1973 Constitution, the Senate has been dissolved alongside the National Assembly. When Zia first introduced a merely consultative and appointed assembly known as the Majlis-E-Shoora in 1982, there was no accompanying Senate. It was resurrected in 1985 through the Revival of Constitution Act.

B. Legislative Process

The structure of bicameralism in Pakistan inscribes the primacy of the popularly-elected lower house in several ways. It is largely from within the National Assembly that the federal government is formed, and this is also the forum for unseating a government through a vote of confidence. Additionally, the lower house retains the sole prerogative of legislating upon financial matters.

Article 91 defines the federal government as being incorporative of a 'Cabinet of Ministers, with the Prime Minister at its head,' to aid and advise the President. The office of the Prime Minister is to be filled by a majority vote of the National Assembly after electing a Speaker and Deputy Speaker. The Prime Minister is required to be a Muslim member of the National Assembly.[6]

In conventional parliamentary terms, the Prime Minister is head of government and usually also the leader of the party that gains a majority of seats in elections. In the absence of a majority win, coalition governments have on occasion been created. With only two dominant parties, the pragmatism of Pakistani politics is reflected in that such coalitions have often been built across deep ideological fissures. The leader of the opposition is also voted in by popular vote of Assembly members, and the person who wins a majority is thus notified.

[6] As a consequence of the system of separate electorates that had existed for much of this time, there was no formal requirement through Article 90 that the Prime Minister be a Muslim in the governments that were constituted in elections between 1985–2008. The Eighteenth Amendment reintroduced this criteria in 2010.

In the Senate, a popular vote takes place every three years to vote in a Chairman. Given that elections to the upper chamber do not coincide with elections to the National Assembly, there is no coincidence of party representation across the assemblies. The position of Chairman is akin to the position of the Speaker in the lower house in terms of regulating debate and ruling on issues of procedure. The Chairperson of the Senate is named as Acting President when the President is unable to discharge his/her duties. The Senate also organises itself on partisan lines so that there is both a majority leader drawn from the governing party in the National Assembly as well as the Leader of the Opposition.

For the composition of the federal government, a Cabinet of ministers is to be appointed by the President, on the binding advice of the Prime Minister. There is no constitutional stipulation about the number of Cabinet positions or the ministerial portfolios to be established. Cabinet ministers are, by specification of Article 92(3), to be members of the National Assembly or the Senate. However, the allowance for appointment of senators is capped at 25 per cent of overall Cabinet positions, although their powers and entitlements are the same as ministers from the National Assembly.[7]

It is stated by way of Article 92(6) that the 'Cabinet, together with the Ministers of State, shall be collectively responsible to the Senate and the National Assembly'. This is a specific alteration dating from the 1985 Eighth Amendment Act and is significant both for formally levelling the powers between Prime Minister and Cabinet members and for ensuring that the executive powers exercised by them are subject to democratic checks. The internal check on governmental functioning is provided in Article 95 as the vote of no-confidence in the Prime Minister. The required trigger is a resolution passed by 20 per cent of the members of the National Assembly calling for such a vote. If then a majority of the assembly members vote in favour, the Prime Minister, and in accord with convention, the Cabinet, cease to hold their offices. Only one no-confidence vote has been initiated under Article 95 and that was against the first government of Benazir Bhutto. It was narrowly defeated in her favour, but both the government and opposition were widely criticised for engaging in extortion and bribery of members of the National Assembly to ensure their vote.

[7] *Ahmadyar v Sartaj Aziz* MLD [1999] Lahore 3341.

Another intended mechanism for oversight of executive functions is provided in the parliamentary committee structure. Since 1992, through alterations to relevant parliamentary rules, the role of parliamentary committees has also become more formalised. The National Assembly and the Senate each have committees that broadly correspond with each ministry, and are meant to provide oversight into their working. In addition, a few special committees exist that are solely concerned with the internal administration of the house, including the Finance Committees of both houses, established by way of Article 88, to regulate their expenditure. The permanent committees of the National Assembly are comprised of 17 members voted in shortly after the inaugural session. Senate committees are also generally reconstituted after an election.

An important role of committees is to scrutinise proposed legislation in the course of parliamentary deliberation. According to the procedural manual of the National Assembly, the 'ever-increasing complexity of a Legislature's role' has resulted in a corresponding increase in reliance on parliamentary committees. Additionally, special committees such as those that drafted the reform package of the Eighteenth Amendment and the currently-functioning electoral reforms committee are tasked with the responsibilities of proposing legislation.[8]

Constitutional provisions establishing legislative procedure are contained in Articles 70–83. These provisions provide that a Bill on any subject-matter contained in the federal legislative list can be initiated in either house of Parliament subject to the exception that money Bills are exclusively to be introduced and passed by the lower house. The Senate has, however, been empowered since 2010 with the power to make recommendations on money Bills. In the case of other Bills, they must be passed by a majority vote of both houses before the assent of the President establishes them as law. In case of failure of one house to pass or make recommendations on a Bill arising in the other house, the Speaker or Chairperson of the other assembly can request that a vote be called to end the delay. For a short period, from 2002 until 2010, a Mediation Committee was put in place to harmonise relations between the houses.

[8] The Parliamentary Committee on Electoral Reforms was constituted in April 2014 amidst the agitation of the Pakistan Tehrik-I-Insaf around the 2013 elections results.

Article 71 enables the President to call for a joint sitting of both houses and this provision is used mostly in instances where quick action is needed and/or debate is sought to be foreshortened. Additionally, in recent times parliamentary committees tasked with oversight of foreign affairs matters have presented their findings to such joint sittings prior to a parliamentary resolution being passed. The passage of Bills, motions and resolutions through joint sessions requires a majority from the combined numbers of overall legislators. This has the effect of diluting the influence of smaller provinces as well of the Senate overall, so the use of Article 71 is often resisted for these reasons.

In terms of actual practice, it is the case that far greater numbers of government Bills are introduced in the National Assembly than in the Senate. There is no such discrepancy with regard to private members Bills, even though fewer Bills on average are introduced in the Senate.

Although of course subject to the qualification that both houses of assembly have been suspended upon a military take-over, there is an aspect of the permanence of the Senate that is of consequence with regard to the processes of legislating. In cases of dissolution of the National Assembly, Bills passed in either house prior to such dissolution will not lapse as a consequence. This is said to provide a 'significant measure of legislative continuity'.[9] This belief is also due to the perception that more 'senior and saner politicians' are to be found in the Senate than in the National Assembly. However, because the manner of election to the Senate requires political parties to nominate their candidates in provincial legislature, the opportunity is availed to dispense patronage or to simply reward loyalists without account of their suitability.[10]

C. President in Parliament

The original 1973 Constitution reflected a consensus about parliamentary structure that cast the head of state, the President, in a mainly

[9] S Baloch, 'Senate Reforms in Pakistan' (2010) *Centre for Civic Education Pakistan* 1.

[10] Zulfiqar Ali, 'Property Tycoon "invests" in Senate Elections' *Dawn News* (19 February 2015) <www.dawn.com/news/1164561>.

ceremonial role. A significant alteration was made when, through a Presidential Order in the lead up to Zia's move to share power with elected representatives, the office of the President was included within the institutions of Parliament in 1985. A set of additional revisions, including the investment in the President of the power to dissolve the lower house, were undertaken and affirmed through the Eighth Amendment Act of 1985 by the Assembly constituted through the popular, although non-party, elections of that year. While some of the Zia-era alterations have been repealed, an array of others continue to be unchanged or only moderately revised.

Searches for judicial aid in favour of returning the constitutional structure to what it had been in the 1973 Constitution have repeatedly failed. A petition filed in 1989, after a second election had taken place under the radically amended Constitution, failed to convince the Sindh High Court that this package of changes was ultra vires for being authored by a military ruler. Rather, the bench cautiously warned that as the 'present legal edifice is based on the amended Constitution, if we take out some amended provisions the superstructure of democracy built on it may collapse'.[11]

It has thus been up to legislators to either work within or modify these alterations. Importantly, the President exercised discretionary authority to call or delay the initial sessions of assemblies until an amendment was made in 2010 to ensure that the National Assembly be convened no later than 21 days after a general election. Additionally, the Revival of the Constitution of 1973 Order of 1985 provided that the President would appoint as Prime Minister whomsoever he felt would command the confidence of a majority in the house. In the Eighth Amendment adopted shortly after by a newly-elected Assembly, this was made subject to the condition that the appointee would gain a vote of confidence from the Assembly within 60 days. These two features of discretionary authority made for heightened political drama in 1988 when the President delayed appointing Benazir Bhutto as Prime Minister in an attempt to engineer a coalition government by establishment-friendly parties. As noted earlier, the situation now is that the Prime Minister is elected by a majority vote in the National Assembly.

[11] *Abdul Mujeeb Pirzada v Federation of Islamic Republic of Pakistan* PLD [1990] Karachi 9.

The further important power that the President wields is that of granting assent to Bills passed in both houses of Parliament, which is the point at which they become law. Presidential assent is a necessary and final step in law making and although the effect of withholding assent has been of shifting consequence, it has never amounted to a veto when the Constitution is in effect.

There was no consequence at all of the President's refusal according to the original articles of the 1973 Constitution, and assent was deemed to be given at the elapse of seven days. In 1985 the period granted for presidential assent was increased to 30 days and an amendment made to enable the President to revert a Bill for a second vote. In exercise of these powers, President Leghari delayed granting assent to a Bill forwarded by the Nawaz Sharif government in the midst of the latter's heightened public rift with the Supreme Court.[12] Chief Justice Sajjad Ali Shah directed the President, through an interlocutory order, to withhold assent on the passage of a contentious Bill on the ground that it was 'unconstitutional'. This was an unprecedented act that was soon reversed by a differently-constituted bench of the Supreme Court. In *Navid Malik v President of Pakistan* Chief Justice Ajmal Mian clarified that the judiciary had no place interfering in the processes of law making, but could only engage its powers of review once a law had been proclaimed.[13]

Since 2010, once a Bill has been passed in both houses, it then travels to the President for assent. The President is required to assent within ten days, but for all Bills other than money Bills, the President can return the Bill unsigned and with or without recommendations to the assemblies. If once again passed in a joint sitting of both houses, it will go back to the President. If the President fails to then sign the Bill into law within ten days, assent will be deemed to have been given.

II. PARTIES AND POLITICIANS

The background rules of parliamentary government, amongst which the legal recognition of political parties and individual political actors

[12] See text in Chapter 5, section VII.

[13] *Navid Malik v President of Pakistan* SCMR [1998] SC 1917.

are a central part, are investigated here. Early precedents set by the first Constituent Assembly to control political outcomes by employing the techniques of bans and disqualifications have been recreated in different forms throughout much of the rest of Pakistan's history. Military governments beginning with Ayub initially endeavoured to proscribe political activity altogether. However, formal prohibitions were only in place until such a time that each, Ayub, Zia and Musharraf, has felt compelled to seek continued legitimacy for rule through the recreation of a representative legislative sphere. This process of 'transforming military rule into a civilian system of administration by employing democratic instruments such as elections and referenda' has engendered a rewriting of rules so that the results are to their advantage.[14] With varied effect, the fundamental right of association has repeatedly been invoked to assert greater independence for a political sphere from the constraints imposed by the military and executive.

A. The Regulation of Political Parties

The hard won dominance of the Muslim League in the lead-up to Partition gave way to the proliferation of parties and programmes soon after Partition. This in turn aroused anxieties and led to restrictive measures on allowable politics. The 1951 ban on the Communist Party of Pakistan reverberated with foreboding of such a narrowing.[15] The ban was part of a larger assault upon leftist politics in the country. Worker militancy immediately after Partition was met with the passage of laws aimed at dissuading collective action; the Essential Services Maintenance Act of 1952 made strikes within certain industries a criminal offence. Popular union leaders were repeatedly detained under preventive detention regimes and further criminalised for 'fomenting trouble among labour in general'.[16]

[14] H Zafarullah and MY Akhter, 'Military Rule, Civilianisation and Electoral Corruption: Pakistan and Bangladesh in Perspective' (2001) 25 *Asian Studies Review* 73.

[15] Estelle Dryland, 'Faiz Ahmed Faiz and The Rawalpindi Conspiracy Case' (1992) 27 *Journal of South Asian Literature* 175; see also *Akbar Khan and Faiz Ahmad Faiz v The* Crown PLD [1954] FC 87.

[16] *Sobho Gyanchandani v Crown* PLD [1952] FC 29.

Ayub first instituted a ban on political parties as 'unlawful organisations' after taking power in 1958, then promulgated the Electoral Bodies Disqualification Order in 1959. It was in these conditions that the first Basic Democracies elections were held.[17] Renewed functioning for political parties was eventually allowed through the passage of the Political Parties Act of 1962 (PPA 1962). Importantly, Ayub also assumed the Presidency of a party comprised of his own loyalists from within the Muslim League, establishing another precedent for both Zia and then Musharraf.

The PPA 1962 established limits to political party activities and also specified that the central government would have the power to ban those parties that took action prejudicial to the integrity or security of Pakistan and were formed at the behest of any foreign government. In *Abula'la Maudoodi v Govt of Pakistan*[18] the Supreme Court determined that the right to association can only be tempered by reasonable restrictions and not denied altogether.[19]

The essentially non-party character of Parliament within the basic democracy system was in contrast to the accelerated pace of political organisation that was taking place outside. Forged often in a protest idiom against authoritarian and military rule, as well as against the perceived injustices of the One Unit, this was a period of political ferment in which the People's Party was formed and in which the Awami Party in the East, and to a lesser extent the Jamaat-e-Islami and the Jamiat Ulema-e-Islam, made significant gains in popular support. They were all young parties insofar as they had not had any significant experience of the workings of the parliamentary system.

When the 1973 Constitution was framed it provided a right of association that was subject to reasonable restrictions. In comparison to previous constitutions, the right was more inclusive for providing citizens the specific liberty to be a member of a political party through Article 17(2). Less than a year later, the First Amendment Act was passed in the National Assembly and made significant alteration to Article 17(1) by specifying that reasonable restrictions were to be read

[17] See text in Chapter 2, section V.

[18] *Saiyyid Abula'la Maudoodi v The Government of West Pakistan* PLD [1964] SC 673.

[19] In addition, see *Tamizzuddin Ahmed v The Government East Pakistan* PLD [1964] Dacca 795. For the *Maudoodi* case, see the discussion in Chapter 7, section I.

'in the interest of the sovereignty or integrity of Pakistan'. It also provided that 'where the Federal Government declare [*sic*] that any political party has been formed or is operating in a manner prejudicial to the sovereignty or integrity of Pakistan' it could refer the matter to the Supreme Court for a final determination.

In February of 1973 the National Awami Party (NAP) government in Balochistan was dismissed by Zulfiqar Bhutto in his role of President and shortly thereafter the NWFP government also resigned in protest at the federal government's actions in Balochistan.[20] Bhutto then disbanded NAP in February of 1975. The reference on the ban was presented to the Supreme Court, which accepted its role as the arbiter on this issue. Justice Hamoodur Rehman upheld the ban on NAP by finding that the promotion of ethnic nationalism was an offence against the sovereignty and integrity of Pakistan.[21] The dissolved party would be refounded in 1978 as the Awami National Party (ANP).

In the anticipation of the elections Zia promised would follow shortly after his assumption of power in 1977, the PPA 1962 was amended to include Islamic ideology and morality as additional grounds for controlling political parties.[22] Additionally, parties were now required to meet certain conditions for the purposes of registering themselves with the Election Commission, a precondition for fielding candidates in an election. These changes were of little consequence for some time, as Zia indefinitely delayed elections and then reconstituted the legislature as an appointed consultative body in 1982.[23] Following the Restoration of the Constitution Order of 1985, national elections were held on a non-party basis. It was in the lead-up to the 1988 elections that the provisions of 1978 were challenged in the courts against the resurrected rights guarantees of the 1973 Constitution.[24]

In *Benazir Bhutto v The Federation* the majority judgment, authored by Chief Justice Mohammad Haleem, held several of the Zia amendments to the PPA 1962 to be contrary to the protections offered by Article 17.[25] They did not find it unduly restrictive for political parties

[20] See text in Chapter 6, section VA.

[21] *Islamic Republic of Pakistan v Abdul Wali Khan* PLD [1976] SC 57.

[22] Ordinance XLI of 1978.

[23] The Assembly at this time was renamed Majlis-e-Shoora.

[24] Rights restored by 'Revival of the Constitution of 1973 Order 1985'.

[25] *Benazir Bhutto v Federation of Pakistan* PLD [1988] SC 416.

to have to abstain from offending Islamic ideology, morality or public order. On this they simply counselled that these be read as constitutive features of the 'sovereignty and integrity of Pakistan', as per Article 17(2). The requirement of registration was, however, held to be contrary to a full realisation of the right of association. This was partly in acknowledgement of the Supreme Court as the only constitutionally mandated forum for making determinations about the banning of parties, as per the changes introduced earlier. Additionally, the vesting of discretionary authority in the Election Commission to refuse recognition to political parties was seen as diminishing the guarantees of Article 17. Participation in elections was deemed to be an essential element of the realisation of the right of association so that 'if the [*sic*] political party is disabled to participate in an election it loses its political texture and to all intents and purposes it will suffer extermination'. This case also provided a number of additional statements about the centrality of the political party apparatus to the form of government anticipated in the Constitution.

In 1993, a presidential dismissal of the first Pakistan Muslim League (PML-N) government under Nawaz Sharif allowed Justice Shafi ur Rehman to identify an Article 17 violation in this act of unjustified dissolution.[26] The Supreme Court decreed that the right 'to form or be a member of a political party' as encompassing not only the rights to constitute a party and contest elections 'but also, after successfully contesting the elections, the right to form the Government if its members', possessed the 'requisite majority'.

The PPA 1962 was repealed and replaced by the Political Parties Order 2002 (PPO 2002). This alteration of law was again in anticipation of the national election that Musharraf was bound by the Supreme Court to call in exchange for a validation of his coup of 1999.[27] Having already ensured that local government elections were conducted on a non-party basis, the PPO 2002 was intended to 'clean up' the political sphere and to ensure that the assembly constituted would be subservient to Musharraf. At this time 'public order' was added alongside sovereignty and integrity of Pakistan as grounds for reducing the rights

[26] *Nawaz Sharif v President of Pakistan* PLD [1993] SC 473.

[27] See text in Chapter 4, section II.

of association under Article 17.[28] Public order provides a lowered threshold for measuring threat, by establishing not only the continued existence of the state but any number of subsidiary criteria as needing protection. Additionally, a sub-Article 17(4) was inserted to read 'Every political party shall, subject to law, hold intra-party elections to elect its office-bearers and party leaders'.

Both changes to Article 17 accorded with innovations made in the regulation of political parties through the 2002 Order; Section 3 placed a prohibition on the promotion of sectarian views, bearing the name of a militant group and fostering militant factions within a party, but removed offences against Islamic ideology as possible grounds for dissolution. Offences to public morality and security were repeated as per the PPA 1962 and the fostering of terrorism was added as a further possible ground for dissolution. Additionally, the conduct of periodic elections to fill high office in political parties was made obligatory for the first time in Pakistan's history. The irony that it was a military dictator who sought to ensure internal democracy within political parties was not lost on politicians.

Beginning in late 2001 a number of organisations, currently totalling 61, were officially banned in Pakistan on evidence of their link to sectarian violence or terror-related offences. These prohibitions were undertaken through the Ministry of the Interior under the Anti-Terrorism Act of 1997.[29] A number of these banned organisations were actively involved in electoral politics through the 1990s. For instance, the *Sipahah-e-Sahaba*, a virulently anti-Shia organisation headquartered in the district of Jhang, was briefly part of a coalition government in Punjab in 1993–1996. Rather than challenge the proscriptions for negating the safeguards of Article 17(2), which would require the Supreme Court to make a final determination, many of these groups have taken the route of rebranding themselves, so that the leadership and infrastructure of these groups reappear under a different name

[28] Legal Frame Order 2002 (Chief Executive Order No 24) had added the said clause (4) to Art 17, with effect from 21 August 2002. Validated by Seventeenth Amendment Act 2003.

[29] APP, '61 Banned Outfits Named by Senate, Jud under Observation' *Dawn* (18 December 2015) <www.dawn.com/news/1227187/61-banned-outfits-named-by-senate-jud-under-observation>.

within the electoral landscape. Most famously, *Lashkar e Taeba* (LeT), banned in 2002, re-emerged as *Jamaat ul Dawa* and contested elections in Kashmir in the year 2005. By styling itself on organisations such as Hizbollah and Hamas, it was able to win greater public acceptance in a new welfare and service-oriented guise. The Mumbai attacks of 2008, in which 164 people were shot in multiple sites of the India city by gunmen, was almost immediately linked to the continued operations of the LeT in the guise of *Jamaat ul Dawa.* International pressure led in turn to the passage of a UN Security Council resolution calling for *Jamaat ul Dawa* to be dissolved. Instead, the Interior Ministry in Pakistan placed it 'under observation'.[30]

In contrast to the show of vigilance against sectarian and militant organsiations, the bar on militant wings of mainstream political parties has never been enforced, even as widespread evidence of the existence and operation of armed sections of a number of parties, particularly those that have a strong electoral base in Karachi, is readily apparent. In *Watan Party v The Federation of Pakistan*, commonly known as the *Karachi Law and Order case of 2011*, the possible recourse to the PPO 2002 provisions was noted, but left for the federal government to utilise.[31] Where the government has intervened, it has been a partisan manner and led to allegations of political victimisation.[32]

These, the 'ground realities' of Pakistan's political sphere, are also reflected in the partial compliance with PPO 2002 requirements necessitating internal party elections. Even amongst political parties that once offered a radical critique of oligarchic power holders, internal succession from within families is an undeniable aspect of their current culture. In fact, in the lead-up to the 2013 elections, a Pakistani news magazine published the results of an empirical study that concluded, 'dynastic politicians belonging to approximately 400 families have been instrumental in shaping policies, programmes and legislation that have impacted the lives of 176 million Pakistani citizens'.[33] Amongst

[30] See text in Chapter 7, section IVB.

[31] *Watan Party v The Federation of Pakistan* PLD [2011] SC 997. See Chapter 6, section VB.

[32] See text in Chapter 6, section VA.

[33] H Javid, A Cheema and MF Nasser, 'The Paradox of Dynastic Politics: Facts, Myths about Political Dynasties in Punjab and Their Implications' *Herald Political Dynasties*, Elections 2013 Special Issue, May 2013, 11.

the large contingent that are feudal or land-holding families, the most famous are the Bhuttos, who have uninterruptedly held top office in the Pakistan People's Party (PPP) for more than 40 years and over three generations.

The holding of non-party elections in 1985 was anticipated to displace feudal elites from power, given the assumption that parties fielded these candidates because they brought with them a vote bank based upon customary loyalties. The election did in fact open the field to an ascendant class of businessmen and the independently wealthy, epitomised in the rise of the Sharif family. The Sharifs are heirs of the Ittefaq group of companies, built up over a generation by their father, and Nawaz Sharif has been leader of the Pakistan Muslim League—Nawaz (PML-N) since its founding in 1988.[34] What the study above also highlights is that in the period since then 'business-owning, trading and professional elites have been as successful as their landowning counterparts, if not more, in forming dynastic families and that the power of capital appears to be as potent as the power of land' in enabling political influence to be concentrated.

In these two major parties, as well as with the Muttahidi Qaumi Mahaz (MQM), Pakistan Tehrik-e-Insaf (PTI) and the Jamiat Ulema-e-Islam (JUI) intra-party elections have been periodically held, but in all, top office holders have contested their seats unopposed. The major exception to this ubiquitous pattern of dynastic control within parties has been the Jamaat-e-Islami. Scoring highest in independent studies of internal democracy, not only for the regularity with which top offices are filled by election, but also in sustaining internal party mechanisms for consultation and deliberation on matters of policy, the Jamaat's practices reflect a long preoccupation with fostering a cadre of ideologically-committed party members. Not surprisingly, where the Jamaat's practices are lagging is in reference to the inclusion of women and minorities indications, in which the PTI and PPP are both better performers.[35]

Although predicated on an abidance of norms of 'good governance' the contradictions of the Musharraf era, which included the continued

[34] Although the Partition-era Muslim League has fractured into many factions, the PMLN is by far the one with the greatest electoral support.

[35] PILDAT, 'Internal Democracy of Major Political Parties of Pakistan 2015' (Pakistan, PILDAT, 2016) 1.

fostering of militant elements by the state itself as well as the quick compromises drawn by Musharraf with a section of the existing political class, ensured that his changes were of minimal transformative impact. The existing political landscape continues to allow extremists space and the internal democracy of parties is far from being realised.

In 2010 the Eighteenth Amendment Act reverted Article 17 to the form it had taken after the passage of the First Constitutional Amendment. The PPO 2002 has been supplemented with some amendments. Significant amongst these amendments is a new provision to ensure that 10 per cent of the candidates fielded on general seats by all parties should be women.

B. Disqualification

A long history of enacting statutes and ordinances aimed at barring individuals from contesting elections for the legislature has been termed the 'doctrine of disqualification' by some commentators. The earliest encoding was by the first Constituent Assembly, which had itself been elected under a limited franchise under the 1935 Government of India Act. The highly centralised and elite composition of the ruling Muslim League under Liaquat Ali Khan sought to immunise itself against public opprobrium for general failures of governance and to punish those expressing regional autonomy or independence of mind against centralised dictate through the Public and Representative Offices (Disqualification) Act 1949 (PRODA).

The Act offered a mechanism for lodging a complaint against a Cabinet minister or an elected member suspected of corruption, nepotism, favouritism or bad management.[36] Until its repeal in 1954, PRODA was primarily made use of by politicians to 'attack their rivals, giving rise to partisan vendettas' and ultimately this made way for the discrediting of the political party system that was capitalised upon by the army and bureaucracy in coming years. However, with a judiciary keen to ensure procedural justice and with the relatively narrow criteria for disqualification, only five politicians were ever effectively debarred.[37]

[36] *MA Khuhro v Federation of Pakistan* PLD [1950] Sindh 49.

[37] C Jafferlot, *A History of Pakistan and Its Origins* (London, Anthem Press, 2004) 64.

Under Ayub, the disqualification of more than 6,000 politicians for the period 1959–1966 under the Electoral Bodies Disqualification Ordinance (EBDO) acted in tandem with the 'restoration of democracy' through the ingenious invention of the basic democracies system. Especially targeted under EBDO were those affiliated with parties that had actively protested the enactment of the One Unit.[38] With subsequent alterations members of the public service could also be charged and the grounds for disqualification were expanded to include any prior indictments under the Security of Pakistan Act. These changes were engineered to ensure that many leading members of the political class, those who had in the past held posts as high as Prime Minister, were in fact 'EBDO'ed'—with disqualifications set to last until 1966.[39]

The transition to democratic government did not do away with attempts to constrain political organisation. Zulfiqar Bhutto's preferred system of undermining rival politicians is detailed in Chapter 7 with regard to detention, but extended beyond that to banning rival political parties such as NAP.[40] In the 1973 Constitution, Articles 62 and 63, entitled Qualification and Disqualification respectively, were incorporated. They were each far more meagre than the current articles, which were expanded by way of Zia's RCO of 1985, and then further supplemented with additional criteria by Musharraf.

The articles passed in the 1973 Constitution detailed qualification criteria that included possession of Pakistani citizenship, the age qualifications of 25 for National Assembly and 30 for the Senate and 'any other requirement that may be mandated by law'. The list of Article 63 disqualifications at the outset included 'being pronounced of unsound mind by a competent court', ceasing to be a citizen, or acquiring citizenship in addition to Pakistan's and being an undeclared insolvent. From the outset it is apparent that these disqualifications were envisioned as being operative both prior to and after an election. In the case of the latter, it was provided in Article 63(2) that the Speaker of the Assembly

[38] S Ahmed, *Bangladesh: Past and Present* (New Delhi, APH Publication Corporation, 2004).

[39] On 30 January 1962 Hussein Shaheed Suhrawardy, Prime Minister in 1956, was arrested in Karachi under the Security of Pakistan Act 1952, which authorised his detention without trial for a year.

[40] For a broader view of the associated mechanisms, see MS Dahiya, 'Mirror Images' (1977) 12 *Economic and Political Weekly* 377, 398.

could choose to acknowledge that a question of disqualification had arisen and refer the matter to the Election Commission.

To the list of original qualifications, Zia added not only that the candidate be a Muslim but also that such person be of 'good character' and not known as 'one who violates Islamic Injunctions' in the package of 1985 reforms.[41] In addition, the person must have 'knowledge of Islamic teachings and practice obligatory duties prescribed by Islam' and be 'sagacious, righteous and non-profligate and honest and *ameen* (righteous)'. These provisions, although widely-assailed for reasons to be discussed further below, have been retained in the Constitution even as other of Zia's innovations were later revised. In part this reflects the general immovability of laws made in the promotion of Islam.[42] It also perhaps suggests that political parties themselves have remained open to maintaining laws through which rivals can be targeted.

Under Zia, numerous criteria were added to the disqualifications of Article 63. Some were framed as safeguards against conflicts of interest, and this included a deepening of the prohibition on the ability of state employees to contest elections.[43] Other new grounds for disqualification included prior convictions for crimes of moral turpitude and for defaming and bringing into ridicule the judiciary or the armed forces of Pakistan under Article 63(1)(g). In this period the list of criteria for disqualification grew to number 18 specific clauses.

In keeping with the generally fractious nature of politics through the 1990s, the disqualification criterion most often used to launch challenges against politicians was that which barred them from electoral contest following service in a state institution. The quick changeover in governments made it a regular occurrence that those displaced from office were seeking re-election in the next election. Broadly though, the systemic logic behind Zia's criteria had no takers in terms of promoting an Islamic, or even corruption-free, political sphere.

This would change when Musharraf assumed power and endeavoured to refashion politics afresh through the Constitution and law. For qualifications, he removed the criteria of Article 62 that one be a Muslim, but retained the criteria related to Islamic knowledge

[41] Constitution of Pakistan 1973, Art 63.

[42] See text in Chapter 8, section IV.

[43] Constitution of Pakistan 1973, Art 63(1)(k) established the bar for two years.

and piety.[44] Musharraf also introduced an educational qualification through the Conduct of General Elections Order of 2002 that required prospective candidates to possess a bachelor's degree. It broadened the list of disqualifications to include default on personal loans and on 'government dues and utility expenses' by either the prospective candidate or 'his spouse or any of his dependents' [*sic*]. Immediately after taking power, Musharraf passed the National Accountability Ordinance, which introduced accountability courts and an investigative and prosecutorial system in the National Accountability Bureau (NAB). Although applicable to all persons and not only public officials, it was in parts oriented to facilitating disqualification. Interestingly, such corruption within the ranks of the military is specifically indemnified from the oversight of the National Accountability Bureau.[45]

The educational qualification impacted vast numbers of politicians and is recounted here in detail both to illustrate the nature of elite anxieties about democracy in the country and also because it is of continuing impact, even though invalidated in 2008. In an early challenge, *PML-Q v The Federation*, the Supreme Court ruled that a minimal educational qualification did not offend against equality guarantees and was a reasonable restriction on the rights of association. The reasonability of this classification was tied to the legitimate object of changing the political culture of Pakistan. Recounting the 'sad tale of failures on the part of the [*sic*] public representatives' in previous episodes of political rule Justice Riaz Ahmed was quick to assume that the acquisition of a university education was a rational stand-in for merit and public-mindedness.[46] There was no corresponding discussion about the vast exclusions that this entailed.

The educational qualification was vigilantly enforced by the officers of the Election Commission in the lead-up to the 2002 elections and resulted in both pre-election disqualifications and, in some cases where false degrees were presented to the Commission during the vetting

[44] Article 62(2) exempts non-Muslims from requirements related to Islamic knowledge and abidance and specifies instead that 'such a person shall have good moral reputation'.

[45] U Javaid, 'Corruption and its Deep Impact on Good Governance in Pakistan' (2010) 48 *Pakistan Economic and Social Review* 123, 125.

[46] *Pakistan Muslim League (Q) v Chief Executive of Islamic Republic of Pakistan* PLD [2002] SC 994.

stage, to disqualifications of sitting members of the Assembly when the fraud was later discovered. However, if the aim of promoting this qualification was to denude the power of career politicians and the feudal class, it often had the converse effect of quickening the entry of a younger generation of heirs-apparent from dynastic political families into electoral politics. Additionally, a certificate of training from a *Madrasa* was considered equivalent to a bachelor's degree, which allowed members of allied religious parties under the banner of the MMA to have a greater comparative advantage in these elections.[47]

When, in 2008, the educational qualification was once again challenged, the Supreme Court found no rational basis for this classification to have been employed.[48] In a complete turnaround from *PML-Q*, the qualification was found to unduly restrict the rights of association.[49] The judges found no evidence that more meritorious and capable legislators had formed the assembly of 2002–2007. In terms of discriminatory impact, the court took notice of the fact that less than 3 per cent of the population possessed the requisite qualification and that this included people currently employed in public service, itself a criteria of disqualification from political contest.

Other than the educational qualification, which continues to have resonance,[50] nearly all the changes introduced to Articles 62 and 63 by Zia and then Musharraf have carried forth. Only minor revisions to some of these were undertaken as a part of the Eighteenth Amendment Act in 2010. Changes at this time included the application of a time limit on disqualification for some of the offences cited under this provision, as well as a standard of evidence requiring a criminal conviction for some of them to become operative.

That the regime of disqualification has expanded and gained great consequence was apparent in one very sensational disqualification in the year 2012, when the Supreme Court acted to force Prime Minister

[47] See text in Chapter 8, section IV.

[48] *Muhammad Nasir Mahmood v Federation of* Pakistan PLD [2009] SC 107.

[49] Relying upon *Benazir Bhutto* and *Nawaz Sharif*, they held that individual rights were co-extensive with the rights accorded to parties; PLD [1988] SC 416 and PLD [1993] SC 473.

[50] *Malik Umar Aslam v Mrs Sumair Malik* SCMR [2014] SC 45; *Muhammad Khan Junejo v Federation of Pakistan* SCMR [2013] SC 1328. Courts have disqualified candidates on the basis of having presented fraudulent degrees in previous contests.

Syed Yousaf Raza Gillani to relinquish his office and seat in Parliament. After convicting Gillani of contempt of court for not pursuing cases of corruption against President Asif Zardari, the Supreme Court notified the Speaker of the Assembly that a question of disqualification on the basis of Article 63(1)(g) had arisen against the Prime Minister.[51] Article 63(2) provides that in such circumstances 'unless he [the Speaker] decides that no such question has arisen', the Speaker must refer this question to the Election Commission within 30 days. In a tense face-off between the Supreme Court and the Peoples Party government, the Speaker refused to make a referral to the Election Commission. The Supreme Court ultimately assumed jurisdiction as per Article 184(3) and decreed that Gillani was indeed disqualified.

Dismay at the disqualification regime grew more acute when, prior to the 2013 elections Zia's pietist Islamic criteria were used by officers of the Election Commission to compile character certificates of potential candidates. For the first time, the ascertainment of whether or not candidates possessed adequate 'knowledge of Islamic teachings and practice obligatory duties prescribed by Islam' was undertaken quite seriously. Resultant disqualifications, when challenged, confronted the appellate authorities 'with no option but to overturn a large number' of them. Some reversals turned on the finding that the junior officers of the Election Commission had overstepped their authority, others on the violation of 'the larger fundamental right to contest elections and still others on the ground that several requirements of Article's 62 and 63 necessitated convictions by a court of law'.[52]

Non-elected rulers have initially always instituted controls over the political party system and expansions of the disqualification regime to restrict the realm of an acceptable politics. It is important to note that these criteria neither reflect popular demand nor is the electorate necessarily respectful of paternalistic dictates on the question of who is fit to govern: the easiest measure of this is that the electorate regularly returns to public office contenders who are known to be financially corrupt. However, that politicians have not sought to reverse or limit these restrictions more effectively and have instead aimed their enforcement

[51] *Mohammad Azhar Siddiqi v Federation of Pakistan* PLD [2012] SC 774.

[52] S Rasool, 'Distilling Eligibility and Virtue: Articles 62 and 63 of the Pakistani Constitution' (2014) 1 *LUMS Law Journal*.

at rivals has reinforced the impression of politics as being waged in a gladiatorial arena, in which the slaying of opponents rather than the realisation of programmes is the end.

In many ways this deep personalisation works to disguise what is in fact a greater convergence between the major parties on the more potent issues of socio-economic policy and national security, amongst others. In the context of what has now long been a two-party system in which third parties have mostly gained their foothold either by reliance upon an ethnic constituency or in appealing to the goal of implanting Shariat, the prospects for new entrants have been low. These convergences in policy are also informed by broader issues, as discussed further below.

III. ELECTORAL SYSTEM

Important for the discussion that follows is the broad ranging challenge launched by the Workers Party in 2012 in which 'certain practices of electioneering as violative of fundamental rights were highlighted'.[53] Coming from a party with few resources, but one that aims to represent the interests of the urban and rural poor, it was less concerned with conduct of particular electoral contests and took broader aim at the system of rules by which embedded disparities continue to be replicated.

A. Elections

A significant demand of the Workers Party petition was of requesting oversight over the duties and responsibilities of the Election Commission, a permanent body whose authority and mandate is defined in Articles 213–221. The office of the President of the Commission and of the four Members of the Commission are to be filled through appointment by the President, for a term of three years after a vetting of candidates through a parliamentary committee hearing of which

[53] *Workers Party Pakistan v Federation of Pakistan* PLD [2012] SC 681, para 7.

the representation is to be equally divided between government and opposition.[54] Article 218 provides that

> it shall be the duty of the Election Commission to organise and conduct the election and to make such arrangements as are necessary to ensure that the election is conducted honestly, justly, fairly and in accordance with law, and that corrupt practices are guarded against.

The statute governing the regulation of elections within Pakistan, and thereby providing the main body of rules and regulations that the Election Commission and its officers are tasked with upholding, is the Representation of the People Act 1976. All of the competencies cited above are defined in this statute. In addition, it lays out the upper limit of campaign spending for individual candidates in their bid for office. For candidates seeking to be members of the national assembly this is set at 1.5 million rupees (approximately $15,000 US). For candidates seeking to be members of provincial legislatures the limit is less, one million rupees ($10,000 US). Such expenditure is expected to be undertaken by the candidates themselves and not the political party which they represent in elections.

The Workers Party asked the court to review the adequacy of these sums. The Workers Party argued that even if effectively policed as the maximal limit, which it has never been, the allowable sum is already a bar to effective participation for those who are themselves not wealthy nor part of a wealthy party apparatus.[55] To this end, they also asked for a declaratory statement that expenditure such as undertaken by party machines through media advertisements, handbills, billboards, sponsorship of large political rallies, etc, constitute a violation of these rules. Not surprisingly, the larger parties who were requested by the court to offer their testimony on these matters differed on the extent to which such controls should be enhanced. They cited 'political expression' and 'democratic practice' as their legitimation for maintaining the status quo. The court saw the present sums as constituting a reasonable limit and ordered only that they be subject to greater policing.

[54] See Twenty-first Amendment Act [2015] for changes to the qualification criteria of Chairman and members and see the Twenty-second Amendment Act [2016].

[55] Actual campaign expenditure is estimated to be as high as $200,000 US for National Assembly contests.

B. Voters/Constituencies

Another issue identified by the Workers Party petition was the Election Commission's record on the maintenance of electoral rolls. These rolls are the record of eligible voters in a given constituency, which must be checked off by officials of the Commission at the time of ballot distribution on election day. The process for the registration of electors and the periodic revision of electoral rolls are laid out in the Electoral Rolls Act of 1974. The requirements for individual registration as well as the maintenance of electoral lists have historically impacted the perception of whether or not a free and fair election has taken place.[56]

Voters in Pakistan are simply those who have attained the age of 18 and are citizens of the country.[57] Voter registration has historically been fraught with problems as various technological means have been found lacking, either giving rise to false votes or in effectively disenfranchising potential voters. Whereas in earlier elections the use of individual state-issued identification cards were the mechanism for verifying votes, Musharraf's claim to be able to computerise electoral rolls prior to the 2002 elections had the effect of excluding approximately 20 million adult voters from those lists, when compared to census data. Constitutional Petition 45 of 2007, brought by the People's Party, resulted in the issuance of a direction to the Election Commission to verify the voters excluded in the 2002 lists and thereby, more than 27 million voters were added to the rolls to vote in 2008.[58] This in turn led to allegations from other parties that a body of 'bogus voters' had been created. The issue was taken up again in Workers Party, and Justice Chaudhry et al directed the Election Commission to 'undertake door-to-door checking of voters' lists and complete the process of updating/revision of the electoral rolls by engaging Army and Frontier Corps to ensure transparency, if need be'.

As the 2013 elections approached, a spate of constitutional petitions were filed asserting that some degree of mismanagement or foul play was at play in the registration of voters. The greatest irregularities were alleged to be taking place in Karachi, where in one instance 669 votes

[56] Mahfuzul Huq, 'Electorates and elections in Pakistan' (1966) 16 *Civilisations* 45, 50.

[57] Constitution of Pakistan 1973, Art 51(2).

[58] Record of order repeated in *Imran Khan v Chief Election Commissioner*. In general see Zafarrullah Khan, 'The Case of Pakistan's "Bogus Voter"' *Newsline* (February 2012) www.newslinemagazine.com/magazine/the-case-of-pakistans-bogus-voters/.

were registered as residing in a small single-family home. It was also alleged that almost 50 per cent of voters had had their votes transferred to other localities.[59] The Supreme Court in *Imran Khan v Election Commission*[60] bemoaned the Election Commission's non-compliance with the directions it issued in *Workers Party* and offered specific directions.

Karachi has been host to a great deal of migrant labour from other regions of Pakistan and the city's shifting demographics threatened the ethnic vote bank which has generally delivered Urdu-speaking voters to the Muttahida Qaumi Mahaz (MQM) and Sindhis to the PPP. Particularly threatening to the MQM is the official recognition of a growing population of Pakhtoon workers, which has enabled the culturally nationalist Pakhtoon-dominated Awami National Party to gain a foothold in the city. Whereas some of the major political parties, especially the Punjabi-dominated Muslim League of Nawaz Sharif, have recognised their electoral limitations in Pakistan's largest city, the election of 2013 threw some new elements into the mix. The newly popular Pakistan Tehreek-I-Insaf imagined itself able to break the ethnic stranglehold of Karachi's politics and filed a number of constitutional petitions in the lead-up to the 2013 elections.

The consequences of such legal agitation were manifest in some changes in policy. Significantly, people were given the choice to register and cast their votes in the locality listed as their 'place of work'.[61] The Supreme Court also issued directions to the Election Commission to establish a mechanism for eight million non-resident ex-pat Pakistanis to be able to vote in coming elections.[62] A broader consequence, however, has been the push to further digitise the compilation of electoral data so that reliance is increasingly placed upon a recently inaugurated programme to compile a database of conventional and biometric data for all Pakistanis. However, problems in execution remain rife and issues of privacy and surveillance are being obscured in the headlong drive towards finding technological means of verifying voters and votes without what many believe to be an adequate legislative framework.

[59] *Imran Khan v Chief Election Commissioner* PLD [2013] SC 120.

[60] ibid.

[61] ibid.

[62] Amir Wasim, 'Overseas Pakistanis can't vote in 2018: ECP' *Dawn* (25 November 2015) <www.dawn.com/news/1222099>.

Also at issue in the failure to compile accurate electoral rolls as well as in the problems of demarcating constituencies has been the unavailability of accurate census data. The last national census was published in 1998. In a country with high levels of population growth and migration as well as rapid urbanisation, the data from that census can only be the basis for projections that are too imprecise to be used in the manner that the Constitution and law mandate for facilitating democratic elections. Article 51(5) provides that constituencies will be divided on the basis of data from the last available census. The last alterations of national and provincial electoral constituencies were undertaken in 2002 while the census results were still relatively fresh. Although successive governments have cited the worsening security situation in the country as reason for the delay, the absence of political will can also be located in a desire not to exacerbate ethnic and regional tensions in the country.[63]

Cases arising from the demarcation of constituency boundaries in reference to local government elections have allowed for the elaboration of certain fundamental principles for the conduct of elections. These principles accord with changes introduced by the Eighteenth and Twentieth Amendments, as well in reference to judicially-elaborated definitions, founded in fundamental rights jurisprudence, about the guarantees of political justice.[64] In *Province of Sindh v MQM*[65] the Supreme Court gave specific political expression to constitutional equality rights guarantees. Against gerrymandering, the court held that to vary the population distribution amongst constituencies is to work against the principle of parity on which a 'one-man, one vote' system relies.

At stake in this case was the discretionary redrawing of constituency boundaries to give sparsely populated 'rural' constituencies an equivalence with more densely populated urban constituencies by the provincial government. The court found evidence that this was amongst the 'attempts to establish a political advantage for a particular party or group by manipulating district boundaries to create partisan advantaged districts'. The exercise was found to be repugnant to the principle of

[63] AM Weiss, 'Much Ado about Counting: The Conflict over Holding a Census in Pakistan (1999) 39 *Asian Survey* 679; see text in Chapter 6, section VB.

[64] *Watan Party v The Federation of Pakistan* PLD [2011] SC 997.

[65] *Province of Sindh v MQM* PLD [2014] SC 531.

'one man one vote' and thereby also contrary to Article 25 equality guarantees in the Constitution.

The direction of the court in the *MQM* case, that the Election Commission bears responsibility for demarcating electoral constituencies for local government elections, was incorporated amongst the changes of the Twenty-second Amendment Act of 2016. In addition to broadening the criteria of qualification for appointment to the Election Commission, two articles of the Constitution were altered to direct the Commission to hold electoral rolls and demarcate constituencies for local government elections.[66]

C. Rigging

Although the issues discussed above hint at ways in which unfair means might be used to influence electoral exercises, there are far more direct modes of intervention that have been at play in instances where elections are rigged. What the political classes, critics of power politics and the general public in Pakistan have realised of late is that controlling or even rigging elections unfold in multiple forms and through mechanics that operate prior to, during and after elections.[67]

Pre-poll rigging is defined thus as the violation of constitutional requirements such as ensuring the neutrality of the caretaker government, the independence of Election Commission and its functionaries, and violation of freedom of media. The use of 'public resources to benefit some contestants' in addition to the foregoing are all readily apparent in each of the episodes of 'managed transition', whereby Pakistan's military governments agreed to devolve some power to civilians through electoral exercises. The election of 1988 became the subject matter of a Supreme Court case, which was filed in 1997 but was not heard until 2014. In this case, extensive evidence of actual transfer of governmental funds to carefully chosen candidates, those who were

[66] The Delimitation of Constituencies Act 1974, s 9 directs the Election Commission to mark the bounds of constituencies to maintain population parity but also to take account of 'existing boundaries of administrative units, facilities of communication and public convenience and other cognate facture'.

[67] IS Gillani, 'How Elections are Stolen and the Will of the People Defeated' (PILDAT Background Paper, 2008) 1.

trusted lieutenants for the army's interests and ideological programme, were brought on board in the creation of a short-lived political party, one which formed the opposition after those elections.[68]

Poll-time rigging is that which is most intuitively related to the subversion of electoral preferences. The stuffing of ballot boxes with false votes, the use of coercion or undue means to influence voting behaviour, and dishonest counting are amongst the acts that constitute such transgressions. Two specific electoral exercises have incited mass protests about their fairness but have yielded very different results. In the case of the 1977 elections, after agitation by an opposition alliance, an independent enquiry was held and it discovered that polling booths had at times remained closed, that there had been armed militia members stationed at some polls, and other such irregularities had in fact taken place. The prolonged agitation, and Bhutto's increasingly heavy-handed mode of dealing with street protestors and opposition leaders, became the pretext of Zia's coup, announcing at that stage that both sides 'were armed to the teeth' and further bloodshed was otherwise imminent.

The allegations that emerged after the 2013 election were similar insofar as all parties, other than the victorious PML-N, made complaints about rigging. However, the PTI was more vociferous and at first demanded a recount in certain constituencies. The government did not cede to this demand and it was only after the PTI's leadership staged a march to Islamabad and camped out there for a full 40 days that the government was brought to the negotiating table and a judicial commission comprised of sitting Supreme Court judges was asked to investigate allegations of rigging. Although the findings of the Commission were not legally binding, it recorded and evaluated evidence of alleged rigging from across the country. In its final report, the Commission cited considerable lapses in organisation on the part of the Election Commission but did not find evidence that the elections failed in providing a 'fair and true mandate of the people'.[69]

[68] *Muhammad Asghar Khan v Mirza Aslam Baig* PLD [2013] SC 1 Human Rights Case No 19 of 1996.

[69] C Almeida, 'Between Hope and Fear' *Dawn* (30 November 2014) <www.dawn.com/news/1147777>.

IV. PARLIAMENTARY DEMOCRACY/PARTIES, CLASS, ETC

The legislative branch of government has faced innumerable obstacles in fulfilling the role outlined in the 1973 Constitution. Additionally, the cyclical turn between militarism and civilian rule has greatly affected the formation and development of the political sphere more broadly. Even when the military has ceded governmental control to representative political actors, their autonomy has been constrained. This is what is meant by the operation of the deep state in Pakistan. It is also the case that working within these constraints has drawn some political regimes and parties into alliance with the military establishment to keep rivals destabilised and suppress popular movements: Bhutto called in the armed forces to quell labour strikes and other sites of unrest;[70] through the 1990s the military was used to control urban militancy in Karachi; in 2015, Nawaz Sharif called the military into Islamabad as Imran Khan and the Pakistan Tehreek-I-Insaf were planning a sit-in outside of parliament.[71] More detailed study of these complex interdependencies and tensions is undertaken in the following chapter.

Here, in concluding this discussion of the legislative branch and the political sphere, the point that needs to be made is that military praetorianism cannot provide a complete answer to the question of why democracy has not found sure footing within Pakistan. In 2007 the leaders of the PPP and PML-N drafted and signed an agreement by which they agreed that, irrespective of who formed the government and who was in the opposition, the role of each would be respected and that neither would seek to have the military intervene in order to destabilise the other. Additionally, they would put an end to political victimisation through the partisan appointments process to national accountability institutions.[72] The 2008 elections returned no clear victor and for some time these two parties entered into a coalition, albeit a short-lived one. Thereafter the assemblies altogether operated in a consensual manner to frame and then pass through the Eighteenth

[70] AH Sayed, *The Discourse and Politics of Zulfikar Ali Bhutto* (New York, St Martin's Press, 1992).

[71] Constitution of Pakistan 1973, Art 245; see also Action in Aid of Civil Power Regulation, 2011.

[72] 'Text of the Charter of Democracy' *Dawn* (16 May 2006) <www.dawn.com/news/192460>.

Amendment Act of 2010. However, this base cooperation soon fell apart and the allegations of rigging from the 2013 elections are emblematic of this.

Some analysts have looked further to suggest that broader failures of representative government are the reciprocal effect of a congenitally underdeveloped social sphere. Factors such as the perpetuation of *biradari* and tribal loyalties, low levels of education and extreme disparities of opportunity are seen as limiting the development of a democratic culture.[73] However, the absence of indicators of a robust or ideal type civil society are also to be understood as the ill-effects of the elite state's deliberate neglect of the vast cumulation of persons who form the subordinate classes of the nation.

The *Workers Party* petition is interesting because it indicts the formal legal apparatus of elections as a site where elite consensus transmogrifies into a popular mandate. It also presents a profound critique of political parties and actual democratic functioning in the country that goes beyond prognostics about the deep state and cultural atavism. The petition quietly pushes the question, 'why have political rhetoric and party policies become so oblivious to the socio-economic needs of the rural and urban poor?' In identifying the coupling of low voter turn-out and the first-past-the post electoral system, the petition draws attention to the fact that the system itself recreates a broader elite hegemony; the capacity of electoral exercises to return majorities in Parliament or enable the creation of coalitions on the basis of horse-trading is related in turn to Parliament's imperviousness to popular demands. The suggested remedies include ballots that offer a choice for 'none of the above', run-off voting in the absence of a conclusive win in any constituency and the introduction of compulsory voting. Emphasis upon on the unfair electioneering practices of wealthy parties and candidates also draws attention to the distinct disjuncture between the lives of legislators and the interests of those they purport to represent.

The disjunct is felt in the neglect of issues of human development by all political regimes in Pakistan. Whereas assemblies through the 1980s and 1990s may have been forestalled from passing any significant legislation by virtue of the extreme fragmentation of the political

[73] M Weiner, *The State, Religion and Ethnic Politics: Afghanistan, Iran and Pakistan* (Syracuse, Syracuse University Press, 1988).

sphere, recent assemblies that exist in a more cooperative environment also show only minimal deviation away from this systemic neglect. In terms of budgetary outlay, along with the government's own administrative funding, military spending continues to be the highest single output and in recent times has increased at an average rate of 11 per cent per year. In contrast, education and health come in pitiably behind, together accounting for less than 5 per cent of the annual budgetary outlay. In replication of what has now long been a pattern of political homogenisation apparent in many different parts of the world, no promises for an economic reform agenda that clashes in any way with the infamous liberalisation agenda pushed as structural adjustment by multilateral donors is on offer from any of the major parties in Pakistan. The dependency yoke of external debt reaches to $7 billion per year in servicing costs and this amongst other features of Pakistan's political economy keeps major political players in a posture of obedience to an agenda that does not seek to redress the extreme wealth and opportunity deficits in the country.

In spite of the many failures of parliamentary democracy, many of which are listed in this chapter, *Workers Party* represents not just these failures but some of the hope that has been built through the steady implantation of democracy over what is now approaching a full decade of uninterrupted Parliamentary rule in Pakistan. Over the course of two consecutive democratic governments, the rules for the holding of elections have grown palpably fairer. Particularly, the Eighteenth and Twentieth Amendments try to ensure a non-partisan character for the Election Commission and also for the interim governments that are appointed. The even more recent Twenty-second Amendment Act extended the Election Commission's oversight to cover the increasingly important realm of local government elections.

The Supreme Court and, to a lesser extent, High Courts throughout the country have finally taken up the mantle of regulating other democratic activities. This includes directing the government to remove obstructions to legitimate political protest by rival parties. They have also mandated the bounds of such protest themselves without an overheavy deference being shown to the internal security paradigm that was the hallmark of courts' functioning in previous decades.[74]

[74] *Haji Lal Muhammad v Federation of Pakistan* PLD [2014] Peshawar 199; *Muhammad Kamran v Federation of Pakistan* CLC [2014] Lahore 1549.

FURTHER READING

I Ahmad and A Rafiq, *Pakistan's Democratic Transition: Change and Persistence* (London, Routledge, 2016).

H Iqtidar *Secularising Islamists? Jamaat-e-Islami and Jamaat-ud-Dawa in Pakistan* (Chicago, University of Chicago Press, 2011).

MM Tudor, *The Promise of Power: The Origins of Democracy in India and Autocracy in Pakistan* (Cambridge, Cambridge University Press, 2013).

4

Executive Government

Civil/Military Relations – Praetoriansim – Presidential Powers – Cabinet Government – Executive Ordinances – Emergency Powers – Actions in Aid of Civil Powers

THE FRAILTY OF democratic institutions and the strength of the armed forces function conjointly throughout Pakistan's history to reinforce a strong executive and disturb any easy mapping of a trichotomous governmental order. As discussed in Chapter 3, the relative strength of the executive branch of government has been bolstered by the fiat exercised by extra-constitutional rulers to reframe the rules with each such assumption of power. This chapter describes exceptional powers, the military executive, the powers of the Prime Minister's office, judicial review of executive action and the executive ordinance powers.

Those who are unacquainted with the structure of the Pakistani Constitution could be forgiven for thinking that the army has a formally prescribed role of power-sharing in government. On the contrary, the ubiquity of the armed forces in the institutions of government has happened in spite of constitutional measures to ensure the army's subservience to civilian rule. Additionally, the expanse of emergency powers that are outlined in the Constitution do not up-end representative government altogether, nor do they provide a formal opening for army intervention. The record of constitutional adjudication on the use of 'actions in aid of civil powers' and emergency provisions of the Constitution shows heightened scrutiny of executive acts that flow from the use of these provisions. Nonetheless, the historical record speaks also to the creation of conditions conducive to military adventurism when they are employed. Additionally, the same judicial actors imposing limits on the use of exceptional powers by democratically-elected governments are quick to validate extra-constitutional acts undertaken by military rulers.

One direct consequence of military rule, at least in the short run, is to coalesce all political power in the executive branch. In the longer run, the two long periods of military rule that followed the enactment of the 1973 Constitution significantly bolstered the powers of the President. Notably, increases in the President's realm of discretionary powers invested the officeholder with the ability to dissolve elected assemblies by the insertion of Article 58(2)(b). The repeated use of these powers was of great consequence in limiting the terms of democratically-elected governments through the 1990s. Cases from these years reveal the wide ambit of discretion accorded to the high executive.

The democratic impulse, when exercised, has been to invest executive powers in the office of the Prime Minister and Cabinet. As section IV, below, illustrates though, democratic officeholders are also prone to compromising the principles and conventions of parliamentary government. In form, they thus end up replicating the heavy centralisations of executive authority that military rulers display. Starting with the record of Zulfiqar Bhutto in the 1970s and then looking at some instances from the 1990s, the acts of successive leaders of government can be understood as attempts to forestall military intervention yet are simultaneously a betrayal of the democratic aspirations of electors.

Through these shifts between a strong President and Prime Minister what remains constant is that the concentration of powers and the vertical linkages of executive rule have deep social reach and impact. Law and order, economic development and a range of fields that structure state/society relations are impacted by the pervasive role of the executive. In recent years, judicial oversight of executive decision-making has grown more elaborate. In the process, a public record of executive functioning is being compiled.

As inherited from colonial rule, the executive ordinance forms an anomalous feature of Pakistan's constitutional structure. The conferral of legislative powers in the office of the President has been of far-reaching consequence. Yet, other than in initial apprehensions voiced about its inclusion in the 1973 Constitution, democratic forces have demonstrated no major desire to see these powers reduced.

I. EXCEPTIONAL POWERS

The exceptional powers regimes provided in the Constitution, although formally indemnified against judicial review, have nonetheless been extensively adjudicated upon by the courts.

A. The Armed Forces within the Constitutional Structure

The drafters of the 1973 Constitution sought to close off the possibility of future military adventurism by criminalising extra-constitutional acts to seize power as treason, retaining powers over appointment of army high command as well as providing a narrow opening for military deployment in the country. That they were unsuccessful is attested to by the two coup d'états engineered in the years 1977 and then 1999. The provisions on treason are described below. This section looks briefly at the constitutional provisions for high military appointments and then elaborates some of the history and the principles forged as response to the invocation of Article 245, which enables the military to be called into service 'in aid of civil powers'.

Article 242 provides that 'Federal Government shall have control and command of the Armed Forces' and that supreme command of the armed forces will 'vest in the President'. Article 242(3) provides that the President, on the advice of the Prime Minister, will appoint a Joint Chief of Staff of the Armed Services and the heads of each of the three forces. A 1976 white paper on army governance advised that more command and control be vested with the civilian government and particularly in the office of the Prime Minister. Subsequent restructuring included the innovation of the office of the Joint Chief of Staff, to be responsible to the government but removed from operational control over the army, navy and air force. The aim was to keep the army in particular in check through internal oversight.[1] This specific change proved to be somewhat misguided, as the Chief of Army Staff (COAS), by retaining operational control over the army, by far the strongest of the three forces, was not much denuded of his powers.

The use of the executive prerogative for appointments to head the three forces has been the cause of much civil/military discontent over

[1] A Shah, *The Army and Democracy* (Cambridge, Harvard University Press, 2014).

the decades. The irony is that the search for the most compliant COAS by civilian leaders has backfired spectacularly; both Zia and Musharraf were picked against norms of seniority to fill this post.

The constitutional provision which provides for the armed forces to intervene in domestic affairs is Article 245. This was, in original form, more circumspect and provided only that 'The Armed Forces shall, under the directions of the Federal Government, defend Pakistan against external aggression or threat of war, and, subject to law, act in aid of civil power when called upon to do so.' Significant changes were made to Article 245 in 1977 when the National Assembly passed the Seventh Amendment Act after the military was called in to quell the Pakistan National Alliance (PNA)-led protests in Pakistan's major cities. Of the two significant alterations that the Seventh Amendment authorised, one was to indemnify the acts of the government and the military, when taken under this provision, against judicial review.[2] Sub-articles were inserted to provide that the validity of any governmental orders invoking Article 245 could not be challenged and that High Court jurisdiction under Article 199 would stand suspended regarding acts of the military when the institution was acting 'in aid of civil powers'.

In a 1977 Sindh High Court judgment that followed the introduction of these changes, the majority accepted that as long as the armed forces acted within the 'pith and substance' of the role defined by Article 245, their actions would not be reviewable.[3] One notable dissent relied extensively upon the 'subject to law' limitation to argue that courts retained jurisdiction to review army acts. In line with Ebrahim J's dissent, a further challenge was launched against the establishment of military courts to try civilians at the Lahore High Court. The majority reasoned that the army was not 'acting in aid of civil power but in derogation or replacement thereof and hence the bar contained in clause (3) of Article 245 of the Constitution was not attracted'.[4]

It was in this legal context that Zia took direct power and brought the army out from even the minimal review powers that had been read into Article 245.[5] The record thereafter of the courts has been mixed.

[2] The second important alteration was the insertion of Article 9A 'Referendum as to confidence in Prime Minister'.

[3] *Niaz Ahmed Khan v Province of Sindh* PLD [1977] Karachi 604.

[4] *Darwesh M Arbey v Federation of Pakistan* PLD [1980] Lahore 206.

[5] See text in Chapter 5, section IIA.

While some judgments display an extreme deference on account of the 'ouster' clause of Article 245(3),[6] a notable case from 1999 reverses this pattern.[7] In *Liaquat Hussain*,[8] Chief Justice Ajmal Mian, in writing the majority position, affirmed that the use by a civilian government of Article 245 'presupposes that the civil power is still there, it is neither supplanted nor effaced out' and that the employment of the armed forces is there to 'invigorate' it. Under Article 245 then the army can 'perform police functions for limited purpose of suppressing riots or preventing threatened disorder or for the purpose of maintaining law and order and security or to assist/help in natural calamities'. They cannot however 'abrogate, abridge or displace civil power of which Judiciary is an important and integral part'. This judgment was authored in February 1999 and months later General Pervez Musharraf would in fact seize power through an extra-legal coup d'état in October of that year.

B. Emergency Powers

Two broad classes of emergencies have been declared in Pakistan's recent history. The first are those proclamations that are issued extra-legally and by the leaders of military coup d'états. These are discussed further in this section as well as throughout the book.[9] The second have the backing of emergency provisions in the Constitution, themselves traceable in form to the Government of India Act 1935. The ambit of emergency powers and the conditions for their invocation are detailed below, with specific attention directed at the extent of allowable rights derogation. Both the extra-legal promulgations of emergency, by Zia and then by Bhutto, have been executed during the pendency of previously declared emergencies under Article 232 by civilian regimes. Put another way, the emergencies invoked by lawful rulers have often flowed into and been the backdrop for extra-legal emergencies.

Constitutional emergencies are to be declared by the President. Articles 232 and 235 describe the conditions that can give rise to such a

[6] For instance, *Akbar Gul Khan v Government of Pakistan* CLC [1995] Lahore 1189.

[7] See text in Chapter 5, section III.

[8] *Sheikh Liaquat Hussain v Federation of Pakistan* PLD [1999] SC 504.

[9] See Chapter 5, section II on military loyalty, and also throughout Chapter 7.

declaration: war or external aggression; an internal disturbance beyond the power of a Provincial Government to control; threats to the economic life, financial stability or credit of Pakistan or any part thereof. The most striking effect of a proclamation of emergency is to centralise decision-making in the federal government and away from provincial governments.[10] In a condition of emergency it is foreseen that the National Assembly may legislate on matters not generally within its competence and that the federal executive will assume the power to issue directives to provincial governments for further execution.

The constitutional emergency powers do not erode the powers of the National Assembly. In fact, the Assembly can both extend its tenure during an emergency and it has the powers to authorise or to nullify an emergency within 30 days of its initial declaration. However, when and if the Assembly passes a resolution to authorise an emergency declared initially by the President, it thereafter has no power to end an emergency.[11] The text of the current provision is absent an original guarantee provided in 1973, which provided for the lapse of an emergency within six months if not ended earlier by presidential proclamation.

The issue of revocation is now only dealt with in Article 236, which declares that 'a proclamation issued under this part can be varied or revoked by a subsequent proclamation'. The logical inference is that it is left to the 'sweet will of the government', or the executive to do this.[12] However, the Supreme Court, in spite of Article 236(b), which bars any court from entertaining a challenge to the validity of a proclamation of emergency, adventurously established its powers of review in the *Farooq Leghari*[13] case, described further below, to include the ability to 'review/re-examine the continuation of Emergency'.

Following upon the declaration of a state of emergency in May of 1998 by President Tarar, a challenge was passed to this Presidential Order by the former President Leghari. The factual background of the emergency was that Pakistan had shortly followed India, the country against which it had already fought three wars, in conducting tests to establish nuclear capabilities and an emergency was imposed in order to counteract the possible effects of international economic sanctions.

[10] *Sardar Farooq Ahmed Khan Leghari v Federation of Pakistan* PLD [1999] SC 57.
[11] *Syed Jalal Mehmood Shah v Federation of Pakistan* PLD [1999] SC 395.
[12] ibid.
[13] *Sardar Farooq Ahmed Khan Leghari v Federation of Pakistan* PLD [1999] SC 57.

The government of Nawaz Sharif additionally cited the possibility of external aggression. In taking up Leghari's petition, the Supreme Court undertook the task of reviewing the correctness of this proclamation and found sufficient justification for the use of Article 232, as the country was found to be facing 'imminent danger' at the time. Treading cautiously, given that Article 236(2) provides another explicit ouster of judicial review, the court did nonetheless review specific laws and executive enactments undertaken on the basis of further elaborated emergency powers.

These further emergency powers are conferred by Article 233 and allow for the suspension of fundamental rights in emergency conditions. Article 233(1) expressly provides that 'nothing contained in Articles 15, 16, 17, 18, 19, and 24 shall, while a proclamation of Emergency is in force, restrict the power of the State to make any law or to take any executive action' contrary to these protections.[14] In contrast, Article 232(2) enables the President to pass an order suspending additional rights for the duration of an emergency. It also specifies both that any order made under the article shall be laid before a sitting of both houses of the Assembly for approval, and that courts will be barred from the enforcement of any of the suspended rights.

While a plain reading of Article 233(1) seems to imply an extension of state powers directly consequent upon the declaration of emergency, whether or not these powers are spontaneously realised was a question posed in the *Farooq Leghari* case. The majority response to the question was that they were not. The court relied upon a range of international treaties and instruments to establish that the suspension of all rights needed to be undertaken with a view to the 'modern jurisprudential theory of proportionality'. Criteria to consider in measuring proportionality included of the severity of causes considered to be threatening 'the life of the nation', good faith of the government and the continued operation of the principle of non-discrimination. The court additionally cited the enshrinement of the principle of non-discrimination under Article 4 of the Constitution to establish the right to be treated according to and with equal protection of the law as a touchstone for valid governmental action in conditions of emergency.[15] Thus, the

[14] These are the rights of movement, assembly, association, speech, trade/business/profession and property.

[15] *Shahid Orakzai v President of Pakistan* SCMR [1999] SC 1598.

rights of speech, assembly and others are liable to be controverted, but a 'direct nexus' for their limitation and the objects desired to be met in the declaration of emergency need also be established.

Liaquat Hussain, the case involving the establishment of military courts under Article 245 also tested the bounds of emergency powers. In it, Chief Justice Ajmal Mian made minimal allowance for rights derogation, as the Constitution itself does not 'visualize that the scope of Article 4, 9, 10, and 25 can be curtailed or diluted'.[16] In the creation of military courts, these rights were all violated, and thereby the offending ordinance was invalidated.[17] Such standards of strict scrutiny were applied again in the *Mian Allah Nawaz* case,[18] where state functionaries were conferred naked and unstructured power.

An account of this judicial record is aided by the acknowledgment that heightened standards of review seem always to be employed by the judiciary when military regimes are tottering and/or when democratic governments are in power. This is amply displayed elsewhere in this book as well as in section V, below, on 'Taming the Executive'.

II. A MILITARISED EXECUTIVE

Political science analysis often classifies Pakistan as a praetorian state. In its historically accurate sense, praetorianism references the pressure exerted by the armed forces upon civilian governments to mould their workings to accord with military objectives. In Pakistan, the armed forces have often directly wielded power, and when General Musharraf relinquished the office of President in 2008, that marked the 32nd year in the country's history that a military officer had held the position of head of state.

While it is outside the ambit of this book to study the direct and indirect forms of praetorianism that define governmental functioning in Pakistan, it is useful to understand that there are a plurality of views on its persistence. One view that has by now been mostly discredited suggests that the congenitally underdeveloped state of the Pakistani

[16] *Manzoor Elahi v Federation of Pakistan* PLD [1975] SC 66.

[17] See text in Chapter 5, section III.

[18] *Shaukat Ali Mian v Federation of Pakistan* CLC [1999] Lahore 607.

political and social sphere impels army intervention in government.[19] Given that the army itself is instrumental in establishing a vast mythography about its own organisational efficiencies, contrary to its record of losses in the battlefield, it is not hard to see why this may guide a public acceptance of such incursions. However, greater explanatory value is had from being acquainted with the vastness of the military's commercial and industrial holdings. Combined with the need to ensure the continuance of a now-established custom of disallowing legislative debate on the vast budgetary outlay to the armed forces, the forces also benefit from governmental measures to ensure monopolistic protections for their industrial and other economic enterprises.[20] In turn, the profitable nature of these enterprises provides extensive autonomy from political oversight for the institution, the possibility of continued post-retirement employment for its rank and file members, and exceedingly comfortable lives for its high officer cadre.

Another factor that has to be given credence is that Pakistan's often crucial geostrategic location has resulted in a manifestation of a preference by important actors in the international state system on bargaining and negotiating with leaders who merge military and governmental controls. While such an explanation may not explain their rise to power, the longevity of rule for Zia and then Musharraf was ultimately and quite apparently tied to the support each lent to the US, first in waging a proxy war against the USSR in Afghanistan during the 1980s and then in the war against Al Qaeda in Afghanistan and within Pakistan's own borders since 2001.

The few comments here on military praetorianism are aimed only at lessening what seems otherwise to be an unbridgeable chasm between the higher law prescriptions of governmental order as per the Constitution and that which has transpired in reality. A fuller discussion of the praetorian elements would be alert to the multi-scalar militarisation that exists in periods of indirect praetorianism, and which gains rapid ground with a military head of state. Tellingly, quotas exist across state educational institutions for the admission of children of military personnel, although there have been some successful challenges to

[19] S Huntington, *The Soldier and the State* (Boston, Harvard University Press, 1957).

[20] See T Ali, 'The Colour Khaki' (2003) 19 *New Left Review* 5, 11. See also A Siddiqua, *Military Inc. Inside Pakistan's Military Economy* (London, Pluto Press, 2007).

the retention of these.[21] Further, a deep militarisation of the broader governmental order happens when military leaders are granted top-tier positions in the bureaucracy, governmental industries and even in public sector universities. All of these reservations and appointments help to recreate the ideological justifications for praetorianism.[22]

Given the role courts have played to keep a broader constitutionalism alive during emergencies, it is a seeming anomaly that the same judicial officers, in many cases, would capitulate so readily in the face of extra-constitutional takeovers. If however constitutionalism is an attempt to ensure that all exercises of power are rule-bound, the furtive search by the courts for such rules follows upon the need to retain their foothold in a given governance scheme. By forging early on a demonstrable fidelity to a pure positivism, which avows that the law is what the sovereign says and that the sovereign is he or she who effectively controls the coercive apparatus of the state, courts have effectively encouraged military dictators to refashion the rules to give cover to their own illimitability.[23] In turn, these rulers have done this both by assumption of constitutionally-sanctioned executive office, as Chief Executive and/or President, as well as by bolstering the powers of the same.

A. Presidential Powers

Interestingly, neither Zia nor Musharraf sought to replace the existing Constitution altogether, as Ayub had done before them. Explanations could be sought in the further reach of Ayub's vision for national development,[24] as opposed to the more perfunctory nature of both Zia and Musharraf's will to power. The immediate history of Zia's takeover of power is described in Chapter 5, in reference the Supreme Court validation of the coup on the basis of the doctrine of state necessity.

[21] *Attiya Bibi Khan v Federation of Pakistan through Secretary of Education* SCMR [2001] SC 1161. The Court decreed that the reservation of seats for medical college entry for doctors' children and army personnel violated Art 25.

[22] For an account of Ministry of Defence Notifications regarding army quotas in bureaucracy see *Major (Retd) Tipu Sultan v Shahzad Hassan* SCMR [2004] SC 1215.

[23] *FB Ali v The State* PLD [1975] SC 506.

[24] See text in Chapter 2, section V.

Here it is important that Zia retained Fazal Elahi Chaudhry as the President after declaring Martial Law on 5 July 1977. Chaudhry was perhaps the only President in Pakistan's history to occupy this role as the figurehead defined in the 1973 Constitution, accepting that the advice of the Prime Minister was binding and that every Presidential Order needed to be countersigned by the Prime Minister.[25] Thereafter, there would be a continuing tussle to codify the expanse of powers accorded to the Prime Minister versus the President. Chaudhry would resign in 1978 due to Zia's unwillingness to hold elections.

Chaudhry's resignation opened up the possibility of transforming the formal powers of the President's office as Zia himself assumed this role. He extended his occupancy in office for an additional five years in 1984 by holding a referendum in which citizens were asked whether or not they wished to see Pakistan governed in accord with Quran and Sunnah under his guidance. In anticipating a transition to managed democracy he expanded the role and competencies of the President to a considerable extent. Amongst the many changes brought in 1985, first through the Revival of the Constitution of 1973 Order (RCO) and then through the Eighth Amendment to the Constitution, Article 90 was altered to read: 'The executive authority of the Federation shall vest in the President and shall be exercised by him, either directly or through officers subordinate to him'. Confusingly, Article 48 also provided the formula that 'the President shall act in accordance with the advice of the Cabinet or the Prime Minister' but with the further qualification that the President then 'reconsider such advice'. Where, however, the President was free to act on his discretion, the validity of such acts 'shall not be called in question on any ground whatsoever'. Additionally, the formula for impeaching a sitting President was revised from the requirement of a simple majority vote of Parliament in cases of mental or physical infirmity or in acting to violate the Constitution to a much more difficult process.[26]

Most importantly, Article 58(2)(b) granted the President the power to dissolve the National Assembly in 'his discretion where in his opinion a

[25] Art 48 of the original elaborated these features.

[26] Art 47 was revised to give the present formula that after notice, investigation and a hearing, the President can only be impeached by a vote of two-thirds for the total membership of both houses of Parliament.

situation has arisen in which the Government of the Federation cannot be carried on in accordance with the provisions of the Constitution and an appeal to the electorate is necessary.' This, as we will see in the following section, was of great consequence in dictating the fortunes of several governments during the democratic interregnum between the Zia and Musharraf regimes.

The second coup engineered in the period after the promulgation of the 1973 Constitution was in October 1999. In conditions discussed below in this chapter, General Parvez Musharraf dismissed the government of Nawaz Sharif, issued a Proclamation of Emergency that declared the Constitution to be temporarily in abeyance and announced the Provisional Constitutional Order (PCO) of 1999. Although the PCO expressly denied the superior courts the jurisdiction to review the validity of Musharraf's acts, the Supreme Court, as in all such previous cases, maintained its claim to an inherent review jurisdiction.[27]

The Musharraf coup and its subsequent review at the Supreme Court revived the application of the 'doctrine of state necessity', but not before the court bemoaned the ways in which the deletion of Article 58(2)(b) two years earlier had necessitated such extra-constitutional action.[28]

In *Zafar Ali Shah v General Pervez Musharraf*, the court validated Musharraf's assumption of the role of Chief Executive, even though this nomenclature for the Prime Minister from the original text of the 1973 Constitution had been removed by way of the Eighth Amendment. Additionally, as the Court had done for Zia, it also offered Musharraf the power to alter law or even Constitution as his reward for holding the Constitution in abeyance rather than having chosen the course of 'abrogation'. However, in this case, certain salient features were presented as defining the limiting conditions on what alterations to constitutional structure could be validly undertaken by Musharraf. These features were named as 'independence of Judiciary, federalism and parliamentary form of government blended with Islamic Provision' (*sic*).[29] Also, the Supreme Court imposed a limit on the duration of the state of necessity, granting the regime three years within which

[27] See text in Chapter 5, section IIA.

[28] *Syed Zafar Ali Shah v General Parvez Musarraf* PLD [2000] SC 869.

[29] See text in Chapter 5, section IIA.

to hold elections for the national legislature on the ground that that was how long it would take for electoral rolls to be compiled afresh.[30]

Unlike Zia before him, Musharraf had ordered the removal of President Tarar, a Nawaz Sharif nominee for President. To validate that there were no other contenders for power as he presided over a caretaker Cabinet also without constitutional authorisation, a presidential referendum was held by Musharraf in 2001 after he first took office under the Presidential Succession Order earlier that year.[31] Challenges to the legality of the referendum failed in the courts[32] and Musharraf secured a high approval rating from an exercise that had no strict constitutional authorisation. Not just blatantly stage-managed, the question that people were asked to vote on was itself 'leading and loaded'.[33] Again, Musharraf stuck to Zia's script in now reinserting Article 58(2)(b) when elections were to be held and the post of President was already his. The altered Article 90 did not reincorporate the designation of Chief Executive for the Prime Minister so that in totality, the balance of powers, especially aided now with additional alterations such as in the creation of the National Security Council, had been tilted back to the President.[34]

Musharraf's alterations were passed through the 2002 elected National Assembly in the form of the Seventeenth Amendment Act. His maintenance of power relied, however, on the wilful and bartered compliance of the judiciary and the legislature. From the latter, a standalone and personalised law authorising Musharraf to retain the dual offices of President and Chief of Army Staff was bought for a period of time.[35] From the former, as demonstrated by the *Pakistan Lawyers Forum* case (2005), challenges to constitutional amendments on the ground that they violated the basic structure of the 1973 Constitution allowed the Court once again to hold that the basic structure was not

[30] See text in Chapter 3, section IIIB.

[31] *Pakistan Lawyers Forum v Federation of Pakistan* PLD [2004] Lahore 130.

[32] *Qazi Hussain Ahmed v General Pervez Musharraf* PLD [2002] SC 853.

[33] V Kukreja and MP Singh, *Pakistan: Democracy, Development and Security Issues* (New Delhi, Sage Publications, 2005) 69.

[34] S Khan, 'Battling Militancy: Government revives National Security Council' *Express Tribune* (23 August 2013) <www.tribune.com.pk/story/594103/battling-militancy-govt-revives-national-security-council/>.

[35] The President to Hold Another Office Act, 2004.

a part of Pakistan's constitutional law and that, in any case, the amendment had been validly passed by the legislature.[36]

By the time Musharraf was close to seeking a re-election as President at the lapse of his five-year term, he was facing a more recalcitrant Supreme Court bench: powers of high executive office were being recast and reshaped in the Supreme Court headed by Chief Justice Chaudhry.[37] In the lead-up to this election, the Supreme Court, through an interim order, enabled Musharraf to contest a scheduled presidential election from within the existing Assembly, but directed the Election Commission to await notification of the results until the court finished deliberating on several challenges that had come forth.[38]

A range of notable court cases were fought or arose from the actions of President General Musharraf, specifically following upon his second declaration of emergency in November 2007, culminating in the nullification of a set of executive orders he issued in this period. What marks the end of Musharraf's reign is an active pursuit initiated by political actors and the judiciary to prosecute Musharraf for suspending the Constitution.

III. COURTS AS REFEREES—ARTICLE 58(2)(B), PRESIDENT v PM

The 1990s in Pakistan are emblematic of the internecine conflict between the President and the Prime Minister in which the former's power to dissolve elected assemblies under Article 58(2)(b) was repeatedly used. There were four dissolutions, one by Zia, two by President Ishaque and then one by President Farooq Leghari in these years.

In reading the cases that fall under the exercise of Article 58(2)(b) the first in 1988 and then through the 1990s, it is apparent that exercise of executive discretion is measured similarly whether the dissolution of an elected government happens by way of constitutional powers or by way of military coup. While the four cases adjudicating the presidential invocations of Article 58(2)(b) demonstrate a strong deference to executive decision-making, they together amount to a resounding cacophony of inconsistency about the extent to which the

[36] *Pakistan Lawyer's Forum v Federation of Pakistan* PLD [2005] SC 719.

[37] See text in Chapter 5, section IV.

[38] *Wajihuddin Ahmed v Chief Election Commissioner* PLD [2008] SC 13.

President's 'satisfaction' should be considered justiciable. Also there are varied standards employed to assess the sufficiency of evidence about whether the decision approached some level of reasonableness.

The first case was heard after the death of General Zia-ul-Haq and tested the lawfulness of his actions to dissolve the Assembly elected on a non-party basis and headed by Muhammad Khan Junejo in 1988.[39] In taking up this case the Lahore High Court established the standard that in spite of Article 58(2)(b) the discretion of the President must be 'based on facts and reasons which are objective realities'.[40] Given that the object had been given in the terms that 'the government cannot be carried on …' the discretion exercised must be justified in relation to material grounds proving this object; the burden was found not to have been met in this case. While this, the *Saifullah* judgment, established a higher threshold of showing governmental breakdown than in subsequent cases, the succeeding cases all follow it in structure but show no consistency on the conditions of breakdown that could give rise to its use. The case was decided after Zia died in an airplane crash and the military high command had already requested the Chairman of the Senate, Ghulam Ishaq Khan to become acting President.[41]

The three subsequent cases were all heard at the Supreme Court and all assumed, once again, the right to exercise revisional and supervisory jurisdiction.[42] In contrast to the sparse order of dissolution that had accompanied Zia's actions in 1988, succeeding dissolution orders were issued with a range of more specific charges against the government to present first a public and then a legal justification for the action being undertaken. Notably, all of these dissolutions cited some form of constitutional stalemate, given the resignation of Cabinet or opposition members, and the consequent inability for the governmental machinery to operate or for legislative action to be undertaken. Further, they all also cited rampant corruption amongst high office holders as impairment on governmental functioning. For the two dissolutions that

[39] *Federation of Pakistan v Muhammad Saifullah Khan* PLD [1989] SC 166.

[40] Fazal Karim, *Judicial Review of Public Actions* (Karachi, Pakistan Law House, 2006).

[41] S Chaitram, 'Toward A Reclassification of Praetorian Rulers: Lessons from the Pakistani Experience' (2010) 27 *Journal of Third World Studies* 63.

[42] *Ahmad Tariq Rahim v Pakistan* PLD [1992] SC 646; *Nawaz Sharif v President of Pakistan* PLD [1993] SC 473; *Mohtarma Benazir Bhutto v President of Pakistan* PLD [1998] SC 388.

affected the government of Benazir Bhutto, the degeneration of the law and order situation in Karachi and the invasion of privacy through telephone wiretapping were also specifically included. The dissolution of the first Nawaz Sharif government followed upon a public speech in which he specifically alleged that President Ghulam Ishaq Khan was undermining his government's authority. In three of these cases, issues of executive or prime ministerial incursions into judicial autonomy were also cited.

In reading these grounds against available evidence, which at times includes the post-hoc availability of press reports, the court veers widely rather than establishing guiding and certain threshold level conditions to establish what might be akin to a constitutional 'emergency' sufficient to warrant dissolution.[43] Rather, the goalposts themselves also change insofar as terms such as 'imminent breakdown', deadlock, impasse and stalemate are used at the same time that failure to protect fundamental rights or to ensure the rule of law are also invoked to try to assess the proper bounds for the exercise of Article 58(2)(b) powers.

These cases are exceedingly important in illustrating the realpolitik of the time, and the continuing impetus to democratic movements and parties to adequately close off possibilities for future presidential adventurism. The quick succession of governments did not create an immediate unity of interests against the 'deep state' though; the very existence of this presidential power was an effective inducement for opposition parties to frustrate and impede the functioning of government so as to precipitate a dissolution and a new round of elections. For this reason and others, the decade of the 1990s is associated with deep fractures in provincial/federal relations and low levels of legislative performance.

Additionally, these cases are also indicative of the ways in which the constitutional system had become ever-more a hybrid one between presidential and parliamentary.[44] This hybridity was itself validated by the Court in the 1997 case of *Mahmood Khan Achakzai*. The basic structure doctrine was once again invoked to assert that the Eighth Amendment and specifically Article 58(2)(b) upset the structure of

[43] See text in Chapter 6, section IV.

[44] *Ahmad Tariq Rahim v Pakistan* PLD [1992] SC 646: it was ruled that the discretion of the President to appoint a caretaker Cabinet cannot be subjected to any restriction.

parliamentary democracy in Pakistan. The Court, in repelling the doctrine and its application in Pakistan, also suggested that the division of powers between constitutional officers was of the order of a political question that it did not feel able to adjudicate upon. Interestingly, it offered justification for its oversight of dissolutions broadly as a power that stemmed from within the constitutional structure.[45]

Following upon General Musharraf's coup in 1998 and in the 'transition' to democracy he engineered in the coming years, he acted under a judicial validation of the coup and self-assumed authority as Chief Executive to reincorporate certain provisions of the Eighth Amendment. While the power of dissolution was one mechanism of vesting ultimate sovereign authority in the office of the President, the Seventeenth Amendment of 2003 also once again increased the subject matters on which the President would exercise discretionary authority. The Eighteenth Amendment, passed in 2010, is the final instrument in this chain and reflects the primacy of an elected executive in the person of the Prime Minister and the role of the President reduced back to what it was in the original 1973 Constitution. Importantly, it repealed Article 58(2)(b).

IV. A PRIME MINISTERIAL EXECUTIVE

While a primary impulse of representative governments has been to invest executive powers in the office of the Prime Minister and Cabinet, the extent to which the Prime Minister's office has accrued far greater powers in the mode of personalised rule tests the claims for democracy that might be made. Such tendencies were exemplified by Zulfiqar Bhutto in the years 1971–1977. The Interim Constitution that his government pushed through the legislature in 1972 installed him in the office of President, an office that was 'more powerful than even the President in the US Constitution'.[46]

In the formulation of the 1973 Constitution, democratic consensus militated for a turn to parliamentary democracy. By the time that

[45] *Mahmood Khan Achakzai v Federation of Pakistan* PLD [1997] SC 426.

[46] SJ Ahmed, 'The Dilemmas of Transition from Military to Civilian Regime: The Making of the 1972 Interim Constitution of Pakistan' (2012) 60 *Journal of the Pakistan Historical Society* 39, 51.

Bhutto was displaced from power he had refashioned the office of the Prime Minister so that it embodied the unitariness of power that he had professed an original preference for. He used the malleability of parliamentary convention to retain powers away from and at the expense of his own appointed Ministers.

A further means of enacting unitary power that had been retained in the new Constitution was the power of promulgating Ordinances. Altogether, over 200 ordinances were enacted in the years 1972–1977. With the aid of a President duly willing to act on his advice, the need for building political consensus, for conferring with Parliament or even ministers in the making of law was circumvented by Bhutto. In fact, Parliament itself was deeply neglected and Bhutto and his Cabinet ministers were said to be rarely in attendance. Additionally, Bhutto engineered a Seventh Amendment Act, inserting a new Article 96A into the Constitution, which allowed the Prime Minister to advise the President to call for a popular referendum to express confidence in the office of the Prime Minister.[47] Although there was no formal clash with the provision laying out the procedure for a parliamentary vote of confidence, it can only be surmised that Bhutto sought, through this, to establish a parallel forum to justify his continuing hold on office as opposition parties aligned in establishing the PNA.[48]

The heavy-handedness with which Bhutto employed executive powers also impelled various reforms to the structure of the bureaucratic-military complex. Towards the army, Bhutto engineered policies of both reform and appeasement. This dualism stemmed from a reliance upon the army to quell labour agitation, regional conflict and, in the final instance, in 1977 in the short-sighted way that Article 245 was invoked to insulate Bhutto against street protest. In contrast he perceived that the self-confidence or arrogance of the bureaucracy needed to be broken if his populist redistributionary policies were to be realised.[49] The intention to reform it was expressed first and foremost by the omission of constitutional protection, in contrast to both

[47] Removed by way of the Revival of the Constitution of 1973 Order, 1985.

[48] See text in Chapter 4, section IA.

[49] CH Kennedy, 'Prestige of Services and Bhutto's Administrative Reform in Pakistan, 1973–1984' (1985) 12 *Asian Affairs* 25.

prior constitutions, for appointment, promotion rank, and so forth, for members of the services.[50]

The reforms of army and bureaucracy were neither unwelcome nor unauthorised within the powers granted to the Prime Minister. However, in combination with the multiple constitutional amendments oriented to altering the terms of service for the judiciary, these acts by Bhutto reinforced a perception that he was enacting personalised rule. Further, the retention of emergency powers under Article 232 for most of his time in power similarly lent credence to apprehensions of his authoritarianism. Notoriously, he also established a secret police service that was responsible only to him, as Prime Minister. While its ambit of operations was limited, its creation was deeply resented amongst the conventional armed forces.

The consolidations of power that Bhutto engineered as Prime Minister and Chief Executive were insufficient nonetheless to keep him installed in office. When his daughter assumed the position of Prime Minster 11 years after his execution, the rules had changed considerably. In Benazir Bhutto's first term in office, she had to take virtual dictation from the army high command about several appointments to her Cabinet as amongst the many conditions imposed for being asked to form the government, even when her party had won the greatest number of seats in the 1988 election. Other clear conditions, those which have thereafter marked a red line of danger when civilian politicians cross at their own peril, were to neither meddle in the promotions of the army nor with matters of foreign affairs and defence.[51]

When the PML-N and Nawaz Sharif won a two-thirds majority in Parliament in 1996, the government ensured the removal of Article 58(2)(b) through the Thirteenth Amendment Act. Sharif also made haste on additional measures and Acts to insulate itself and this included passage of the Fourteenth Amendment to the Constitution, in 1997[52] which barred floor-crossing. While the Amendment came to

[50] S Maheshwari, 'Administrative reforms in Pakistan' (1974) 35 *The Indian Journal of Political Science* 144.

[51] See A Jalal, *The Struggle for Pakistan* (Cambridge, Harvard University Press, 2014) 305–306.

[52] Text of Fourteenth Amendment—by way of inclusion of Art 63A 'Disqualification on ground of defection, etc'.

be at issue in much of the breakdown of relations between Sharif and the Supreme Court and then between Sharif and President Leghari,[53] it was upheld against a challenge at the Supreme Court.[54]

Sharif also shrouded his drive towards further executive and legislative powers within the office of the Prime Minister under the rubric of furthering the Islamisation of the legal system.[55] The Fifteenth Amendment proposed only a few changes to the existing Constitution but these proposals aroused great anxiety about Sharif's dictatorial aspirations. To speed up Islamisation, the executive was being empowered to issue directives, which had no other constitutional authorisation. Furthermore, the constitutional amendment formula was to be made more lenient for measures oriented to Islamisation. Just as Zia had renamed the National Assembly Majlis-I-Shoora to signify that it was a body for consultation, so it seemed that Sharif was aiming for a similar demotion of parliamentary institutions. The Fifteenth Amendment was passed by the lower house and was in the Senate when Musharraf's November 1999 coup disturbed this advance.[56]

Backed by a two-thirds majority in Parliament, Sharif had built up a mistaken notion of immovability from power, given this historic mandate. Additionally, in a hawkish public environment, he had also gained some public stature for having undertaken the step of testing to establish Pakistan's nuclear capabilities. Several missteps would, however, place him on the other side of the red line that marked danger for civilian rulers in Pakistan. In October 1998, the army high command had initiated a military operation to regain the Kargil Valley from Indian occupation. Vast casualties ensued on both sides as, counter to Pakistani calculations, the Indian army and public was willing to put up a significant fight. By all reliable accounts, Sharif had been kept in the dark through the planning and original invasion, posing

53 See text in Chapter 5, section VII.

54 *Wukula Mahazv Baraiv Tahafaz Dastoor v Federation of Pakistan* PLD [1998] SC 1263.

55 A Jan, 'Pakistan on the Precipice' (1999) 39 *Asian Survey* 699.

56 The Fifteenth Amendment Act sought to introduce an Art 2B, which would establish the Supremacy of Quran and Sunnah. The Fifteenth Amendment Act text is available online at <www.pakistani.org/pakistan/constitution/amendments/15amendment_new.html>.

the distinct quandary that, 'An army chief acting unilaterally poses serious questions of legality, while the Prime Minister's complicity in the Kargil episode raises concerns about his credibility, months after the two nuclear rivals had signed an agreement in February 1999'.[57] Under significant international, particularly American, pressure Sharif agreed to a unilateral withdrawal while maintaining that the invasion was not in fact undertaken by army regulars. The terms and timing of the withdrawal enraged the army high command. Later in the same year, Sharif sought to displace General Musharraf as Chief of Army Staff while the latter was on a trip to Sri Lanka. This became the pretext for the staging of Musharraf's coup, Sharif's trial for hijacking and an eventual negotiated plea bargain that allowed Sharif to retreat, in exile to Saudi Arabia.[58]

With Nawaz Sharif as Prime Minister of a majority government since 2013, there has been a perceptible centralisation of powers once again, but not with the aid of Constitutional Amendments. With a hand-picked President, a majority PML-N Assembly at the centre, as well as a PML-N government with his brother as Chief Minister in Punjab, the only effective threats to this power has been exercised indirectly by the military.[59]

V. TAMING THE EXECUTIVE

Whereas earlier attempts to tame the executive by the judiciary followed a more circuitous route, what happened under the Chaudhry court—and which excited a vast retributive reaction against it—was a much more direct assault on what were considered unassailable prerogative powers by executive functionaries of the state. By erecting itself in some ways as the 'regulator' of state action broadly, the court began a process of calling into account both the elected and unelected sections of the executive branch.

[57] Jalal, *The Struggle for Pakistan.*

[58] C Baxter, *Pakistan on the Brink, Politics Economics and Society* (Lanham, Lexington, 2004) 56.

[59] It was widely reported that the anti-rigging protests staged by the PTI were an instance of pressure being exerted upon the PML-N government.

A. Military Adventurism Ended?

The Sindh High Court Bar Association[60] case is the judicial response to the last historical attempt to instantiate a new body of laws by executive fiat in Pakistan. Through it, alterations made to the Constitution from the declaration of a 2007 emergency onwards were declared void.

In the unanimous decision authored by Chief Justice Chaudhry, a long history of judicial acquiescence in the face of unconstitutional takeovers and power aggrandisements was declared as having always been wrong in law. In contrast to the harkening for a higher law in the form of protected principles that the basic structure doctrine necessitates, this judgment sought to find safeguards for the future within the 'four corners of the constitutional text'. Thus, the issue of army takeovers was related to the existing Article 6 which describes as 'high treason' any acts to abrogate, subvert or hold in abeyance the Constitution. Further, that Article 245(b) provides the only possible means where the military can perform a role in civilian life and that too 'in aid of' and as requested by civil powers. In labouring over this judgment, the court sought to warn high army officers and their aiders and abettors that they should seek to gain power only at their own peril. Additionally, the judgment prescribed a procedural conformity with the constitutional text insofar as the amendment formula as described in Articles 237 and 238 provide the sole criterion by which to measure an amendment as valid. Those amendments undertaken as Presidential Ordinances were thereby declared invalid. Thus, although the invalidation impacted only those 'legal bridges' Musharraf contrived in his last months in power, the sheer fact that such a thorough review was undertaken followed through with the aims of the *Asma Jilani* judgment of 1973.

In April 2014 Musharraf was charged with high treason under Article 6 of the Constitution and its enabling law.[61] The charge sheet was framed in reference to five specific acts undertaken in and around the 2007 declaration of emergency. These included the proclamation of emergency itself, the administration of oath of office to judges and attempts to amend the Constitution by Presidential Order and by incorporation of Article 270AAA into the constitutional text.

[60] *Sindh High Court Bar Association v Federation of Pakistan* PLD [2009] SC 879.
[61] High Treason Punishment Act, 1973.

While the court case continues and a variety of charges have been framed for a number of Musharraf's associates and accomplices, including the Prime Minister of the time, Shaukat Aziz, the outcome is yet uncertain. It seems to be one of the pieces on the chessboard of civil/military relations, such that it is reputed that attempts to destabilise the Nawaz Sharif regime by the military are due to the affront the institution feels at having one of its own brought to account. The delays in delivering a verdict include Musharraf's ability to seek and be granted permission of the court to undergo medical treatment outside the country for a range of dubious ailments. Again, this indicates to the average Pakistani the high-handedness of the military in ensuring that the case does not achieve conclusion and conviction.

B. Democratic Executive and Prerogative Powers Reviewed

A range of petitions ranged at the high offices of the Prime Minister and his Cabinet were taken up in the years after 2008. These included high-value corruption cases implicating the elected executive. Importantly, the *Rental Power Plant* case[62] of 2012 was heard and resulted eventually in the issuance of an arrest warrant for Prime Minister Raja Pervaiz Ashraf. As Minister of Water and Power, Ashraf had been responsible for the enforcement of a policy first outlined in the latter days of a Musharraf presidency. The policy was aimed at providing a quick fix to alleviate acute energy shortages in the country.

Against evidence published by the Asian Development Bank of significant governmental financing of private investors and negligible electricity production, the Supreme Court took notice. Sticking close to a script of judicial review of administrative action that it had authored in the earlier *Steel Mills Privatisation* case,[63] the Court looked at the reasonableness, legality and transparency of the government's actions. In fact, it read this violation of transparency as a compromise of both fundamental rights to 'life and liberty' as well as security of property. The fact that the Court read the provision of electricity as amongst the constitutive base for a fundamental right to life is in keeping with

[62] *Alleged Corruption in Rental Power Plants* SCMR [2012] SC 773.

[63] *Watan Party v Federation of Pakistan* PLD [206] SC 697.

a range of other cases it investigated in these years to uncover executive maladministration in the provisioning of basic utilities.[64] It thereby boldly trod into the domain of making directions about allocation of resources.[65]

In addition, the idea of a fundamental collective right to resources also underlay the court's reasoning in the *Reko Diq* case.[66] This case involved a considerable mining concession to a consortium of foreign companies in the province of Balochistan.

The Chaudhry court refused to cede jurisdiction to hear the case in spite of a range of arguments urging restraint. To this end, the case for the Australian/Canadian and Chilean mining consortium seemed to present something akin to a 'doctrine of globalisation'. Overarching principles of international commercial law, evidence of an arbitration clause and Pakistan's ratification of a range of bilateral investment treaties were the important features of such advocacy. The Court countered these with a range of principles from international public law treaties governing corruption. Although no specific charges of corruption have been laid from this case, evidence of conflicts of interest amongst several parties and possible corruption was brought on record. Coupled with a range of procedural irregularities involved in the grant of the concession, the court determined that contracts contrary to domestic law would not be enforced. Additionally evidence of non-enforcement of existing rules and the absence of transparency led the court to declare the whole of the agreement *void ab initio*.

In *Reko Diq* the court also made forceful recommendations in an area that has remained within the domain of executive prerogative: the signing of international instruments and treaties. The court provided the forceful recommendation that the federal government must consult all provinces before becoming signatory to such treaties. Citing the fact that the compensatory regimes established by way of bilateral investment treaties for direct and indirect expropriation are 'expanding to include even delay in decision of the court, change in legislation and adverse decision of domestic court', the court directed that the federal government must consider the impact that the ratification of such

[64] *Engineer Iqbal Zafar Jhagra v Federation of Pakistan* [2009] SCMR 1399.

[65] *Engineer Iqbal Zafar Jhagra and Senator Rukhsana Zuberi v Federation of Pakistan* PTD [2014] SC 243.

[66] *Maulana Abdul Haq Baloch v Government of Balochistan* PLD [2013] SC 641.

treaties has upon the constitutional principle of 'independence of the judiciary'. Although it was not ultimately passed into law, a proposed Ratification of Treaties Bill was introduced shortly thereafter as a private members Bill in Parliament.

While the resource nationalism displayed in the *Reko Diq* case ensured wide-ranging, though far from universal, favour in the realm of public opinion, another set of cases, also putatively tied to issues of endemic corruption, were more susceptible to charges of judicial overreach.[67] These involved the court directly intervening in the matter of appointments to public sector organisations and high-level bureaucratic positions. As noted elsewhere, the bureaucracy in Pakistan exercises considerable power and as the functional executor of policy and executive decision-making, bureaucrats are necessary intermediaries in many forms of developmental and transactional activity. Individually and as a class, they are much scrutinised for displaying any vestige of unjust enrichment or politicisation.

However, the longer history of what now appears as endemic and systemic 'corruption' arises partially from the changes that impacted the structure of the civil services of Pakistan through the 1973 Constitution. It has been argued that the restructuring carried out by Bhutto, by allowing for greater political control to be exercised over promotions and terms of service, has caused palpable deterioration in the services rendered by the bureaucracy.[68] It was in this context that the Chaudhry court, upon a petition by a member of the PML-N, devised a formula of appointment that was extremely contentious.

In the *Khawaja Asif* case,[69] the court recommended that a 'Code of Practice' be devised and under it an independent commission be established to oversee all high-level bureaucratic appointments. However, in exercise of its revisional jurisdiction, a bench headed by one of Chaudhry's successor chief justices has held that this recommendation does not hold the status of law and that in fact it erred in non-consideration of Article 90 of the Constitution. Chief Justice Nasir-ul-Mulk

[67] See F Siddiqi, 'Public Interest Litigation: Predictable Continuity and Radical Departures' in MH Cheema and IS Gilani (eds), *The Politics and Jurisprudence of the Chaudhry Court 2005–2013* (Karachi, Oxford University Press, 2015); see also text in Chapter 5, section V.

[68] CH Kennedy, *Bureaucracy in Pakistan* (Oxford, Oxford University Press, 1987).

[69] *Khawaja Muhammad Asif v Federation of Pakistan* SCMR [2013] SC 1205.

restated a principle that has in fact guided the judiciary for the longer duration of its operations, in that it is 'settled law that the Courts should ordinarily refrain from interfering in policy making domain of the Executive'.[70] In short, the Chief Justice displayed a fidelity to more conventional views of the trichotomy of powers with clearly delineated and rule-bound abidance of existing rules and laws. However, he stated that the principle of judicial deference will only apply where the executive is seen to be complying with existing laws and in abidance of the principle that 'where appointments are to be made in exercise of discretionary powers, such powers are to be employed in a reasonable manner'.

VI. PRESIDENTIAL ORDINANCES

Article 89 of the Constitution firmly accords legislative powers to the President. In contrast to the elevated forms of contest that have been played out in reference to other executive and presidential powers, the grant of ordinance-making powers has rarely been the subject of controversy. While the discussion surrounding the reincorporation of Executive Ordinances through the 1973 parliamentary debates was at times heated, all attempts to amend or abolish these powers were defeated by the government. Some previous PPP stalwarts who had lost favour with Bhutto argued from the position that the ordinance power was itself a 'relic' of our imperial history; amendments were tabled that would limit the exercise of Presidential Ordinances to the pendency of war and other disorder sufficient to constitute an emergency. On another pole, the need for ordinances to meet substantive conformity with Quran and Sunnah was also tabled.

In many ways the more important amendment that also failed at this time was one seeking to restrict the use of the ordinance power against the making of laws that imposed new taxes.[71] It was against this proposed delimitation that Bhutto's law and finance ministers both spoke to the need to rein-in rapacious capitalism, for which the rapid

[70] *Ghulam Rasool v Government of Pakistan* PLD [2015] SC 6.

[71] Pakistan National Assembly Debates, 1st Parliamentary Year, Second Session, 13 March 1973,Volume II, No 19, pp 1131–1176.

fire action of the executive ordinance was a necessary complement.[72] The original article as passed at this time has in fact no express delimitations on the substantive matters which can be legislated upon by the President. However, Presidential Order No 20 of 1985 introduced the change that a Presidential Ordinance that deals with any or all matters listed as describing the quality of a money Bill shall have to be considered by the National Assembly. This is in strict conformity with the process of money Bills more broadly being introduced and debated within the lower house after and recommendatory powers of the Senate regarding the same.

In the case of all ordinances, it is held that they will be valid for up to four months, and if at that point are either not voted into Acts of Parliament or extended for one additional period of 120 days, they will be considered to have been 'repealed'.[73] Built into the constitutional structure are specific directives about the impact of repeal in Article 264. It has been held that these consequences apply when Parliament has repealed but not necessarily when an ordinance has been held to be ultra vires through judicial review.[74]

Although the current Article 48 provides that in all 'his functions' the President shall act on the advice of the Prime Minister, whether or not there are explicit fetters on the President for the exercise of this legislative power remains somewhat unsettled. In a somewhat roundabout discussion, it has been suggested that where an assembly stands dissolved and a caretaker government is brought into being, there is ample reason to believe that ordinance powers are also nullified.[75] This seems to be in accord with what might be considered to be the original intent of constitutional framers who vociferously argued against detractors of the ordinance powers by citing 'the whole of the constitutional instrument' in which minimum numbers of days was prescribed for parliament to be 'in session', leaving very few days for exercise of the ordinance powers. Although two subsequent military coups and the two army generals' refusal to constitute Parliament according to

[72] Pakistan National Assembly Debates, 1st Parliamentary Year, Second Session, 22 March 1973, Volume II, No 26, p 1826.

[73] Constitution of Pakistan 1973, Art 264: Effect or repeal of laws.

[74] *Federation of Pakistan v Dr Mubashir Hassan* PLD [2012] SC 106.

[75] Karim, *Judicial Review of Public Actions.*

constitutional guarantees have proven them incorrect, it can only be surmised that the possibility of the Assembly being in session was a condition precedent for the exercise of ordinance powers granted in the 1973 Constitution.

Additionally, the criteria that circumstances necessitating immediate action must be in existence is the second of the conditions that might be construed to subject the exercise of ordinance-making powers to judicial review. Integrally, this is related to questions of whether an act of President's satisfaction itself can be reviewed. It has, in general, been the rule that mala fide intent will not be attributed to a governmental official. However, by the same token, given that the rule for testing satisfaction extends to ensuring that it is well beyond mere opinion, the rule in general seems to be that this forms one mode of invoking judicial review.[76]

In spite of what might seem to be a situation whereby ordinance powers are limited, by lapse or by the conditions constitutional defined as necessary for their operation, the expanse of law in this country proves that a far more permissive environment has prevailed. Additionally, their extension or normalisation into law has happened during the pendency of military rule through Articles 270A and 270AA. These provisions provide for the 'Affirmation of Presidents' Orders' and 'Declaration and Continuance of Laws' for Zia- and Musharraf-era ordinances. Even otherwise, ordinances have often assumed a permanent character, as in the many passed by Ayub and Bhutto. The *Sindh Lawyers Forum* case, however, sought to close off possibilities of such further incorporations.[77]

FURTHER READING

A Jalal, *The State of Martial Rule: The Origins of Pakistan's Political Economy of Defence* (Cambridge, Cambridge University Press, 1990).

HA Rizvi, *The Military and Politics in Pakistan, 1947–86*, 3rd edn (Lahore, Progressive Publishers, 1986).

A Shah, *The Army and Democracy: Military Politics in Pakistan* (Cambridge, Harvard University Press, 2014).

[76] ibid 222.

[77] *Sindh High Court Bar Association v Federation of Pakistan* PLD [2009] SC 879.

5

The Judiciary

Superior Judiciary – Jurisdiction – *Suo Moto* Powers – Public Interest Litigation – Judicial Activism – Judicial Independence – Judicial Appointments – Basic Structure

ALREADY APPARENT FROM the two preceding chapters is the centrality of Pakistan's higher judiciary for maintaining a bare subsistence of legality through great upheavals. The cost of doing this has, however, been a loss of public prestige for a judiciary perceived as compromising on basic principles of judicial independence. This chapter first details the structure and powers of the judicial system as laid out in the Constitution of 1973. There are then two concerns instrumental to the organisation of the sections that follow. The first is to address the judiciary's ambit of action or its jurisdiction within de facto and de jure constitutionalism. The second concern is to understand the criteria by which judicial independence has been measured historically and leading to an increasingly narrow preoccupation with the processes for judicial appointment.

The judicial response to the disruption of formal constitutionalism in 1977 provides some indication of the challenges faced when a coup is staged and an extra-constitutional legality is being delivered. A detailed examination of the judicial role in General Zia's ability to retain power is undertaken along with a description of the blatant illegalities that preceded the execution of Zulfiqar Bhutto under his regime. When thereafter freed from some of the fetters of the Zia regime, members of the higher judiciary set out on a restorative path, garnering public prestige while also seeking to redress a range of social problems that had historically fallen outside the system of justice. By creative adaptation of a programme of social reform through public interest litigation and also in more vigilant enforcement of fundamental rights the judiciary charted a fairly novel role for itself in the decade of the 1990s. This path was interrupted by another military coup in 1999, also subsequently validated by the Supreme Court. However, that the parliamentary system was restored by 2002 was amongst the conditions that allowed for a reinvigoration of judicial review practices that sought more intensively to redress rights violations and earned the Supreme Court under Chief Justice Iftikhar Chaudhry the reputation of being the most activist bench to date. The judiciary's search for legitimacy, from this point forward, was to be ever more intricately intertwined with the second major concern of this chapter, the establishment of judicial independence.

The suspension of Chaudhry in 2007 by President Musharraf was a flagrant breach of the principle of judicial independence, enshrined as an aspiration as far back as 1949 in the Objectives Resolution. However, an equally long history of partisan and politicised decision-making in reference to judicial appointment, tenure and removal from service has encumbered its realisation. All of this was indicted in the protest movement that would last for nearly two years before Chaudhry's restoration.

Thereafter, the striving for independence has taken on additional expressions. It has marked the field of constitutional interpretation both in the definition of a broader jurisdictional ambit and a more aggressive posture towards policing other branches of government. In the context that Musharraf had been removed and a fuller flourishing of democracy was at hand, certain actions of the court in this era incited a battle for primacy between the principles of rule of law and the striving for democracy. This was counterbalanced at times by a marked reticence to seek inspiration from transplanted doctrines of constitutional interpretation by the Supreme Court. Overwhelming in the recent record of judicial assertion is its keen oversight over the judicial appointments process; in many ways, this interest indicates that the higher judiciary has seemed to identify the judicial appointment process as the emblematic feature of judicial independence.

I. HISTORY AND STRUCTURE OF THE POST-INDEPENDENCE JUDICIARY

Close to Independence and Partition, nationalist leaders in India, particularly those of a Gandhian persuasion would counsel reform of the justice sector in order to bring it more in line with indigenous, pre-colonial systems. 'Modernisers' resisted this.[1] The formal justice system as it is had developed under colonial rule, although permeated by a deference to existing social hierarchies in local sites and a reliance upon customary codes for dispensing justice, had nonetheless generated new social classes, themselves stakeholders in its functioning. These included growing numbers of lawyers and the collectivities in which they were organised. Thus, a dominant strain of the movement for independence viewed the struggle against British rule as completion of the struggle for liberalism, of which the maintenance of the formal British system of justice was a necessary component.

At Partition, much of the court system was inherited and vested with the range of powers given within the 1935 Government of India Act. A High Court was established for the province of East Bengal and then the 1950 Abolition of Privy Council Act was passed by the Constituent Assembly to direct final appellate authority to the Federal Court. The next major alteration to the structure of the judicial system occurred with the broader administrative merger of the One Unit system and was meant to ensure a simplification of the cumbersome multi-graded lower courts.[2] In addition, the repeal of special laws based on cultural specificity was aimed at bringing all areas other than those given special constitutional protection as 'tribal areas' within the fold of High Court jurisdiction.[3]

In the 1956 Constitution, the conditions for the realisation of judicial independence from the executive included an appointment, tenure and removal policy that was intended to be impervious to political influence. The 1962 Constitution, however, provided a process of judicial appointment that was heavily controlled by the executive. It also established the Supreme Judicial Council as a forum to address

[1] See, generally, M Galanter, 'The Aborted Restoration of Indigenous Law in India' (1972) 14 *Comparative Studies in Society and History* 53; see also MD Peers and N Gooptu, *India and the British Empire* (Oxford, Oxford University Press, 2012).

[2] The structure of civil courts in the country was further altered through the West Pakistan Civil courts Ordinance of 1962.

[3] Laws repealed included, the Dastoor-ul-Amal Diwani State Kalat 1952. Also, the same was accomplished later through the Presidential Order No 11 of 1961, the Special Areas (Restoration of Jurisdiction) Order, 1961. For a detailed historical summation see *Malik Taj Mohammad v Bibi Jano* SCMR [1992] SC 1431.

complaints of ineptitude and wrongdoing by members of the Higher Judiciary, to be comprised by the Chief Justice of the Supreme Court and other senior members of the judiciary.

With a few exceptions, the judiciary to this point was mostly accommodative of heavy executive control and when Yahya Khan abrogated the Constitution of 1962 and also thereby 'declared that all proceedings pending in any court for the enforcement' of fundamental rights would be suspended, he was dealing with a judiciary that took his decisions 'quietly and lightly'.[4] By the time that the 1973 Constitution was being written, there seemed to be fuller political consensus that a formally independent judiciary needed to be established. Below, the structure of the superior judiciary is described, with particular attention paid to its jurisdictional bounds as well as the safeguards for independence contained within the 1973 Constitution.

A. Judicial Structure

The 'judicature' is given form in the 1973 Constitution through Articles 175–209. Article 175 provides that 'there shall be a Supreme Court of Pakistan, a High Court for each Province and such other courts as may be established by law.' While the 17-judge Supreme Court is at the apex of the appellate system, it does not have any administrative control over the High Courts nor the Subordinate Court system. The subordinate judiciary is organised through provincial statutes, and the powers to supervise and superintend its functioning are vested in the High Courts through Articles 202 and 203 of the Constitution.

The formal definition of jurisdiction is contained in Article 175(2) and provides that 'no court shall have any jurisdiction' other than in accordance with the 'Constitution or by or under any law'. For the Supreme Court, jurisdiction is comprehensively elaborated within the Constitution; it exercises original, appellate, advisory and revisional jurisdictions. In contrast, there is a more circumspect set of provisions provided for the High Courts.

Appeals arising from the decisions of district and session courts go to one of the four High Courts, which are located in the provincial

[4] H Khan, *A History of the Judiciary in Pakistan* (Karachi, Oxford University Press, 2016).

capitals but have additional benches through the provinces.[5] The Supreme Court can entertain appeals from the High Courts in both civil and criminal trials as well as in cases where a substantial question of law pertaining to interpretation of the Constitution arises. This level of appeal is not by right and the court has to grant leave to appeal.

In addition to serving as courts of appeal, the superior courts exercise additional original jurisdiction under the Constitution. Article 184(3) grants the Supreme Court the capacity to take up any matter of 'public importance' pertaining to the enforcement of fundamental rights and grant a suitably fashioned remedy. Article 184 also establishes that the Supreme Court has original or initial jurisdiction in cases of conflict between two or more governments, in which case it can deliver a declaratory or non-binding judgment. Under Article 199, the High Courts are empowered to entertain writs against public functionaries and provide remedies to make them 'refrain from doing' what they are not permitted to do, declare unlawful an act of a public functionary or to require a person 'purporting to hold a public office to show under what authority of law' they claim to hold that office. In other words, the array of prerogative or extraordinary writ remedies are specifically available for the High Courts to award in their original jurisdiction. The High Courts can also give an(y) order to any person for the enforcement of any of the fundamental rights upon the petition of an 'aggrieved person.' This limiting clause means that the High Courts have lesser leeway to accord remedies through public interest litigation, discussed further in this chapter, often brought by organisations or groups that are not directly affected by a rights violation. In other cases, the absence of a 'public interest' nexus for entertaining rights claims makes this a more hospitable forum for such petitions.

The advisory jurisdiction of the Supreme Court can be activated by the President, who may 'obtain the opinion of the Supreme Court on any question of law which he considers of public importance'. Lastly, the revisional jurisdiction of the Supreme Court allows it to review any judgment pronounced or any order made by it or any court in the land.[6]

In terms of territorial jurisdiction, the expanse of the Supreme Court's authority extends across the federation[7] and its judgments are

[5] Constitution of Pakistan 1973, Art 198.

[6] Constitution of Pakistan 1973, Art 185.

[7] Constitution of Pakistan 1973, Art 184.

binding throughout.[8] The four High Courts for each of the provinces exercise jurisdiction over their territories. Additionally, a fifth High Court was created for the federal capital, Islamabad, in 2010 and its jurisdiction extends within the capital's borders.[9]

Questions of jurisdiction are to be settled by way of the Constitution, or by other laws, and in the case of other courts established under the law, jurisdiction for them is also settled by and in accordance with law.[10] Provincial statutes govern the multiply-graded subordinate judicial structure. There is an array of specialised tribunals that are established in accordance with legislative lists defining federal and provincial legislative jurisdiction.

Important for the sections that follow is that certain articles of the Constitution contain ouster clauses directing that official action taken under them will not be reviewable in any court. In addition to the emergency provisions discussed in the previous chapter,[11] these include administrative acts in tribal areas and constitutional amendments passed according to the formula given in Article 239. Additionally, the mechanics of putting the Constitution in abeyance by both Zia and Musharraf have involved the swearing of an oath under the Provisional Constitutional Orders (PCO) that each promulgated. In Zia's case, the oath was preceded by the declaration of martial law and the Laws Continuance in Force Order (LCFO), which specifically directed that no court could challenge the proclamation, or issue any order against Zia as Chief Martial Law Administrator. In Musharraf's case, while the PCO issued two days after his 1999 coup was less draconian insofar as it neither proclaimed martial law nor suspended the enforcement of all fundamental rights, it did contain mirror provisions to the 1977 LCFO, directing that no court would challenge the seizure of power nor any orders issued by Chief Executive, Musharraf.

These formal limitations on jurisdiction have not altogether ring-fenced judicial agency. In recent years, greater numbers of judges have been willing to forgo their place in the system when basic principles of independence are compromised.

As noted earlier, a major encumbrance to judicial independence until 1973 had been the over-heavy controls exercised by the executive

[8] Constitution of Pakistan 1973, Art 189.

[9] Constitution of Pakistan 1973, Art 175.

[10] Constitution of Pakistan 1973, Art 175(2).

[11] See text in Chapter 4, sections IA and IB.

over appointments, transfer and tenure as well as in the allocation of resources. The original 1973 Constitution provided a guarantee that 'the judiciary shall be separated progressively from the executive within ten years from the commencing date'.[12] A law commission report in the following year made recommendations for how this would be accomplished.[13] However, in spite of these hopeful signs, the courts were simultaneously being chastened through the First, Fourth and Fifth Constitutional Amendments passed by the Bhutto regime. These restricted the jurisdiction of courts by removing charges of preventative detention from their review and thus limited a key enforcement mechanism against the executive. The Fifth Constitutional Amendment also allowed for the transfer of judges without their consent between benches. Additionally, the age of retirement for Chief Justices was extended so as to enable compliant judges to retain office longer. All mentions of succession by seniority were removed.[14]

In addition to the constrictions on jurisdiction, the formal guarantees of independence were further eroded through a range of martial law orders from 1977–1985. Importantly, the prospective date of separating the judiciary from the executive branch was delayed so as not be realised until 1995. Further changes from Zia's rule included the introduction of a rule that if a judge refused a presidential transfer to another branch, he/she would be 'deemed' to have retired.[15] Additionally, a strategy pursued in earnest well into the 1990s was the appointment of ad hoc judges in place of permanent judges to the higher benches. Without the fuller benefits of tenure, these judges were more beholden to the government and this was reflected in their judgments. As described in section II, below, the courts, in spite of the prohibition of the LCFO, repeatedly entertained challenges to General Zia's martial law in the early years.

As described in section VII, below, executive controls only whittled away with forcible judicial orders through the 1990s. In *Sharaf Faridi*, Justice Ajmal Mian, writing for the majority, provided that any executive control or oversight over members of the judiciary, is 'against the

[12] Constitution of Pakistan 1973, Art 175(3).

[13] The High Powered Law Reform Committee 1974.

[14] Arts 180 and 196 of the 1973 Constitution specified that acting chief justices would in all cases be the senior most ranking judge on a bench.

[15] Presidential Order No 24 of 1984 amendment to Art 200(4).

concept of separation and independence of judiciary as envisaged by Article 175 of the Constitution and the Objectives Resolution'.[16] This was shortly followed by the *Al Jehad* case,[17] which elaborated significant principles for appointment, transfer and tenure. *Al Jehad* was authored amidst intense institutional in-fighting amongst governmental actors. The move to codify many of the recommendations and principles of *Al-Jehad* would come many years later through the Eighteenth Amendment Act of 2010. The alterations since then and the nature of continuing conflict are described in section VII, below.

II. MILITARY LOYALTY

Zia-ul-Haq's coup of 1977 allowed for the continuance of laws and for the functioning of the judiciary but put the Constitution in abeyance. When Zulfiqar Bhutto and a number of close associates were arrested by the martial law regime and Bhutto's wife challenged this detention at the Supreme Court, the courts were in a bind given the formal restrictions placed on them. When the courts contrived to exercise an inherent jurisdiction in this case, they also opened the door to a judicial validation of Zia's extra-constitutional assumption of power.

While Chief Justice Anwar-ul-Haq would later claim to have been betrayed by the endless deferrals of elections and other promises made by the dictator at the time that the *Nusrat Bhutto case*[18] was being heard, Zia was bolstered by Haq's judgment in manifold ways. Zia thereafter perpetrated more aggressive assaults on rights, political parties, civil society members and the judiciary itself. The Supreme Court judgment in *Nusrat Bhutto* cited the General's promise to rule the country as 'nearly as may be, in accordance with the Constitution' as a reason to accord him latitude in returning the country to a 'peaceful atmosphere for the holding of elections and restoration of democratic intuitions'.[19] Perhaps not anticipating this, the regime's council argued at the outset that the Court's jurisdiction had been ousted by way of the 1977 LCFO. The orders issued at the moment of the coup were presented

[16] *Sharaf Faridi v Federation of Islamic Republic of Pakistan* PLD [1989] Karachi 404.

[17] *Al Jehad Trust v Federation of Pakistan* PLD [1996] SC 324.

[18] *Begum Nusrat Bhutto v Chief of Army Staff* PLD [1977] SC 657.

[19] AG Shariffudin Pirzada; martial rule in the given circumstances is envisioned to be of a temporary nature.

as 'supra-constitutional'. Against this contention, the Court retained for itself the powers vested through Article 199 of the Constitution as fundamental to the maintenance of the 'legal order' that would be reverted to and for which it would be the hinge. In addition to affirming that Zia's assumption of power represented a limited 'constitutional deviation', the court also accepted that the conditions of unrest that prevailed at that time were such as to validate the proposition of *salus lex populi*. In other words, the doctrine of state necessity was revived from the *Governor-General's reference* 1955 to validate this takeover of power.[20]

Powers of judicial review were discovered as untouched by the circumstances of the state of necessity that mandated martial law. For instance, Justice Haq writes that while the executive and legislature are combined in the office of the Chief Martial Law Administrator (CMLA) 'for the reason that these two organs of the State had lost their constitutional and moral authority in the circumstances', the judiciary remained unaffected.

The *Nusrat Bhutto* case gave wide-ranging powers to the CMLA, including the ability to amend the Constitution itself, but circumscribed by the doctrine of necessity as it applied to the factual scenario of unrest in the country, as well as subject to the retention of judicial review powers. However, early on, the structure of independence for the courts was already undermined insofar as the existing four Chief Justices of the Provincial High Courts had all agreed to act as Governors for their respective provinces. In addition, Post-Proclamation Order No 2 of 1977 allowed the President to appoint, on his discretion, acting Chief Justices to replace the permanent Chief Justices who had accepted executive office. Thus, Maulvi Mushtaq Hussain, made infamous in his role as the author of the initial order for Zulfiqar Bhutto's execution, was so elevated. The same order enabled the President to transfer judges between High Courts. In spite of these formal assumptions of powers over the judiciary, provincial High Courts fought back against encroachments of rights, particularly in reference to the detention of political prisoners.

The Second Amendment Order of 1979 inserted Article 212A into the Constitution and allowed the CMLA to establish 'one or more Military Courts or Tribunals for the trial of offences punishable under the Martial Law Regulations or Martial Law Orders' or under any other special laws. It maintained the Supreme Court as a court of appeal

[20] See text in Chapter 2, section I.

for cases tried by military courts but nullified any jurisdiction of the High Courts for cases taken to military courts. The following year a further alteration was made to the Constitution, now to Article 199 by the insertion of three sub-clauses.[21] If read strictly, the effect of these would have been to nullify altogether powers of judicial review that the Supreme Court had protected for itself in the *Nusrat Bhutto* case. The amended article indemnified all martial law orders or regulations, all orders or judgments of the military courts and declared all acts of the CMLA and his subordinates as valid with retrospective effect dating to Zia's initial assumption of power. The much more expansive assault on the structure of judicial independence as well as of judicial review would come in 1981 with the re-swearing of an oath of allegiance by members of the superior judiciary under the Provisional Constitutional Order 1981. While a few judges chose at this juncture not to take the oath and thereby publicly alluded some fidelity to higher principles of independence or rule of law, others were simply not invited to do so by Zia. Thus, 19 judges were summarily dismissed and a pervasive fear established amongst members of the judiciary.

The issue of the oath is one that judges have dilated upon in their memoirs, seemingly always to rectify the notion that they were somehow traitors to their office in having sworn it. One such account is given by Ajmal Mian (Chief Justice of the Supreme Court from December 1997 to June 1999), when he recounts a discussion had between himself and another member of the Sindh High Court, who were both offered the opportunity to continue in service on the condition of swearing Zia's oath.[22] Acknowledging that he and his colleague were appointees after 1977, they both agreed that their initial judicial oath was sworn under the existing dispensation of 'law' and not the 'Constitution'. This thereby accorded consistency to their acts if they were to take the further oath, which they did. However, the same memoir also records an unending spiral of executive meddling through the mechanisms of transfer, reappointment, and so forth, all of which are impliedly decried. The retrospective turn has also been taken by authors of the *Nusrat Bhutto* judgment. Dorab Patel would lament having granted the right to constitutional amendment, although the power was circumscribed and subject further to the condition that Zia would

[21] Presidents Order No. 1 of 1980.

[22] A Mian, *A Judge Speaks Out* (Karachi, Oxford University Press, 2004).

act in matters in order to 'advance or promote the good of the people'. Dorab Patel later wrote that this was also a 'very vague concept'.[23]

The evidence of constitutional mutilation largely suggests that the Zia regime would not brook 'legalistic procedural rules and rights above the rapid achievement of desired substantive outcomes'.[24] While not extensive, there is some evidence that the retention of the powers to structure and channel social conflict amongst independent actors and between them and the state would lend the judiciary some support in the future authoritarian heavy-handedness. In *Yaqoob Ali*, the Sindh High Court stated explicitly that military orders under the doctrine of necessity could be held to be justiciable.[25] It was not an untrammelled right for the CMLA to exercise an arbitrary will of one.

Nonetheless, in its everyday functioning the judiciary was exceptionally constrained during this period. Until the formal passage of the RCO in 1985, fundamental rights had been unavailable for legal enforcement. Additionally, there were two realms of contest that Zia defined for the coming years as of continuing relevance to the constitutional landscape of the country. Both of them bear heavily upon the structure and jurisprudence of the courts in the country. The first was the establishment of the Federal Shariat Court, discussed further in Chapter 8. The second was the passage of the Eighth Amendment to the Constitution, discussed extensively in Chapters 3 and 4.

A. Bhutto Murder Trial

In spite of the exertions of some judges to maintain autonomy during Zia's reign, the institution as a whole was cloaked with ignominy for the events that led to Zulfiqar Bhutto's execution. Following upon the declaration of martial law, an allegation of murder made against Bhutto in 1974 was opened up and formal charges laid. This would

[23] P Dorab, *Testament of a Liberal* (Karachi, Oxford University Press, 2000) 155.

[24] CN Tate 'Why the Expansion of Judicial Power?' in CN Tate and T Vallinder (eds), *The Global Expansion of Judicial Power* (New York, New York University Press, 1995) 28–29; see also CN Tate 'Courts and Crisis Regimes: A Theory Sketch with Asian Case Studies' (1993) 46 *Political Research Quarterly* 311.

[25] *Yaqoob Ali v Presiding Officer, Summary Military Court, Karachi* PLD [1985] Karachi 243.

lead to a lengthy and secret trial, a finding of guilt and Bhutto's eventual hanging. Bhutto was initially found guilty by a unanimous verdict of five judges of the Lahore High Court. On appeal, his conviction and sentence were upheld by the Supreme Court, with three of the seven judges dissenting.

It has been remarked that simply reading the judgments for this case 'can give the wrong impression that the evidence was bulky and voluminous, "in reality the trial was based mainly on the testimony of Masood Mahmood, the Director-General of the Federal Security Force (FSF), who turned approver"'.[26] An approver is, in the tradition of colonial justice, usually a co-accused who turns state witness. In this case, other members of the FSF had been arrested and a range of charges about their extra-legal activity were being framed. The over-heavy reliance upon Mahmood's testimony was not the only irregularity in the trials: the acting Chief Justice of the Lahore High Court, Maulvi Mushtaq Hussein, was at the time of the trial known to have locked horns with Bhutto on numerous previous occasions. On appeal, Bhutto faced a Chief Justice whom he had denied promotion a year earlier.

Benazir Bhutto termed the whole episode a 'judicial murder' of her father, even as blame for Bhutto's displacement from power extended in many directions, including towards the US and other Western powers who found some of Bhutto's allegiances with the Soviet bloc unpalatable.[27] Amongst the judges on the bench of the Supreme Court who denied Bhutto's appeal was the future Chief Justice Nasim Hassan Shah. Seen as someone who had 'obeyed' martial law, after his retirement from service he gave an interview on live television hinting both that there had been higher direction given to hang Bhutto and that, in fact, the punishment could have been mitigated given that the charge was of abetment.[28] This led to a filing of a reference to reopen the case during the 1990s and it has been pending at the Supreme Court since then, with only periodic hearings taking place.[29]

[26] TW Rajaratnam, *A Judiciary in Crisis: The Trial of Zulfiqar Ali Bhutto* (Madras, Kaanthalakam, 1988) 9.

[27] V Shofield, *Bhutto: Trial and Execution* (London, Cassell, 1979).

[28] 'Bhutto's Judicial Murder: Some Stray Thoughts' *The News International* (9 April 2011) www.thenews.com.pk/Todays-News-13-5187-Bhutto%E2%80%99s-judicial-murder-some-stray-thoughts.

[29] 'Justice Nasim Shah: An upright Judge' *The Nation* (4 February 2015) <www.nation.com.pk/lahore/04-Feb-2015/justice-nasim-hassan-an-upright-judge>.

III. THE 1990s JUDICIARY

Until the RCO of 1985 was passed, a chief effect of the post-*Nusrat Bhutto* dispensation had been the suspension of fundamental rights in the country. The Chief Justice Mohammad Haleem (1981–1989) sought to alter this record in the aftermath of democratic restoration by drawing upon the example of neighbouring India, where public interest litigation was expanding. Whilst not anywhere near as dramatically realised, a motivation for this turn in Pakistan mirrored the Indian judiciary's desire to regain some of the popular legitimacy it had lost in being seen to have capitulated to Indira Gandhi's heavy handed imposition of emergency in the years 1975–1977.[30]

An additional feature of this time was that human rights compliance had begun to be monitored through a burgeoning non-governmental sector. Along with a push to align adjudicatory practices to take account of international rights statements, the latent powers of the judiciary were being rediscovered. The strong judicial review powers of the 1973 Constitution, as per Article 184(3), provided mechanisms for redress of rights violation that were broader than would have been allowed under a strictly adversarial system. This enabled the courts to push in the direction of loosening the requirements of standing to allow petitions from people and groups not directly affected or harmed by the denial of rights. Starting from the proposition that matters of a public nature are themselves of public importance,[31] and that those affected by the denial of rights may not themselves be able to petition the courts for redress, the court provided propitious conditions for testing the expansiveness of fundamental rights guarantees in the country.[32]

What was also notable was that, starting with the *Darshan Masih* case[33] in 1990, the powers of *suo moto* jurisdiction were activated as under Article 184(3). In that case the Supreme Court converted a telegram detailing rights abuse in the form of forced labour into a constitutional petition.[34]

[30] *Benazir Bhutto v Federation of Pakistan* PLD [1988] SC 416.

[31] *Shirin Munir v Govt of Punjab* PLD [1990] SC 295.

[32] Nasim Hasan Shah, *Public Interest Litigation As a Means of Social Justice*, PLD [1993] Journal 31; see also W Menski, AR Alam and MK Raza, *Public Interest Litigation in Pakistan* (London, Platinum Publishing Ltd, 2000); see also *Benazir Bhutto v Federation of Pakistan* PLD [1988] SC 416.

[33] *Darshan Masih v The State* PLD [1990] SC 513.

[34] Bonded Labour System (Abolition) Rules, 1995.

Analogous to what had been the pattern in India in the previous decade, a novel body of rights was being fashioned by reference to existing constitutional provisions. The use of Article 9, which guarantees 'No person shall be deprived of life or liberty save in accordance with law' was the basis for broadening the ambit of rights considered justiciable. Thus, in the *Shehla Zia* case,[35] residents of an Islamabad neighbourhood who sought to forestall the construction and operation of an electrical grid station that they alleged would compromise their health were offered relief. This propelled the passage of the Environmental Protection Act in 1997. Additionally, by suggesting that the constitutional guarantee was of life beyond its 'mere vegetative' state, the Court opened the door to varied assertions about what those other conducive conditions were and the extent to which the state was responsible for their guarantee.[36]

This more activist and aggressive posture of the court would extend in some cases to the invalidation of legislative acts in this period. For instance, in *Mehram Ali*, specific provisions of the Anti-Terror Act establishing a parallel justice system, which relaxed the evidentiary rules for trial and presumed to bypass the regular court system, were directed to be altered so as to be brought in line 'with the rules and procedures of the existing constitutionally established judicial system'.[37] While Nawaz Sharif's government complied with court directions from that case, it shortly thereafter issued an Ordinance which went much further in terms of establishing a parallel judicial system to try to control a spiralling escalation of violence in Sindh and then the rest of the country. The Pakistan Armed Forces (Acting in Aid of Civil Power) Ordinance, 1998 was passed after the declaration of Governor's rule in Sindh province. It specifically called upon the army to 'convene as many courts as may be deemed necessary to try offenders'. In the *Liaquat Hussain* case,[38] the court fought back against this Ordinance, which had also created a completely novel offence of 'civil commotion', for which

[35] *Shehla Zia v WAPDA* PLD [1994] SC 693.

[36] See text in Chapter 7, section II.

[37] *Mehram Ali v Federation of Pakistan* PLD [1998] SC 1445; see also C Kennedy, 'The Creation and Development of Pakistan's anti-terrorism Regime 1997–2002' in SP Limaye, M Malik and RG Wirsing (eds), *Religious Radicalism and Security in South Asia* (Homolulu, Asia-Pacific Center for Security Studies, 2004) 391.

[38] *Sheikh Liaquat Hussain v. Federation of Pakistan* PLD [1999] SC 504.

sentences of 'rigorous imprisonment' of up to seven years could be awarded.[39] The whole of the Ordinance was declared to be of 'no legal effect' in a unanimous decision of a nine-member bench.

Finally, in what is a line of similar cases that looked into the vires of the government's aggressive anti-terror posture and agenda, the *Jamaat-e-Islami* case of 2000 invalidated certain provisions of the amended Anti-Terror Act on the touchstone of individual rights protections.[40] Specific measures enabling law enforcement to shoot on sight, and on the grounds of mere suspicion of a person being involved in the commission of a scheduled offence, were declared invalid and against rights guarantees. Additionally, in order to make the least possible incursion upon constitutionally-protected rights, particularly of association, the court declared that aspects of collective actions could only be tried under anti-terror laws if their commission was demonstrably related to elements of terrorist activity.[41]

The Supreme Court also undertook in this period to extend its jurisdictional sway over the constitutionally-defined tribal areas. In spite of Article 247(7), which specifically bars the Supreme and High Courts from exercising 'any jurisdiction under the Constitution in relation to a Tribal Area', challenges to administrative actions in these areas were admitted. For instance, the restoration of tribal justice under the Frontier Crimes Regulation Act in the province of Baluchistan was found to be contrary to constitutional equality guarantees[42] and the ascription of 'tribal' was found to be of questionable validity with regard to the residents of this province. Additionally, in an important case involving the administration of a provincially-administered tribal area, the prior judicial view of the Frontier Crimes Regulation, that it is not 'law' but the working of administrative action which is 'concerned more largely with the vindication of public interest than with the enforcement of private rights'[43] was tempered by the guarantee that all administrative

[39] The Pakistan Penal Code, s 53 differentiates between simple and rigorous imprisonment and provides that the latter is accompanied by hard labour. For an early colonial history of penal servitude, see D Arnold 'Labouring for the Raj: Convict Work Regimes in Colonial India 1836–1839' in CG De Vito and A Lichtenstein (eds), *Global Convict Labour* (Leiden, Brill, 2015) 199.

[40] *Jamat-i-Islami Pakistan v Federation of Pakistan* PLD [2000] SC 111.

[41] *Mehram Ali v Federation of Pakistan* PLD [1998] SC 1445.

[42] *Government of Balochistan v Azizullah Memon* PLD [1993] SC 341.

[43] *Manzoor Elahi v Federation of Pakistan* PLD [1975] SC 66.

action should be conducive to the 'peace and good government' of these areas, as provided in Article 247(5).[44]

IV. CHIEF JUSTICE IFTIKHAR CHAUDHRY AND EXTENSIVE REVIEW

The person who would become most deeply associated with carrying forward the jurisprudential innovations of the 1990s was also a direct and immediate beneficiary of General Musharraf's seizure of power. When the first PCO was announced in early 2000, 6 of the 13 judges of the Supreme Court declined to take oath upon it and were subsequently retired from service. The Chief Justice of the time, Saeeduzuman Siddiqi, was amongst them. Shortly after, new appointments were made and Iftikhar Chaudhry, only months after being promoted to the position of Chief Justice of the Balochistan High Court, was amongst the appointees. Not immediately spurning the benefits conferred, he also thereafter signed his name to judgments that 'validated the military takeover by Gen Musharraf, his referendum, his legal framework order (LFO) and the 17th constitutional amendment that gave the president additional powers and allowed him to continue as the army chief.'[45] He proceeded quickly in terms of seniority through the denuded bench to become Pakistan's youngest ever Chief Justice in 2005.

In a turnaround from this early record, Chaudhry was reborn as an activist judge upon becoming Chief Justice. Early in his tenure, a human rights cell was set up at the Supreme Court. A novel innovation, 'it receives applications relating to human rights violations either through post, fax, telegram, email or through use of court box available in the Supreme Court or on the basis of print and electronic media reports'.[46] A staff of intermediaries then prepares fact sheets on the basis of which the court can initiate *suo moto* cases. The process

[44] *NWFP v Muhammad Irshad* PLD [1995] SC 281. See text in Chapter 6, section II.

[45] 'Profile: Pakistan's Chief Justice Iftikhar Chaudhry' *BBC News* (14 June 2012) <www.bbc.com/news/world-asia-18425141>.

[46] Supreme Court Human Rights Cell: <www.supremecourt.gov.pk/web/user_files/File/pb_dg_hrcell_dt_20.02.2014.pdf>.

enabled over 6,000 human rights cases until the year 2007 to be decided for affected parties without, often, the expenses involved in retaining counsel themselves.[47]

Such cases received regular publicity in the national media and made the person of the Chief Justice as well as the institution of the Supreme Court increasingly popular amongst a broad swathe of Pakistani society. The Supreme Court frequently targeted situations in which the local political elites were implicated. These included the recovery of kidnap victims in which politicians had been involved. Additionally, cases of police brutality, as well as of violence against women, were taken up.[48]

In addition to these human rights cases, the court began to elaborate a doctrine of 'transparency', whereby executive action was to be tested against procedural criteria derived from broader administrative law principles.[49] By early 2007, the court had rolled back the privatisation of the Pakistan Steel Mills under such scrutiny and also incurred some official wrath for daring to call in high officials of the security establishment in its pursuit of missing persons petitions.[50]

However, as the following section indicates, there was only a brief moment of what seemed to be unanimous public support for the activism that was associated with the Chaudhry court. In turn, even Chaudhry in his later years as Chief Justice and certainly those who have followed him in office have been more circumspect in the use of *suo moto* powers and in employing some of the other innovations of public interest litigation. Thereafter the redressal of individual rights violations was tied somewhat to reinvigorating all levels of the judicial structure to become forums where these issues could be tried. The National Judicial Policy of 2009, authored by Chief Justice Iftikhar Chaudhry counseled reforms through to the lowest levels of the judiciary to close off possibilities of political capture and corruption.[51] Additionally, those operating the human rights cell were instructed to redirect individual petitions back to the district and sessions court level

[47] See MA Munir, *Public Interest Litigation in Supreme Court of Pakistan* (Punjab Judicial Academy, 2007) 136–37. SCMR [2006] SC 1780.

[48] Human Rights Case No 13-L of 2006 SCMR [2006] SC 1769; Human Rights Case No 3062 of 2006 SCMR [2006] SC 1780; Criminal Miscellaneous Application No 189 of 2006 SCMR [2006] SC 1805. For representative sample see www.supremecourt.gov.pk/web/page.asp?id=1759.

[49] See text in Chapter 4, section VB.

[50] See text in Chapter 7, section IVC.

[51] OL Bouvier and F Cosadia, 'Pakistan—A long march for democracy and the rule of law 2007–2008' (2009) *International Federation for Human Rights* 1.

and thereby lessen the burden upon the Supreme Court to exercise its original *suo moto* jurisdiction.

V. THE LAWYERS' MOVEMENT AND JUDICIALISATION OF POLITICS

This section details the rise and fall of the lawyers' movement in Pakistan (2007–2009). Stages in the movement provide an opportunity to chart the at times conjoint and at other times radically opposed fortunes of democracy and rule of law in this country. The movement arose spontaneously in defence of judicial independence when Chief Justice Chaudhry was asked by General Musharraf to tender his resignation in March 2007. When Chaudhry declined to do so, Musharraf acted against the constitutionally-mandated procedure for investigating any alleged wrongdoing by a member of the Superior Judiciary through the Supreme Judicial Council, and made Chaudhry non-effective by official presidential order.[52] This excited the creation and sustenance of a protest movement spearheaded by a unified coalition of bar associations and councils and the lawyers they represented.

A dramatic restoration for the Chief Justice was undertaken when the existing Supreme Court declared Musharraf's acts illegal and deemed that Chaudhry had been the rightful Chief Justice throughout his suspension.[53] Thereafter, the Supreme Court under Chaudhry was obstinate in pursuing cases of high political importance. For instance, the court threatened to nullify General Musharraf's re-election to the office of President.[54] This in turn precipitated the imposition of an 'emergency' designed to replace the recalcitrant benches of the Supreme Court and the High Courts with a compliant superior judiciary. Members of the superior judiciary were now invited to take a second oath under the PCO of 2007. Fifty-three out of ninety-five[55]

[52] S Ghias, 'Miscarriage of Chief Justice: Judicial Power and the Legal Complex in Pakistan' in TC Halliday, L Karpik, and MM Freeley (eds), *Fates of Political Liberalism in the British Post-colony: The Politics of the Legal Complex* (Cambridge, Cambridge University Press, 2012).

[53] *Chief Justice of Pakistan Iftikhar Muhammad Chaudhry v President of Pakistan* PLD [2010] SC 61.

[54] See text in Chapter 4, section II.

[55] Khan, *A History of the Judiciary in Pakistan* 502–505.

judges refused. People once again braved an increasingly authoritarian state's displeasure by taking to the streets in defence of this beleaguered judiciary.

In the sphere of public perception, the impact of lawyers acting in concert, without discernible self-interest in the outcome of their struggle and in defence of the judiciary, was of profound effect. Even as the protest movement broadened its ambitions in later days, a steadfast narration of lawyers as embodying the deeper principles of fairness and justice underlying an otherwise impersonal and, to most, incomprehensible body of laws was cultivated through their adherence to the demand for 'judicial independence' right from the outset. In many ways it was a conservative agenda powered by the notion that an efficiently functioning judiciary grafted onto a free market could meet equity concerns for Pakistan's vast population of dispossessed. For others, Chaudhry had simply become a repository for hopes of justice that had nowhere else to rest.

The lawyers' movement thus remained unified and was even able to draw in the support of the major political parties as long as it was staged in opposition to a military ruler. However, as Musharraf took to restoring some legitimacy for his own rule by going ahead with elections scheduled for January 2008, leaders of major political parties and lawyers associations considered whether an overall boycott should take place. Soon after though, the movement would fissure on the grounds of whether the rule of law standard, for which the Chief Justice's restoration set a threshold of compliance, or the pro-democracy goal of partaking in the scheduled elections would have primacy.

The major political parties tied their fortunes to the outcome of the elections, even as some of the smaller ones abided by the boycott in protest against the continuing post-emergency suspension of the Chief Justice. In December 2007, whilst exiting a campaign rally, Benazir Bhutto was assassinated. The elections were delayed somewhat and when held in February 2008 returned a coalition government between the PPP and PML-N. Defying promises they made, including through signing the multi-party Charter of Democracy which promised to protect judicial independence and militate for the restoration of judges who had not signed the PCO, the PPP delayed the restoration of the pre-emergency judiciary.

The People's Party government had much to lose with the restoration of a judiciary that had tied its fortunes to a strict rule of law standard. Just prior to the declaration of emergency and Bhutto's assassination, the National Reconciliation Ordinance (NRO) had been enacted. Through it, existing criminal and civil cases registered against a list comprising hundreds of persons, all of whom had been elected members of the National Assembly at some prior stage, were to be nullified. Amongst the chief beneficiaries of the NRO were Benazir Bhutto and her husband Asif Ali Zardari, who was elected President in 2008. Although delayed, Zardari did order the restoration of the Chief Justice in March 2009. Zardari's political fate became subject to grave uncertainty when the Supreme Court nullified the NRO itself. Furthermore, the Court directed that the national accountability bureau reopen cases against Zardari, which had been pending in Switzerland.

Prime Minister Yousaf Raza Gillani stalled and pleaded on behalf of Zardari the defence of presidential immunity, as established under international customary law. To this defence the court responded:

> The Respondent's stand amounts to saying that the order of 'this Court is non-implementable' and if accepted such an argument 'would set a dangerous precedent and anyone would then successfully flout the orders of the Courts by pleading that according to his interpretation they are not in accord with the law'.[56]

The further convolutions that followed are detailed elsewhere in this volume.[57] This was the beginning, however, of a growing antipathy towards Chaudhry for compromising democracy in the retention of a strict rule of law standard.

A case that further called into question the Chaudhry Court's judgment, turned on the public leak of the contents of a proposal submitted to the US high command through diplomatic channels by the Zardari government.[58] The memorandum itself promised a purging of military officers who were acting in collusion with Islamist militants, such as through the safe harbouring of Osama Bin Laden until 2010. Under Article 184(3) the court established jurisdiction on the basis of the fundamental rights to life, dignity of man and rights to information.[59]

[56] *Suo Motu Case No 4 of 2010*, PLD [2012] SC 553.

[57] See text in Chapter 3, section IIB.

[58] *Watan Party v Federation of Pakistan* PLD [2012] SC 292: Constitution Petition under Article 184(3) of the Constitution regarding alleged Memorandum to Admiral Mike Mullen by Mr Husain Haqqani, former Ambassador of Pakistan to the United States of America.

[59] ibid.

The claims on jurisdiction were problematic, as they suggested that the right to life for any individual is tied inextricably to the security of the state. The court directed that a judicial commission comprising high level jurors be established in order to adduce culpability for what, seemingly to their minds, was a prospective surrender of sovereignty by the democratic government to the USA.

This case excited extreme furor in Pakistan amongst those who wished to see democracy flourish. Academic commentaries have also impugned the judges for not having understood, in their zeal, that judicial autonomy should not be about maintaining a 'maximalist position'. Rather, that it needs to coexist in an 'institutionalist matrix' in which the broader goals of parliamentary democracy and constitutionalism need to be fostered. *Memogate,* as the whole incident came to be known, was used by detractors of the Chaudhry Court to suggest that the Court was continuing its historical role of complicity with the military and the executive against the interest of Parliament.[60] In contrast, defenders of the Chaudhry court have argued that it was serving as ombudsman for the country, restoring faith in the system as a whole.

Even a seemingly egregious political judgment such as the *Memogate* case can be seen to have done pro-democracy work. The judicial commission established to investigate the authorship of the memo eventually assigned culpability to one individual, whose resignation was sought by the political government.[61] Speculation was rife that the leaked memo would have otherwise become the catalyst for a direct military takeover. The logic is perhaps sound. Given that military governments have rarely been resisted, at least at the beginning of their tenure, and that there is a culture in general of reviling politicians in the country, the court directed its moral legitimacy to providing a bulwark against military intervention for the duration of its term. It was a staged and complicated affair, necessarily giving the impression of flouting a putative division of powers doctrine and engineering a judicialisation of politics.

[60] Anil Kalhan, 'Gray Zone Constitutionalism and the Dilemma of Judicial Independence in Pakistan' (2003) 46 *Vanderbilt Journal of Transnational Law* 1.

[61] BS Mirza, 'The Chaudhry Doctrine: A Small-c Constitutional Perspective' in MH Cheema and IS Gilani (eds), *The Politics and Jurisprudence of the Chaudhry Court 2005–2013* (Karachi, Oxford University Press, 2015).

In these years the court's jurisprudence certainly did intersect with a range of issues that have been termed the domain of 'mega-politics'.[62] In many ways the Court's advance was such as to outpace the standard judicial review practices that have been held to be indicative of a judicialisation of politics in much of the world. This notion of judicialisation implies that rather than being left to the domain of democratic decision-making, the review of far-reaching political questions such as involving 'electoral processes and outcomes … regime legitimacy, executive prerogatives, collective identity, and nation building' is undertaken by the judicial branch. There is no doubt that from July 2007 until the end of Chaudhry's tenure this was the case in Pakistan. What is interesting to note, however, is that the court ardently resisted some vestiges of judicialisation that are indigenous to South Asia broadly.

VI. BASIC STRUCTURE

The basic structure doctrine, discussed in various places throughout this book, was first forged by judges of the Indian Supreme Court to review constitutional amendments. There is a specific higher law and higher morality basis to the basic structure doctrine, as it provides that the constitutional dispensation must, in all cases, maintain fidelity to a set of transcendental principles. In the Indian case, these were originally elaborated as parliamentary democracy, federalism, independence of the judiciary and minority rights, although the list has grown further. Employment of the basic structure doctrine enables the judiciary to act as the guarantor of these principles and strike down a constitutional amendment, even where validly passed by a legislature, if it derogates from or impinges upon the realisation of these principles.[63]

Through Chief Justice Chaudhry's tenure, and earlier, several cases arose in which the basic structure doctrine could have provided an easy fix for constitutional deviations engineered by Musharraf.

[62] R Hirschl, 'The New Constitution and the Judicialization of Pure Politics Worldwide' (2006) 75 *Fordham Law Review* 721.

[63] See M Mate, 'Two Paths to Judicial Power: The Basic Structure Doctrine and Public Interest Litigation in Comparative Perspective' (2010) 12 *San Diego International Law Journal* 175. See also Sudhir Krishnaswamy, *Democracy and Constitutionalism in India: A Study of the Basic Structure Doctrine* (New Delhi, Oxford University Press, 2010).

In spite of the court repeatedly hearing petitions that employed the doctrine to challenge such deviations, the court did not affirm basic structure as valid law in Pakistan. In a way this was simply in keeping with precedent; while insufficient for challenging a constitutional amendment, it was used in some fashion nonetheless to elaborate a set of proscriptive guidelines on the kinds of amendment that could be framed by a non-elected government, such as in the *Zafar Ali Shah* case.[64] However, given how far the Chaudhry court had veered from past practice in many ways, this cannot serve as a full explanation of why the basic structure doctrine was resisted for the most part.

A more roundabout explanation might be had in seeking greater clarity about the aims pursued by Chaudhry and allies on his bench including Jawad Khwaja, who himself was Chief Justice for a short period in mid-2015. A recent volume dedicated to excavating these aims and the patterns established during Chaudhry's reign as Chief Justice begins with a foreword by Justice Khwaja, in which he rejects the need to rely upon doctrines from other jurisdictions.[65] He goes on to acknowledge his own transformation into a more publically-minded judge as a consequence of the power available to the Supreme Court to redress broad-scale social and governance problems. In other words, there was no shame in being described as a political court and in fact, the court was self-aware in cultivating a constituency amongst a broader public that was dissatisfied with the performance of its government.

However, as the various contributors in the volume go on to illustrate, a political orientation for the court necessitated the need to appease other actors, including a legal community with an entrenched conservative and formalist outlook. Rather than seek a 'law of laws' to regulate governmental conduct, the court sought to efface the distinction between the constitution and constitutional interpretation.[66] In its most important political decisions the court shows a strict fidelity to finding guidance and coherence from within the 'four corners'

[64] See text in Chapter 4, section II.

[65] Cheema and Gilani, *Politics and Jurisprudence of the Chaudhry Court.*

[66] F Siddiqi, 'Public Interest Litigation: Predictable Continuity and Radical Departures' in Cheema and Gilani (eds), *Politics of Jurisprudence of the Chaudhry Court* 77–130.

of the constitutional text rather than through an invocation of higher level principles.[67] Where a bench including Chaudhry would utilise the opaquely interpretive basic structure doctrine was in seeking parliamentary reconsideration of the judicial appointments structured through the Eighteenth Amendment as described in the following section.

In early 2015, sometime after Chaudhry had retired from his seat, a major reversal in the highest courts' posture towards the basic structure doctrine was authored. In what is generally known as the *Twenty-first Amendment* case a majority of the Supreme Court's full bench affirmed the right to strike down a constitutional amendment, even where validly passed by an Assembly, if found to be contrary to the basic and salient features of the 1973 Constitution. At issue, the case was the authorisation for trial of suspected terrorists through the mechanism of military court martials as provided firstly through an amendment to the Army Act of 1952. It is believed the 'deep state', the army, in various ways strong-armed the democratic Parliament to provide fuller protection by incorporation into the Constitution, although subject to elapse at the end of two years.

While the 'basic features' cited as worthy of protection vary amongst the judges who rely upon the basic structure doctrine, one criteria that is uniformly upheld is that judicial power can only be exercised by the judiciary, not the army. Notably, Khwaja, who was a member of the full bench on the *Twenty-first Amendment* case[68] authored a note which provided courts with the power to strike down a constitutional amendment but not in reliance upon the basic structure doctrine. Again, it was through a close reading of the Preamble combined with a reading down of constitutional provisions that had been enshrined by dictators that this was accomplished by Khwaja.

Ultimately though, the affirmation of the basic structure doctrine was not sufficient in itself to sway the majority of the members to declare the Twenty-first Amendment ultra vires. This majority voted that the particular provisions of the amendment were insufficiently violative of rights guarantees to be invalidated. In their reasons these judges found the measures to meet a proportionality test given the 'scourge of terrorism' in the country and the emergency character of the amendment. Those opposed to these military courts cited the absence of due process and the existing anti-terror courts

[67] See *Sindh High Court Bar Association v Federation of Pakistan* PLD [2009] SC 879.
[68] *District Bar Association Rawalpindi v Federation of Pakistan* PLD [2015] SC 401.

as the correct forum. The effective impact of the judgment is that the court established itself as a proper forum of appeal, albeit on limited grounds, for convictions arising from military judgments.

VII. JUDICIAL INDEPENDENCE

The 1973 Constitution prescribed a formula for the appointment of judges that was heavily weighted in favour of the executive. When the Eighth Amendment passed by Zia shifted the effective powers of the executive to the President, it was to this office holder that the Chief Justice of the Supreme Court was required to recommend a list of nominees.[69] However, as greater affective powers were seized by the Prime Minister of the 1990s, a terrain of acute and persistent struggle was created between the elected executive and the judicial branch.

Both of the elected Prime Ministers in the 1990s showed great inclination to flout established conventions for maintaining judicial independence. Most notable in this regard is Benazir Bhutto's disregard for the constitutional tradition of appointing the senior most judge on the Supreme Court as Chief Justice; she instead appointed Justice Sajjad Ali Shah and thereby superseded two more senior judges in 1994. Benazir had Shah's lone dissent against the restoration of the first Nawaz Sharif government as indication of loyalty to her party. In his dissent he famously referred to the ethnic divide in the court by which Punjabi politicians were restored and Sindhi's disqualified,[70] thereby objecting to the different treatment meted out to Sharif and Bhutto respectively.

In spite of the blatant favouritism shown towards him, it was also widely rumoured that the Bhutto regime intended to keep Shah deeply beholden to it and that Shah had signed a prospective letter of resignation to be used at some future date.[71] Nonetheless, having earned the ire of other judges on the bench, Shah soon found himself in the unenviable position of leading a court that enshrined principles of appointment that starkly illustrated the irregularity in his own appointment process.

[69] S Ijaz, 'Judicial Appointments in Pakistan: Coming Full Circle' (2015) 1 *LUMS Law Journal*.

[70] *Mohtarma Benazir Bhutto v President of Pakistan* PLD [1998] SC 38.

[71] Khan, *A History of the Judiciary in Pakistan* 502–505.

In her second term in office, Benazir Bhutto was keen to find and appoint other judges who were her sympathisers. Rushed attempts to do just that led, however, to legal challenges being launched against these appointments. One consequence was the *Al-Jehad Trust* case, in which the Supreme Court elaborated key principles to be abided by in the appointment process.[72] Although initially reluctant, Shah ultimately signed the majority opinion authored by Ajmal Mian J.

Al-Jehad interpreted the stipulation of Article 175 that the President make judicial appointments 'after consultation' as meaning that 'the consultation should be effective, meaningful, purposive, consensus oriented, leaving no room for complaint of arbitrariness'. It also held that the 'opinion of the Chief Justice of Pakistan and the Chief Justice of a High Court as to the fitness and suitability of a candidate for judgeship is entitled to be accepted in the absence of very sound reasons to be recorded by the President.' The Court further granted veto powers to the concerned Chief Justices in the matter of appointment of judges of superior courts. The judgment enshrined the principle of seniority for elevation to the office of Chief Justice, as well as limiting other possible violations of tenure. These stipulations and conditions became standard bearers for the establishment of 'judicial independence' into the future.

Bhutto felt herself betrayed by the *Al-Jehad* judgment and this opened conflict between her and President Leghari as well as with Chief Justice Shah. Citing this and additional grounds of governmental breakdown, in 1996 President Leghari proceeded to order her government's dissolution under Article 58(2)(b). The next government of Nawaz Sharif also went against the spirit of the *Al-Jehad* judgment in not finalising appointments recommended by Chief Justice Shah.

Surely not without the use of inducements, but also as a continuing consequence of his initial appointment, there was an effective mutiny against the Chief Justice within the Supreme Court. Sitting in regional benches of the Supreme Court, two judges accepted petitions challenging Shah's continuation in office in the aftermath of the *Al Jehad* judgment and granted an interim order suspending him from performance of his functions.[73] Shah refused to accept these restraints. He also

[72] *Al Jehad Trust v Federation of Pakistan* PLD [1996] SC 324.

[73] Khan, *A History of the Judiciary in Pakistan* 79–81.

widened the breach between himself and Prime Minister Nawaz Sharif by issuing contempt of court notices against Sharif and some of his ministers. Ultimately, the Supreme Court was itself physically assaulted by members of Sharif's PML Party in November 1997.

This attack did not incite any popular support for the institution and thereby presents a stark contrast to the ways in which a large public came out in support of Iftikhar Chaudhry a decade later. More importantly here, the public support of Chaudhry allowed the judiciary to build upon the principles elaborated earlier in *Al-Jehad*.

Interestingly, the 2007 declaration of emergency provided a necessary pivot to regaining judicial power of this sort. When emergency was declared on 3 November 2007 a seven-member bench of the Supreme Court convened an emergency meeting and declared Musharraf's acts illegal. This changed thereby the assessment, upon later review, of the act of the many judges who swore upon the second PCO oath that Musharraf administered under that Oath of Office (Judges Order 2007). In the *Hasnat Khan* case, the act of taking the oath was given the status of being a nullity in law. The court, once again headed by Chief Justice Chaudhry, declared that the judges who had taken an oath under the second PCO would not only cease to hold their office but that the judgments that they had authored would also be nullified. Furthermore, revisiting the *Al-Jehad case* for support, they decided that the appointments undertaken whilst Abdul Hameed Dogar was the Chief Justice (3 November 2007–21 March 2009) were in violation of the strict requirement for meaningful consultation with a validly-appointed Chief Justice.[74]

The popular reaction to this case was mixed, and some critics assailed the courts for innovating an extra-constitutional mechanism for retiring judges from service. Undeterred, the Chaudhry court went even further in bolstering its powers over appointments. The Eighteenth Amendment Act of 2010 had introduced a new Article 175A to the Constitution, which would provide for a Parliamentary Committee and a Judicial Committee to operate in tandem to vet nominations to the Higher Judiciary. The Court thus undertook to review a constitutional amendment and direct the legislature to reconsider its ambition to be a part of this process. On the basis of upholding judicial independence, a

[74] *Justice Hasnat Ahmed Khan v Federation of Pakistan* PLD [2011] SC 680.

principle that was part and parcel of a basic structure doctrine not fully avowed to this point, the Court under Chaudhry referred the matter back to Parliament for 'reconsideration', with recommendations regarding the changes that need to be introduced to the appointment process under Article 175A. There was more or less a wholesale incorporation of these recommendations in the new Article 175A that was introduced through the Nineteenth Amendment Act in 2011. While the committee structure still stands, the balance has tipped towards the judicial branch in terms of effective power.

The new article has been the subject of substantial litigation on the issue of the exact division of power it imagines between the Judicial Commission and the Parliamentary Committee, and their relationship with each other.[75] In cases that have arisen under Article 175A, it seems to be that the legal aptitude and suitability of the proposed candidate will be exclusively considered by the Judicial Commission, while the Parliamentary Committee's ambit is limited to considering the integrity and personal conduct of the candidate. Moreover, denial by the Parliamentary Committee of a recommendation made by the Judicial Commission requires 'compelling reasons based on irrefutable evidence against the nominated person', which can further be subjected to judicial review.[76]

As a closing note on the issue of judicial independence, it is necessary to point out that the record of appointment of women to the highest courts is hugely inadequate. In fact, while five women were appointed during Benazir Bhutto's first term as High Court judges in benches across the country, all of them failed to be appointed as either Chief Justices or be elevated to the Supreme Court. In at least one instance, a court case ensued on the basis of alleged gender-based discrimination. In two others, significant meddling such as in the appointment of these judges to alternate tribunals against their wishes interfered with their career trajectory within the superior judiciary.[77] Members of the

[75] *Munir Hussain Bhatti v Federation of Pakistan* PLD [2011] SC 407; *Federation of Pakistan v Munir Hussain Bhatti* PLD [2011] SC 752; *Federation of Pakistan v Sindh High Court Bar Association* PLD [2012] SC 1067.

[76] *High Court Bar Association, Bahawalpur v Federation of Pakistan* PLD [2015] Lahore 317, paras 17–18.

[77] Adil Najam, 'Why is there no woman on our Supreme Court?' *The News International* (8 October 2015) <www.thenews.com.pk/print/66589-why-is-there-no-woman-on-our-supreme-court>.

higher judiciary have remained exceedingly silent in the face of criticism. Some legislative measures have been proposed but not adopted for introducing a gender quota for appointment to the higher benches. However, where the higher judiciary has assumed powers of appointment for itself, it will have to be the forum to provide guarantees that equity concerns such as this will be addressed.

FURTHER READING

M Azeem, *Law, State and Inequality in Pakistan: Explaining the Rise of the Judiciary* (Singapore, Springer, 2017).

M Cheema and IS Gilani (eds), *The Politics and Jurisprudence of the Chaudhry Court 2005–2013* (Karachi, Oxford University Press, 2015).

T Halliday, L Karpik and MM Freeley (eds), *Fates of Political Liberalism in the British Post-colony: The Politics of the Legal Complex* (Cambridge University Press, 2012).

H Khan, *A History of the Judiciary in Pakistan* (Karachi, Oxford University Press, 2016).

S Krishnaswamy, *Democracy and Constitutionalism in India: A Study of the Basic Structure Doctrine* (New Delhi, Oxford University Press, 2010).

M Mate, 'Two Paths to Judicial Power: The Basic Structure Doctrine and Public Interest Litigation in Comparative Perspective' (2010) 12 *San Diego International Law Journal* 175.

PR Newberg, *Judging the State: Courts and Constitutional Politics in Pakistan* (New York, Cambridge University Press, 1995).

6

Federalism

Tribal Areas – Kashmir and Northern Areas – Fiscal Federalism – Legislative Powers – Provincial Emergencies – Ethnic Conflict – Muhajir – Balochistan – National Finance Commission Award – Eighteenth Amendment – Local Government

IN 1970 BALOCHISTAN was declared a Governor's province and with the dissolution of the One Unit the borders and boundaries were restored for Sindh, Punjab and the North West Frontier Province (NWFP) to what they had been under the Government of India Act 1935. Following the secession of Bangladesh in 1971 there was a distinct desire to invigorate this federalism in design and spirit to a more authentic and organic union between the remaining provincial units. In the making of the 1973 Constitution certain vestiges of highly-centralised control and oversight, such as had been the hallmark of the One Unit plan, were done away with. Additionally, whereas the counter-majoritarianism of the first two decades was oriented to the maintenance of parity between East and West,[1] in this design, the principle was employed to bolster the representation of interests by the smaller provinces.

This chapter begins with a look at the political structure of federalism, including provincial representation at the level of the federal government, the structure of provincial governments and the system of rule for non-provincial territorial entities as provided in the 1973 Constitution. Following that are three further sections: the first looks

[1] See text in Chapter 2, section II.

at the division of legislative and executive powers between provinces and the federation; the second investigates two instances of continuing ethnic conflict in Pakistan and their relation to the formal structures of federalism; the last looks at the constitutional guarantee of local government introduced in 2010 and the extent of its realisation.

Issues related to federalism have in many ways been the bane of statecraft in Pakistan. The federal formula contrived in 1973 has eventually been considered a failure by all of the federating units other than the Punjab. Owing partly to the centralising imperative of recurrent and lengthy military rule, the devolution promised in 1973 was never realised. In 2010 a package of far-reaching reforms in the Eighteenth Amendment Act received unanimous assent in the National Assembly and a range of provisions aimed at eroding both legislative and executive centralisation were incorporated into the Constitution. Importantly, the package also renamed the NWFP as Khyber Pakhtunkhwa (KP). In each part of this chapter, an attempt is made to mark the changes introduced by the Eighteenth Amendment and to gauge their impact thus far.

I. POLITICAL STRUCTURE OF FEDERALISM

The political structure of the 1973 Constitution promises a bicameral legislature at the centre and is described further, with particular attention paid to the relations between the National Assembly and Senate, earlier in this volume.[2] Notable for this discussion is that the population-based constituency mapping of the National Assembly reflects the heavy majoritarianism of the Punjab and that the design of the Senate is strictly counter-majoritarian. Each senator has a term of six years and is formally a direct representative of a province, given that she/he is elected from a provincial Assembly.

Provincial legislatures are all unicameral assemblies that follow an electoral formula that mirrors that of the federal Assembly; women's and minority seats are determined on the same proportionate basis as for the National Assembly.[3] Elections for provincial assemblies are

[2] See text in Chapter 3, section IB.
[3] See text in Chapter 3, section IF.

held on the same day as a federal election and electors thereby signal their choice for both levels of government simultaneously. The head of government for provinces is the Chief Minister, who is directly elected from the Assembly, along with Speaker and Deputy Speaker, usually on first sitting. In contrast to provisions for the National Assembly, no constitutional minimum is imposed upon the provincial Assemblies for the numbers of sittings that each Assembly must record. Other matters of Assembly functioning are Westminsterian in general form and include provisions for a vote of no-confidence by the Assembly. The executive authority in the province, by way of Article 129, is to be exercised in 'in the name of the Governor by the Provincial Government, consisting of the Chief Minister and Provincial Ministers'.[4]

The President of the Federation appoints a Governor for each of the provinces as the federation's representative. While the Governor is to act on the advice of the Chief Minister, or the head of the provincial government, he/she also has, in the tradition of colonial governance, a range of discretionary powers to exercise. By repeated amendments to the Constitution, the executive powers of provincial governments have formally shifted between the appointed Governor and the elected Chief Minister and Cabinet. The instruments are the same as those which have enacted this alteration for the federal executive: the Eighth and Seventeenth Amendments granted greater executive powers to the Governor, and the Thirteenth and Eighteenth Amendments shifted these back to the elected Chief Executive and Cabinet.

Governors are required to ratify Bills passed by the Assembly and can send a Bill back with suggestions for alteration. However, where the Assembly once again assents to the Bill, with or without incorporation of the Governor's advice, the Governor's assent will be deemed to have been given. In addition, Governors have the power to issue Ordinances in times when the provincial Assembly is not in session and where the Governor is 'satisfied that circumstances exist which render it necessary to take immediate action'.[5] These powers are a direct corollary of the Federal Ordinance powers that are elaborately discussed in an earlier chapter of this book.[6]

[4] See *Aurangzeb Shah Burki v Province of Punjab* PLD [2011] Lahore 198.

[5] See Constitution of Pakistan 1973, Art 128.

[6] See text in Chapter 4, section VI.

A further set of institutional mechanisms were forged in the 1973 Constitution to enjoin the two levels of government in cooperating towards developing a common economic policy and in resolving inter-provincial disputes in certain areas. The National Economic Council (NEC) and the Council of Common Interests (CCI) each comprise the membership of the Prime Minister and the Chief Ministers of the four provinces, as well as some additional nominated members. The NEC was intended to form a platform for cooperative economic planning and the CCI was to facilitate policy-setting in areas within the concurrent list and after the Eighteenth Amendment, in matters reduced down to those enumerated within Article 142(b).[7] Additionally, by a majority vote, inter-provincial disputes arising in reference to water and electricity use and distribution are to be settled in the CCI.[8]

II. EXCEPTIONS TO THE FEDERAL FORMULA

There are a number of territorial entities in Pakistan that do not have the status of provinces and therefore are excluded to varying degrees from constitutional rights and protections.

Article 246 of the Constitution redescribes units that have a long history of administration as tribal areas within the provincial bounds of Khyber Pakhtunkhwa as Federally and Provincially Administered Tribal Areas (FATA and PATA respectively). Article 247 prescribes that the 'executive authority' of the federation will extend into these areas and that Parliament cannot legislate for them. In the case of PATA the President can make directions that are to be enforced by the Governor of KP. These also prescribe that 'neither the Supreme Court nor any High Court will exercise jurisdiction' in the Tribal Areas unless Parliament so prescribes by law. While FATA is guaranteed representation at the centre, these representatives cannot legislate for their constituents, owing to a bar contained in Article 247. Popular elections have been the mechanism for choosing representatives since 1996, although it was

7 These are criminal law, criminal procedure and evidence.

8 *Gadoon Textile Mills v WAPDA* SCMR [1997] SC 641: this case upholds the powers of the CCI to a significant extent, allowing for the setting of electricity rates through this forum.

only through the 2002 Political Parties Act that political parties were enabled to field candidates for these elections.

The administrative acts promulgated by the federal or provincial governments escaped judicial review both by way of the bar contained in Article 247 as well as by the fashioning of doctrine that these Acts did not constitute law until 1995. A Supreme Court case in that year introduced the principle that such Acts would be justiciable on the guarantee that they are conducive to the peace and good governance of these areas.[9] Since then, the US campaign of drone warfare against the populace of FATA in particular has inspired challenges to the formal denial of fundamental rights protection under Article 247.

In the context that the Khyber Pakhtunkhwa Assembly 'adopted a resolution urging the president and the federal government to ensure [an] amendment to the Constitution for extending the Supreme and High Court jurisdictions to the Federally Administered Tribal Areas', the Peshawar High Court gave a powerful ruling decrying the continuance of drone attacks by the United States which had resulted in thousands of deaths by 2011.[10] Specifically citing the court's obligation 'to safeguard and protect the life and property of the citizens of Pakistan and any person for the time being in Pakistan' as a part of the jurisdiction conferred by way of Article 199, Chief Justice Dost Muhammad Khan provided further directions to the government to safeguard the sovereignty of all of Pakistan's territory. Importantly thus, fundamental rights guarantees were extended by this ruling to the people of FATA.[11] In contrast, the Supreme Court refused to admit petitions related to drone attacks, citing its own lack of jurisdiction on issues of defence, security and foreign policy, and deemed executive action in these areas to be non-justiciable.

[9] *NWFP v Muhammad Irshad* PLD [1995] SC 281; see text in Chapter 5, section III.

[10] SA Shah, *International Law and Drone Strikes in Pakistan: The Legal and Socio-political Aspects* (New York, Routledge, 2014) 150; although methodologies for calculating deaths caused from drone strikes vary, the author is relying upon data compiled by the Bureau for Investigative Journalism at <www.thebureauinvestigates.com/projects/drone-war>.

[11] *Foundation for Fundamental Rights v Federation of Pakistan* PLD [2013] Peshawar 94. See M Ashfaq, 'KP Assembly Resolution: Courts be Extended to Fata' *Dawn News* (7 May 2013).

FATA and PATA continue thus to be situated outside formal constitutional cover; systems of government and rule as well as the prevailing criminal law are provided by the 1901 Frontier Crimes Regulation (FCR). However, even the somewhat stable system of governance that was in place through the intermediation of a centrally-appointed Political Agent as per the FCR has undergone extreme fragmentation as a consequence of militant activity on the one hand, and the official war on terror, on the other.[12]

As noted in Chapter 2, the Northern Areas and Azad Jammu and Kashmir (AJK) have had a tenuous incorporation into the Pakistani state. Between them, the demands of the AJK population for representative government have been more readily agreed to by the Pakistani government. In 1974 a parliamentary system was established there. However, a Council for Kashmir Affairs with the PM of Pakistan and the PM of Azad Kashmir enjoying joint helmsmanship has also been vested with inordinate legislative and executive powers.[13] Nonetheless, an Assembly, a system of judicature and a Constitution replete with fundamental rights are the guarantee of the semi-sovereignty of AJK.

On the other hand, the status of the Northern Areas has generally been of living under heavy executive control via the auspices of the Minister of Kashmir Affairs and Northern Affairs. Some vestiges of indigenous legal systems have continued to operate.[14] After the 1974 Constitution for Kashmir was promulgated, residents of the Northern Areas also sought redress through that legal system. This situation altogether prompted a judgment from the Kashmir High Court[15] calling for the effective merger of Northern Areas within Kashmir and relied upon their once joined status to do so. This was overturned at the AJK Supreme Court[16] and thereafter, in 1999 the *Al Jehad* case[17] at

[12] 'Matters of jurisdiction: High court seeks petitioner's assistance in case against drone strikes' *The Express Tribune* (30 October 2014) <www.tribune.com.pk/story/783711/matters-of-jurisdiction-high-court-seeks-petitioners-assistance-in-case-against-drone-strikes>.

[13] The Azad Jammu and Kashmir Interim Constitution Act 1974, Art 21.

[14] C Hong, 'Liminality and Resistance in Gilgit-Baltistan: Legal Working Paper Series on Legal Empowerment for Sustainable Development' (2012) *Centre for International Sustainable Development Law* 1.

[15] *Malik Muhammad Miskeen v Government of Pakistan* PLD [1993] Azad J&K 1.

[16] *Federation of Pakistan v Malik Muhammad Miskeen* PLD [1995] SC AJ&K 1.

[17] *Al-Jehad Trust v Federation of Pakistan* SCMR [1999] SC 1379.

the Supreme Court of Pakistan extended cover of fundamental rights for residents of the Northern Areas and directed the central government to enact constitutional amendments to provide the people of the Northern Areas with the means to realise an elected Assembly and an independent judicial structure. A decade later, the Gilgit-Baltistan (Empowerment and Self-Governance) Order, 2009 provides for a replication of the structure of government of Azad Kashmir with some differences that more closely mirror the structure of government for the provinces. There is a centrally-appointed Governor, who is, along with the Prime Minister, a member of the Gilgit-Baltistan Council,[18] which has expansive legislative powers.

III. FEDERAL/PROVINCIAL POWERS

The complicated nature of power sharing between the federal and provincial tiers of government is described below in terms of the formula by which legislative powers are divided between them.

A. Legislative Powers

Through Article 141, the territorial bounds of legislative jurisdiction for the centre and provinces are established: the federal Assembly may make laws, including laws having extra-territorial jurisdiction, for the whole or any part of Pakistan. Provincial Assemblies are enabled to make laws for the whole or any part of a province.[19] As units within a larger federation, provinces have more circumscribed territorial jurisdiction. On the other hand, there are no territorial limitations on laws made by the federal government and there are pockets of territory within provinces that are directly administered by the federal government. For instance, the federal territory of Islamabad is geographically within the Province of Punjab but the laws of the province are of no effect within it.[20] FATA is similarly situated within

[18] Gilgit-Baltistan (Empowerment and Self-Governance) Order, 2009, Art 22 and Art 23.

[19] *KESC v NIRC* PLD [2014] Sindh 553.

[20] *Hashwani Hotels Ltd, Karachi v Government of the Punjab* PLD [1981] Lahore 211.

Khyber Pakhtunkhwa and ruled wholly through the FCR and federal government.[21]

Subject matter jurisdiction has been carried over through a list system as first introduced in the 1935 Government of India Act. This system is the complicating feature of federal-provincial power sharing. Until the coming into force of the Eighteenth Amendment Act of 2010, Article 142 provided that there would be two specific subject matter lists, the federal and the concurrent and for the latter, both provinces and the federal government would have the power to legislate. In contrast to the minimalist list of six points that Mujib had suggested be retained with the federal government in the lead-up to the secession of East Pakistan, the federal list as articulated in Schedule 4 to the 1973 Constitution was far more extensive, containing 111 subjects of exclusive federal legislative powers.

The concurrent list contained 47 subject matters and included law and order, education and health policy. Additionally, provincial Assemblies, as well as holding legislative powers for items contained on the concurrent list, were vested with residual jurisdiction for subject matters falling outside of the federal and concurrent lists. The 1973 Constitution had no provincial list per se. The very existence of the concurrent list was controversial in the making of the 1973 Constitution and it was anticipated then that the powers on the concurrent list would devolve to provincial competence within ten years. The Zia-ul-Haq coup of 1977 and the subsequent arrogations of power at the centre that followed in his reign are mostly blamed for the non-realisation of this aim. The Eighteenth Amendment, with some reservations, finally did away with the concurrent list in 2010. The impact of this will be discussed further below, after the following description of the ways in which both residual and concurrent jurisdiction were assessed by the courts prior to this alteration.

In a system that was conceived as one of cooperative federalism, the courts are accorded the formal role of settling conflict between these two tiers of government. In a far-reaching judicial statement, the powers of each tier were said to be constrained only to the extent that they must not violate or transgress upon the power of the other Assembly and must abide by other constitutional limitations, including

[21] See FCR discussion in Chapter 1, section IVA.

fundamental rights guarantees.[22] The first condition was made the basis of judicial arbitration both in reference to the overlapping jurisdiction established by the concurrent list and in gleaning the proper ambit of residuary jurisdiction falling to the provinces.

The adjudication of conflicts between centre and provinces for matters on the concurrent list led in instances to the courts repeating the platitudinous sentiment that their respective powers are coextensive and equal.[23] However, the substantive thrust of the greater number of judgments was in fact to uphold the supremacy of federal powers in the case of such conflicts. Much of the jurisprudence that investigated the overlapping powers of the federal and provincial assemblies arose in reference to Article 143, which clearly provides that where the federal parliament is competent to enact law, and where a provincial Assembly enacts a law which is in whole or in part repugnant to the federal law, the provincial law, to the extent of the repugnance, will be held to be void. Thus, in addition to the explicit enumeration of domains of central legislative exclusivity, the concurrent list also established domains of federal legislative primacy in accord with a plain reading of Article 143.

As Article 143 provided for voidability in case of repugnancy, a broad array of situations have been described as sufficient for such a finding.[24] Repugnancy can be found by inference in situations where obedience to one code could interfere with obedience to the other and also where the other can take away rights conferred by one code. Most elaborately, taking their cue from a long history of federalism case law in India, something akin to a doctrine of 'occupied field' informed the adjudication of conflicts about legislative power-sharing in Pakistan.[25] Such a principle suggests that even where the federal law was not intended to be exhaustive, its existence within a specific field is sufficient to render the provincial statute within that field as repugnant.[26]

[22] *Messrs Elahi Cotton Mills v Federation of Pakistan* PLD [1997] SC 582.

[23] *Quetta Textile Mills Ltd v Province of Sindh* PLD [2005] Karachi 55.

[24] *Water and Power Development Authority v Mian Muhammad Riaz* PLD [1995] Lahore 56.

[25] *Zaverbhai Amaidas v State of Bombay* AIR [1954] SC 752; *State of Assam v Horizon Union* AIR [1967] SC 442. See also *Tika Ramji v State of Uttar Pradesh* AIR [1956] SC 676 and *Deep Chand v State of UP* AIR [1959] SC 648.

[26] ibid.

This is not without exception, however, and in other cases the need for actual conflict, particularly in reference to defining residuary jurisdiction for provinces, was necessitated.[27]

In findings of repugnancy the remedies awarded have included the striking down of provincial statutes, their reading down or limitation of their application.[28] Such a 'plain reading' of Article 143 was repeatedly upheld in cases in the fields of labour and industrial relations in particular.[29]

Given the interwoven nature of these realms, a great deal of conflict and thereby ample opportunity for courts to determine the jurisdiction of each rung of government arose. The rights and duties prescribed under social security schemes, mostly administrated by the provinces, have been read down or altogether negated in specific cases as a consequence of the court upholding federal supremacy.[30]

In *Elahi Cotton*,[31] Justice Ajmal Mian defined interpretative principles for ascertaining the expanse of legislative competences implied by specific subjects in legislative lists. Given the absence of a provincial list per se, this worked to expand the manoeuvre accorded to the *Majlis-E-Shoora* in reference to the federal list. By expounding the need for 'liberal construction', Mian was able to arrive at the 'cardinal rule of interpretation' that 'each general word should be held to extend to all ancillary or subsidiary matters which can fairly and reasonably be said to be comprehended in it'. Given the precedential value of this case and others like it, it is easy to see how the field of provincial competence might narrow.[32] It is the record of such narrowing that has led in parts to an alteration and renewal in terms of the formal jurisdictional divides that the Eighteenth Amendment package of reforms promised.

[27] *Shamas Textile Mills Ltd v The Province of Punjab* SCMR [1999] SC 1477; *Messrs Quetta Textile Mills Limited v Province of Sindh* PLD [2005] Karachi 55.

[28] *Chaudhry Muhammad Siddique v Government of Pakistan* PLD [2005] SC 1.

[29] *Pakistan Telecommunication Company Ltd v Member NIRC* SCMR [2014] SC 535.

[30] *Sui Northern Gas Pipelines Limited Lahore v Government of the Punjab* PLC (CS) [2001] Lahore 383.

[31] *Messrs Elahi Cotton Mills Ltd v Federation of Pakistan* PLD [1997] SC 582.

[32] ibid.

B. Jurisdiction after the Eighteenth Amendment

After the Eighteenth Amendment, Article 142 now only provides that there will be a federal list, to be contained in the Fourth Schedule to the Constitution. Although the 47-item concurrent list was mostly done away with, the revised Article 142(b) in fact provides a set of areas, namely 'criminal law, criminal procedure and evidence' for which Parliament and the provincial Assemblies shall 'both have power to make laws'. The current Article 142(c) provides that the proper domain for the exercise of provincial legislative powers is inclusive of all matters that are neither in the federal legislative list nor contained in Article 142(b). In this vein, there has been a significant devolution of powers to the provincial level. However, Article 143 remains unaltered and as a consequence, the possibility of the centre holding a trump to the provinces' legislative actions remains.

A recent case at the Peshawar High Court illustrated, however, that the very act of abolishing the concurrent list has impacted the reasoning of the courts so that such primacy is no longer a foregone conclusion. This case tested the vires of a law against corruption-related offences by public officials in the province of Khyber Pakhtunkhwa.[33] The federal government had itself reframed prior accountability and anti-corruption legislation to pass the National Accountability Ordinance in 1999. The petitioners sought nullification of the provincial statute on the basis that the federal law had 'exhaustively covered the field of corruption and corrupt practices for all of Pakistan and importantly, that the doctrine of occupied field was a necessary part of federalism case law in Pakistan.' The court differed and held in fact that the scope of the occupied field doctrine had narrowed considerably after the abolition of the concurrent list. It could not be the measure of valid legislation promulgated under the authorisation of Article 142(b), the new 'mini-concurrent list'. More stringent tests for repugnancy were needed to assess whether and to what extent provincial and federal laws for these subjects could be reconciled. The reasoning in this case could be a boon to those who have sought a way into cooperative federalism.

Nonetheless, the record of post-Eighteenth Amendment litigation suggests that broad areas of uncertainty persist. Still generating some

[33] *Noor Daraz Khan v Federation of Pakistan* PLD [2016] Peshawar 114.

significant litigation has been the domain of labour laws. Industrial relations and employment standards were both areas that had historically been legislated upon by the federal government, but which were transferred to provincial competence after 2010. The two larger provinces, Sindh and Punjab, were quick to enact industrial relations legislation and other labour legislation, whereas the smaller provinces faced a definite lag. The federal government also seized certain jurisdiction in passing an industrial relations statute to cover the federal territory of Islamabad as well as to regulate the creation and conduct of trade unions for industries located in two or more provinces.

The federal government's actions were challenged at the Supreme Court in the 2011 *Air League of PIAC Employees* case. The court articulated something akin to a watertight compartmentalisation test to protect the provincial prerogative to legislate against federal incursions.[34] It did this on the back of Article 144, which was introduced in 2010. Article 144 provides that the federal government can legislate in a subject area within the provincial legislative domain when expressly asked to do so by one or more provincial legislatures. While acknowledging that there are 'institutions/corporations which have their branches all over the country' and concomitantly that trade unions may wish to be registered at the national level in such institutions, thereby necessitating federal level legislation, the court under Chief Justice Iftikhar Muhammad Chaudhry sees a full solution presented in Article 144, thereby necessitating that provincial Assemblies request such action by the federal government.

A later case from the Karachi High Court differed, by seeing the passage by the national legislature of the Industrial Relations Act of 2012 as a necessary step to allowing workers to realise their Article 17-guaranteed fundamental right of association.[35] The court accepted that the national legislature must necessarily step in to provide a mechanism for this realisation where workers are employed by companies established in two or more provinces because fundamental rights cannot be abridged other than for enumerated reasons. The Court found further support for its determination in item 58 of the federal list, which reads 'Matters which under the Constitution are

[34] *Air League of PIAC Employees v Federation of Pakistan* SCMR [2011] SC 1254.
[35] *KESC v NIRC* PLD [2014] Sindh 553.

within the legislative competence of Majlis-e-Shoora (Parliament) or relate to the Federation.' The court separated this specific mandate into parts, so that the words 'relate to the federation' were interpreted as being inclusive of all matters that it would be beyond the territorial bounds of a provincial legislature to enact laws for. Thus, the delimitation of the territorial jurisdiction of provincial legislative powers was made central to the reasoning in this case. Item 58 was presented as the panacea where provinces can only provide the enabling mechanism for the realisation of the right to association within their territorial borders and where, presumably, a uniformity of rights protection is necessitated in specific organisational or occupational fields beyond these borders.[36]

The joining together of the expanse of fundamental rights guarantees and item 58 authorisation for federal action, if upheld at further appeal at the level of the Supreme Court will certainly do much to damage the effective devolution of legislative powers that were promised under the Eighteenth Amendment. However, perhaps a greater problem with the division of legislative competence anticipated after the Eighteenth Amendment is the capacity shortfall that is being experienced by provincial governments.

The fiscal burden of this transfer already indicates a resource lag owing to several design features of actually existing federalism in Pakistan. Taxation heads have increased for the provinces, but in a country where it is notoriously difficult to expand the tax base beyond those who are taxed at source, this means an added infrastructural cost to the provinces that is not currently being managed. A chief corollary of all this is that the smaller provinces have been unwilling or unable to legislate or define policy in many areas. In the areas of labour relations and management, health and education, Balochistan, KP and Sindh have shown a definite lag. In addition, the acquisitive federal bureaucracy is unwilling to devolve ownership of some not insubstantial social welfare insurance schemes to the provinces for their management. As per a continuing history, the only province that was able to fully

[36] At issue in *Air League* was the validity of a 2008 Industrial Relations Act, which lapsed in any case in 2011. In 2012 the federal government promulgated another Industrial Relations Act, which in all material respects was the same as the 2008 Act, but nonetheless Faisal Arab J deemed this was sufficient grounds to distinguish this case from *Air League*.

incorporate the changes and show compliance with the 'demands' that accompany devolution to the provinces is Punjab.

C. Federal Powers and the Executive

The distributions of executive powers in the federation are defined by Articles 97 and 137 of the Constitution. Article 97 provides that the executive authority of the federation 'shall extend to the matters with respect to which the *Majlis-e-Shoora* has power to make laws. Article 137 mirrors this in providing that the executive authority of the provinces shall extend over those matters for which the provincial assemblies have power to make laws. It seems to be anticipated that the legislative and executive authority of the various levels of government are coextensive.

Ever the pragmatists, however, the framers of the Constitution also included mechanisms for subjecting the provincial executive to the supremacy of the federal executive on several grounds. Article 148 provides the more circumspect direction that the executive authority of the province shall be exercised so as to secure compliance with federal laws. However, Article 149 confers greater powers upon the federal bureaucracy to provide directions to the provinces in a range of matters. Included in them are any situations thought to be necessary so as not to 'impede or prejudice' the functioning of the federal executive. Additionally, Articles 149(b) and (c) provide for the federal executive to give directions to the provinces for establishing communication and transportation links in, as well as 'for the purpose of preventing any grave menace to the peace or tranquility or economic life of Pakistan or any part thereof.'

The quid pro quo for these possible encroachments on provincial powers is the correlative 'duty' placed upon the federation in Article 148(c) 'to protect every Province against external aggression and internal disturbances and to ensure that the Government of every Province is carried on in accordance with the provisions of the Constitution.' Coupled with the powers of presidential dissolution under Article 234, this article has been the mechanism for the more overt central interference in provincial government, as discussed below.

While the drive towards a unitary consolidation of the executive function has been described in another chapter, the principles and formal guarantees of federal power-sharing have also had to co-exist in a persistent environment of tension. The retention of a fairly broad set of emergency powers provisions, as well as the maintenance of the office of the Governor as the centre's representative at the provincial level have been amongst the means by which the unitariness of executive rule has been felt in the furthest reaches of the federation.

IV. EMERGENCY

As detailed earlier, the federal powers of emergency under Article 232 impose extensive limits on the powers of the provincial government. In light of these, the question of whether or not provincial assemblies could be barred from meeting during the promulgation of a national emergency came up to be determined in 1999. The Supreme Court held that the federal government can assume the powers vested in or exercisable by any body or authority in the province other than the Assembly and that an order barring the Sindh Assembly from meeting was held was contrary to the constitutional rights of Assembly members.[37]

In the same Emergency chapter of the Constitution, there is a clearer delegation of powers to the President to dissolve provincial assemblies: under Article 234, the President can declare a provincial Assembly non-functional and revert the province in question to Governor's rule for a period of two months. The condition for invocation of these powers is that the President be 'satisfied that a situation has arisen in which the Government of the Province cannot be carried on in accordance with the provisions of the Constitution' to direct the Governor to assume powers on the President's behalf. The Governor thereby assumes power over 'all or any of the functions of the Government of the Province, and all or any of the powers vested in, or exercisable by, anybody or authority in the Province, other than the Provincial Assembly'. The President's powers are themselves activated by the advice given by the Governor.

It was after the return of electoral and parliamentary democracy that the exact nature of the executive's powers to tread into provincial parliamentary affairs would be tested through judicial review. Beginning in

37 *Syed Jalal Mehmood Shah v Federation of Pakistan* PLD [1999] SC 395.

1990 and carrying on through the decade, a number of instances arose wherein provincial governments were formed by parties that were the official opposition within the central legislature. As a consequence, significant amounts of meddling, exacerbated by the Governor's role as central appointee, worked to destabilise provincial governments. One illustrative and important instance involves the coalition government under the Pakistan Muslim League of Sabir Shah in the NWFP. In that case,[38] the government at the centre was Benazir Bhutto's and the President and Governor were both also members of her party. A presidential proclamation was issued, declaring Governor's rule, once advice had been tendered suggesting that a constitutional deadlock or impasse had been reached in the province. The details of the alleged impasse included inter-party defections and the frustration by the Speaker of the Assembly of a call for a vote of confidence as well as the near incitement to violence of student groups aligned to the major parties in a way that threatened the working of the provincial government. Against this scenario the court held that the President's proclamation was issued for sound reasons and was within the ambit of what might be termed a constitutional emergency.

In a later case,[39] the conditions of a constitutional emergency were strictly parsed and delineated and that a number of ministers within the ruling coalition had resigned from their seats was held not to be sufficient to prove a constitutional emergency. Further, the court more explicitly dilated upon the implications for the federal principle. Reflecting upon the peculiarity of the federal powers of intervention, which in the case of Pakistan and also India are available beyond conditions simply of external aggression or civil unrest, but also extend to constitutional emergencies, the court cautioned that these powers should be used sparingly.

After the Eighteenth Amendment of 2010 the executive power to suspend Assemblies is mediated by the following preconditions: the Governor of a province, upon receipt of an act of Parliament signaling its inability to exercise effective control may request the President to intervene. Alternately, both houses of Parliament must separately pass a resolution demanding the imposition of such an emergency.

[38] *Sabir Shah v Federation of Pakistan* PLD [1994] SC 738.

[39] *Manzoor Ahmed Wattoo v Federation of Pakistan* PLD [1997] Lahore 38.

This latter condition thus ensures that the Senate, given its representation of the federating units, has some influence on opposing a resolution that would be held to be against the interests of the lesser provinces. The enforcement mechanisms at the disposal of the executive during Emergency Rule remain entirely intact and include the suspension of fundamental rights.

A range of situations have arisen in recent times whereby a time-bound Governor's rule has been operationalised under Article 234. In 2009, citing the 'unprecedented and unique constitutional void' left in the Province of Punjab as the sitting Chief Minister was retroactively disqualified from holding the post of MPA, President Zardari declared Governor's rule there.[40] In 2013, after a spate of killings of the minority Hazara community by sectarian anti-Shia militias, the 'centre' caved in to popular demands that the provincial Assembly be suspended and Governor's rule be established.[41] The popular pressure arose probably in anticipation that direct executive rule would be less encumbered in seeking out and bringing to account the perpetrators of such violence. In actuality, no charges were laid.

V. ETHNIC CONFLICT AND THE FEDERAL FORMULA

While it is commonplace to state that Pakistan is a multiethnic society, it is also true that different ethnic identities have organised at different points in ways that reflect aspirations for either subsumption within the broader scheme of the Pakistani nation or as emergent nations themselves. The tendency amongst a group or a people to see themselves as autonomous and distinct, or as dependent, exploited, and disaffected, is reflective of a range of ways in which ethnic identification is made within the seams of national policy, including the formal features of federalism as well as other fields of political and economic development.[42]

[40] 'President Imposes Governor's Rule on PM`s Advice' *Dawn News* (26 February 2009) <www.dawn.com/news/446826/president-imposes-governoraes-rule-on-pmaes-advice>.

[41] 'Governor's rule to be imposed in Balochistan' *Dawn News* (14 January 2013) <www.dawn.com/news/778500/governor-rule-possible-raisani-ready-to-resign>.

[42] C Jaffrelot and RB Rais, 'Interpreting Ethnic Movements in Pakistan' (1998) 37 *The Pakistan Development Review* 153.

A. Ethnic Conflict in the Federation

Although it is impossible to account for the range of ethnic conflicts that continue to plague the project of federalism in Pakistan, two of these are described below. In Sindh, and to a great measure centred in Karachi, the province's Urdu-speaking *Muhajir* community, which migrated at Partition, has been in an intractable conflict with the Sindhi population as well as newer migrants to the province. The aggregative logic of a federal formula that ascribes a unitary ethnic character to each of the provinces exacerbates tensions in Sindh. An absence of accounting for large minorities is reflected in other provinces as well, but with the salient difference that the *Muhajir* community has experienced a precipitous decline in its fortunes from Partition when all indicators suggested that it was a dominant minority within the federation. In its more organised forms it has employed militancy and also sought a meaningful role in politics at all governmental levels within the federation to counteract the effects of such decline.

Ethnic strife in Balochistan has been of a different nature. In Balochistan, the primary conflict has been between ethnic Baloch and the state security apparatus, which is instrumental to the processes of resource-extraction and appropriation. However, as with Sindh, the native Baloch have fostered grievances against Punjabi and Pukhtoon settlers and residents and this has also erupted into violence. The Pakistani state has indirectly, by refusing to acknowledge features of systemic inequality, and directly, by the recurrent use of force to quell nationalist politics, treated the people of Balochistan as a secessionist threat.

As noted in Chapter 2, several ethnic conflicts were brewing in West Pakistan at the same time that grievances in East Pakistan were gaining heightened expression. The economic development plans authored during the Ayub era had accepted the premise of functional inequality and not sought to mediate widening disparities even when they articulated with the existing sense of marginalisation by ethnically- and regionally-defined groups. The One Unit plan was oriented to the subsumption of minority groups and the fostering of a national culture that accepted the de facto dominance of a Punjabi-*Muhajir* alliance of power. Thus, groups in the West questioned the very basis of the federal compact as vehemently as it was being suspected in the East.

Immediately prior to the dissolution of the One Unit formula, both intra-group rivalry and greater organisation of peripheral groups and regions was impacting politics in West Pakistan. The Sindhi Language Movement, organised after the *Muhajir* migration at Partition, was a response to the cultural chauvinism that reinscribed the primacy of the *Muhajir's* mother tongue, Urdu, in avenues of education and employment. While the tensions building in the rivalry between Sindhi and *Muhajir* would blow over into violent riots in the early 1970s, the ferment for group recognition was building in other parts of West Pakistan as well.

In the late 1960s popular regional leaders visited East Pakistan and agreed to militate for Mujibur Rahman's six-point agenda calling for a limitation of federal powers. With the dissolution of the One Unit and the announcement of elections in 1970, a profusion of regionalist political parties looking to enter the electoral contest were established.[43] A number of these, including the *Jeay Sindh Naujawan Mahaz* merged a left-ideological orientation and a promotion of cultural rights. More consequentially, the National Awami Party (NAP), a party further to the left of the spectrum than Bhutto's Peoples Party, won sufficient seats to allow them to establish coalition governments in Balochistan and NWFP and operate as a significant pressure group at the centre.

The NAP-headed government in Balochistan acted quickly on passing a reformative agenda inclusive of measures to enact affirmative action and development in aid of the native Baloch population. It also abolished the *Sardari* system in name although what that meant in practice was not fully clear.[44] When the government began to bargain for greater control over its plentiful natural resources, Bhutto tried surreptitious forms of meddling to disturb the functioning of what had been an allied party to that point. Considerable unrest was taking place in Balochistan, particularly in Quetta where nationalist students were leading a campaign against Punjabi settlers. In 1973 the discovery of an arms cache in the Iraqi embassy in Islamabad, purportedly destined for Balochistan to aid in a planned insurrection against the

[43] M Rashiduzzaman, 'The National Awami Party of Pakistan: Leftist Politics in Crisis' (1970) 43 *Pacific Affairs* 394.

[44] See text in Chapter 1, section IVC and fn 43; see also Himayatullah Yaqubi, 'Leftist Politics in British India: A Case Study of the Muslim Majority Provinces' (2013) 34 *Pakistan Journal of History and Culture* 63.

central government, led Bhutto to dismiss the NAP government, dissolve the party and accelerate a military operation in Balochistan.[45] Another NAP government, this time in the NWFP, resigned in protest at Bhutto's actions in Balochistan. This and succeeding events aided the dissipation of secular and progressive forces in these parts of the country. The Supreme Court upheld the ban on NAP, reflecting heavy central bias against political action organised on ethnic grounds.[46]

The executive and judiciary have acted in synchronicity with one another to police the expressions of political grievance in regionalist terms. The regime of preventive detention was used extensively against figures such as GM Syed of Sindh and Abdul Ghaffar Khan of the NWFP. The act of organising on an ethnic basis was condemned as introducing fissiparous tendencies into the polity and the exercise of expressive and political rights readily negated when oriented to 'liquidating the democratic state that has bestowed that liberty'.[47] Such collusion ensured that these spokespersons of distinct brands of ethno-nationalism were kept in jail and away from politics for much of their lives.

Such policies of containment continued post-1973, so that many of the regionalist parties, aligned in an odd mishmash with religious and other rightist parties as the Pakistan National Alliance (PNA) to call for Bhutto's removal.[48] This then set the stage for their pacification by Zia after he assumed power from Bhutto in 1977. Such a pacification took different forms; the robust army action against Baloch nationalist insurgents was called off; other Baloch, Pakhtun and Sindhi nationalists, although freed from jail by Zia, thereafter either lay low or went into exile. In Sindh though, tensions rose nonetheless and the stage was set for a spiral of violence that continues to date.

These tensions were getting ever more stark through Bhutto's reign, as Sindhis had enjoyed patronage by their ethnic kinsman,[49] whereas

[45] *Manzoor Elahi v Federation of Pakistan* PLD [1975] SC 66; see text in Chapter 3, section IIA.

[46] *Islamic Republic of Pakistan v Abdul Wali Khan* PLD [1976] SC 57.

[47] *The State v Abdul Ghaffar Khan* PLD [1957] (WP) Lahore 142. See also text in Chapter 2, section II and Chapter 7, section IV.

[48] See text in Chapter 4, section IA.

[49] Note that Mumtaz Bhutto, cousin of Zulfiqar Bhutto, held the position of Chief Minister of Sindh from May 1972–December 1973 and was succeeded by Ghulam Mustafa Jatoi, also a large Sindhi landowner.

the fortunes of *Muhajirs* were perceived as being in inexorable decline. Zia's regime faced its most potent sites of resistance amongst Sindhi's who came out to the streets in incredible numbers when the movement for the Restoration of Democracy made its protest calls in the early 1980s. On the other hand, *Muhajireen* youth disaffection organised in the call for an end to quotas for university admissions and official employment. In 1984 the *Muhajir Quami Mahaz* (MQM) was launched from what had been a student-based insurrectionary movement in promotion of greater *Muhajir* representation.[50] Some 'circumstantial evidence' has linked the founding of the MQM to military funding and support.

The MQM[51] was a formidable force when it entered the electoral arena in 1988, and yet the mainstreaming of the MQM and its associated demands did not result in the deradicalisation of its militant wings. In 1994 the army was called in to break the MQM's hold in pockets, where its powers were said to approximate that of a 'state within a state'. Through combined police, paramilitary and army action, a few years of street warfare ensued in some of Karachi's poorer areas. The state agencies were accused of extra-judicial killings and the infamous 'encounter', in which a 'staged' police action disguises such a killing, was widely performed in these years. In addition to assertions about the lawlessness of MQM leaders in general, a plot to establish an independent state for *Muhajirs* by the name of Jinnahpur was either uncovered or fabricated by the military.[52] In either case, the wide-ranging military operation of these years was not widely decried in Pakistan, although attempts to introduce more far-reaching changes to anti-terror laws coupled in with this action were invalidated by the Supreme Court.[53]

[50] See L Gayer, 'Guns, Slums, and "Yellow Devils": A genealogy of urban conflicts in Karachi, Pakistan' (2007) 41 *Modern Asian Studies* 515; see also Nicola Khan, 'Mobilisation and Political Violence in the Mohajir Community of Karachi' (2007) 42 *Economic and Political Weekly* 2435.

[51] The party changed its name to Muttahida Qaumi Mahaz in 1997 to signal a move away from representing a single constituency.

[52] '"Muhajir Republican Army" is another gaffe after "Jinnahpur": Altaf Hussain' *The Express Tribune* (30 August 2013) <www.tribune.com.pk/story/597470/muhajir-republican-army-is-another-gaffe-after-jinnahpur-altaf-hussain/>; 'Of anti-MQM narratives' *The Nation* (9 December 2015) <www.nation.com.pk/columns/09-Dec-2015/of-anti-mqm-narratives>.

[53] See text in Chapter 5, section III.

The loss of life has been and continues to be considerable in the many interfaces of factional intra-MQM strife as well as in conflict involving *Muhajirs*, Sindhis and, to an increasing extent, Pakhtun and Afghan populations that migrated to the city in the last two decades.

As was also the case in Sindh, the freeing of political space and the restoration of democracy in the 1990s allowed nationalist parties and leaders to move into the mainstream for some time in Balochistan. However, they were less effective than the MQM in gaining political concessions at the centre so that the historical causes of insurgency, the highest unemployment and mortality rates and the lowest literacy and access to basic provisions, including healthcare and electricity, have continued in place.[54] With renewed army rule under Musharraf, the 'development' of Balochistan through the intensive exploitation of its natural resources, backed increasingly by foreign investment, picked up pace. While state forces disengenously blame the *sardars* for keeping the province's wealth to themselves and perpetuating the deprivation of the broader population, it is these same state forces that are enacting a silent war against the Baloch in this last decade through a campaign of murder and enforced disappearance.[55]

B. Formal Federalism and Ethnic Conflict

Having cited these two major ethnic/regional conflicts and their continued play in Pakistan, we can also juxtapose some of the constitutional mechanisms that perpetuate rather than ameliorate these tensions.

Pure proportionality is a principle used repeatedly and to ill effect in some of the formal instruments of federalism in Pakistan. In a country where the population imbalance between different federating units is so vast that the most populous, Punjab, houses 55.63 per cent

[54] The infant mortality rate for Balochistan in 2009–2010 was 72 deaths per 1,000 live births and the 10+ literacy rate in Balochistan stands at only 45%, half the national MDG target of 88%. For more data see UNDP 'Balochistan Millennium Development Goals (MDG) Report 2011'.

[55] See Balochistan Missing Persons case Human Right case no 29388-K of 2013 Supreme Court of Pakistan. See also A Khan, 'Renewed Ethnonationalist Insurgency in Balochistan, Pakistan: The Militarized State and Continuing Economic Deprivation' (2009) 49 *Asian Survey* 1071.

of the population and the least populous, Balochistan, is home to only 4.96 per cent, an adherence to this principle has yielded frightening consequences. In between these two, Sindh has 23 per cent and Khyber Pakhtunkhwa 13.4 per cent of the overall population. Furthermore, in spite of all evidence, an underlying assumption of national policy makers that each of the provinces has a homogenous ethnic character and no other cleavages worthy of recognition, is written into the quota regime as well as the fiscal resource scheme managed by the federal centre. Both of these have had direct impact on the continuance of the conflicts cited above as well as others that cannot be described here.

The quota regime presents something of a bridge between the formal and political aspects of federalism in Pakistan. This has been an issue of great political importance, as it impacts heavily on the composition of the bureaucratic wing of what is an oligarchic power structure that includes, in addition, the military. While there was a push to align general army recruitment with ethnic representation at the national level, no formal 'quota' has been announced, nor has this kind of representation been realised. The Punjabi and Pushtoon preponderance is attested to by the fact of there being 'no senior Sindhi or Baloch officers in the armed forces'.[56]

Quotas for the bureaucracy confer the impression of reconciling diversity in this multi-ethnic state, but in fact fail to do so for the reasons elaborated below. Following the secession of East Bengal and in tandem with the promulgation with the 1973 Constitution, this scheme was reframed in the following terms: 10 per cent merit; 50 per cent Punjab (including Islamabad); 7.6 per cent urban Sind (Karachi, Sukkur, and Hyderabad); 11.4 per cent rural Sind (areas in Sind other than those above); 11.5 per cent NWFP; 3.5 per cent Baluchistan; 4 per cent Northern Areas and FATA; and 2 per cent Azad Kashmir. As noted by Charles Kennedy, the reason why 'this particular formula was chosen is open to conjecture'.[57] Presumably it reflected the same politics of containment that had sought to dispense marginal bits of effective power and representation to provincial elites rather than seeking broader representation. Originally passed for the duration of a

[56] F Ahmed, 'Ethnicity, Class and State in Pakistan' (1996) 31 *Economic and Political Weekly* 3050, 3052.

[57] CH Kennedy, 'Policies of Ethnic Preference in Pakistan' (1984) 24 *Asian Survey* 688, 693.

decade, this quota has been renewed every decade thereafter. In 2014, an official memorandum revised the formula so that the 'Merit quota' was decreased to 7.5% and Balochistan's quota increased to 6%, whilst the other figures remained constant.

This national quota system enjoys constitutional indemnification against challenge in a somewhat roundabout way. Article 27 both bars discrimination in service and allows for ameliorative measures, yet nowhere specifically mentions ethnicity in either case. The first clause of Article 27 specifies that no citizen 'otherwise qualified for appointment in the service of Pakistan shall be discriminated against' on the grounds 'only of race, religion, caste, sex, residence or place of birth'. An exemption was provided, originally only for 20 years but in 1999 extended to 40 years, for posts to be reserved for 'any class or area to secure their adequate representation in the service of Pakistan'. The official quota system of proportional representation was therefore the adequate level of representation being sought and thereby protected against challenge. Recently, through the Eighteenth Amendment Act, an additional clause enabling the *Majlis-e-Shoora* to enact any law to redress the under-representation of 'any class or area' has been added to Article 27. While no such legislative measures have been passed, it will be interesting to see whether and to what extent more robust initiatives to redress historical under-representation of minority groups, ethnically or otherwise, will be enacted in consequence of this allowance.

Thus far, the quota regime has failed to redress the grievances of the groups discussed above. In the case of *Muhajirs*, the official regime has been cited as a means to diminish their position in the federation. Spokespersons cite the lowering of the merit quota, which was 20 per cent prior to 1973, and the drawing of a distinction between urban and rural Sindh as means of shutting them out of positions in which they were historically over-represented. It is certainly the case that with a higher pure merit intake and with an aggregative rather than divided quota this primarily urban population was once more visibly a part of the governmental apparatus. For the Baloch, the fact of there having been significant internal migration within the country entails that a Punjabi or Pakhtoon person residing in Balochistan can take advantage of the quota which works on a geographical and not an ethnic basis. Without a specific counter-majoritarian intent in any case, the extreme marginalisation of the Baloch from centralised administration and policy-making will necessarily persist.

However, other important quota regimes exist officially at the level of provincial governmental services and at the point of entry to government-funded educational institutions. These more varied regimes have faced numerous constitutional challenges. Recently upheld at the Supreme Court in a case originating in Balochistan, reserved university seats for applicants from rural areas were deemed to be lawful. Although the judgment does not acknowledge the ethnic line as such, the logic of the ruling follows the establishment of the divided quota from Sindh, which provides an implicit acknowledgement that Sindhis reside in greater concentrations in rural rather than urban areas of the province.[58] Across other provinces as well the representation of 'disadvantaged' groups is sought to be enacted through quotas that seek district-level representation or in other cases employ the category of a 'tagged areas' to demarcate sub-provincial regions considered backwards or impoverished.[59] The constitutional safeguard for ensuring proportionate representation for the federal services is employed broadly in judicial reasoning to affirm that these classifications are in fact reasonable ones.

The fiscal transfer regime between the centre and the provinces has, until recently, followed a formula of population-based proportionality alone. This, the National Finance Award (NFC) is to be devised every five years by the National Finance Commission, established by way of Article 160. The taxation formula between the federal and provincial governments is outlined in the same provision and heavily favours the central government, which collects income tax, excise duties, import duties etc. In total, this has meant that the centre generates '90.7% of the total tax revenue with the remaining 9.7% collected in roughly equal proportion by the provinces and local governments'.[60] With some variation dependent upon which headings of revenue collection are classified as capable of disbursement back to the provinces, the formula has been that close to 60 per cent of the central government's

[58] *Miss Shazia Batool v Government of Balochistan* SCMR [2007] SC 410.

[59] *Dr Abdul Rasheed v Government of Balochistan* PLD [2014] Quetta 186; *Huma Saad v Chairman, Joint Admission Committee, Medical/Dental Colleges, KPK, Peshawar* CLC [2012] Peshawar 891; *Mst Attiyya Bibi Khan v Federation of Pakistan* SCMR [2001] SC 1161.

[60] See R Broadway and A Shah, *Fiscal Federalism* (London, Cambridge University Press, 2009).

total revenue collection is kept for its own uses and the remainder divided and transferred to the provinces.

As the pace was quickening towards an expansion of provincial powers and the reallocations set in train with the Eighteenth Amendment, the formula for the NFC was also revised away from strict proportionality. From 2009 onwards the new formula provided that 82 per cent of resources allocated to the provinces were distributed according to population, 10.3 per cent for poverty/backwardness, 5 per cent for revenue generation and collection, and 2.7 per cent to account for the greater costs of development associated with low population density. The revised formula resulted in a 5.6 per cent reduction of the share of Punjab from the last consensus award of 1996. Punjab received 51.7 per cent, there was a 1.3 per cent increase in Sindh's allocation to 24.6 per cent, a 1.1 per cent increase in KP's share to 14.6 per cent, and a 3.8 per cent increase in Balochistan's share, to 9.1 per cent.[61]

The NFC reward provides the bulk of the revenue for the basic administrative functioning and the provisioning of services in line with matters over which the provinces exercise jurisdiction under the provincial legislative lists. To varying degrees, the complaint that the mechanisms of resource consolidation and transfer that the NFC represents constitutes a drain upon the *Muhajir* and Baloch communities, has been expressed by these groups. Although tax generation remains abysmally low across the federation, it is nonetheless the case that the feudal character of the national political elite has ensured the maintenance of a broad exemption for the imposition of a tax on agricultural income. This protectionist bias in favour of agriculturalists maps easily onto the sense of grievance that the urbane *Muhajir* foster. In the case of Balochistan, the inadequacy of an NFC award that measured population without accounting for poverty or for the expansiveness of territory was finally addressed in 2009. What meshes somewhat with the NFC transfer is the question of natural resource ownership and the enforcement of a formula for profit-sharing between centre and province.

The resource historically at issue for the Baloch has been natural gas, of which it is the largest and oldest supplier in Pakistan. The bulk

[61] 'Draft Report of 7th NFC Finalised' *The Nation* (21 February 2010) <www.nation.com.pk/politics/21-Feb-2010/Draft-report-of-7th-NFC-finalised>.

of this is used up by the power sector but large shares also go towards powering industry and in general household consumption. Domestic supplies of energy resources in Pakistan fall far short of consumption needs and the cash-strapped central government has resorted to maintaining domestic supplies by a variety of coercive means.[62] When the NAP government attempted to wrest this resource for provincial ownership in 1972, this served as a major provocation for Bhutto's dissolution of the government. The Constitution of the following year offered the accommodation that there would be a direct repatriation of excise tax collected on gas resources back to the source province in Article 161. Further, Article 158 also provided that the source province would have 'precedence over other parts of Pakistan in meeting the requirements' of that province subject to 'commitments and obligations' already undertaken prior to the date of the Constitution's promulgation. However, in reality, the resource has been on a succession of long leases to a consortium of centrally-owned governmental companies, with purchasing rates set at an inordinately low rate. The central government has failed to pay the direct transfers that should have transpired from application of Article 161 and the payment of dues under the leases are 'in arrears to the extent of tens of billions of rupees'.[63]

In the year prior to the passage of the Eighteenth Amendment, the government engaged in an act of reconciliation through formal means and negotiations to ensure the *Aghaaz-e-Haqooq-e-Balochistan* (The Beginning of Rights for Balochistan). For months, a process of consultation, which was limited by the unwillingness to talk with members of nationalist parties, but claimed nonetheless fair representation accorded to 'stakeholders', was staged so as to render what would pass for a compromise solution to Balochistan's reincorporation in the federation. While it made some acknowledgement of army heavy-handedness in dealing with the issue of missing persons, the centre nonetheless did not concede to a withdrawal of forces or even a curtailment in the long run of further construction of cantonments in the province. This, along with the emphasis placed on the development of the port town of Gwadar as a Special Economic Zone, and the initiation of mega

[62] M Khwaja, Abid Suleri 'Natural Resource Allocation in Balochistan and NWFP: Reasons for Discontent' (Sustainable Development Policy Institute, 2009).

[63] ibid 7.

projects including the building of dams, provides a truer indication of the manner in which the national elite political class still understands the incorporation of Balochistan to be as a region for the appropriation of resources and wealth towards an aggregate national good.

Nonetheless, with the passage of the Eighteenth Amendment in 2010, an altered Article 172 now provides that any new discoveries of gas or mineral reserves will be equally shared between the centre and that province. This seems a specific concession to the Baloch given the ongoing discovery of copper, iron and other mineral resources within its territory. Nonetheless, for concessions already in place, and especially those that have attracted foreign investment, the central government has still struck bargains that offer the Baloch a nominal share of the earnings and profits.[64] In an analogous case arising out of Sindh, the court provided only limited leeway to that province in light of pre-existing contracts and undertakings.[65]

Thus altogether, the federal formula in the case of Pakistan has shown limited capacity to mitigate ethnic and regional inequity and conflict that is consequent upon it. The obstinacy of maintaining an official 'blindness' to inequality experienced by ethnic minorities moulds the working of other institutional technologies of governance, including the census. It has been noted that 'Pakistan's ethnic arithmetic is difficult to establish in precise terms because the official census has not contained a specific question concerning the mother tongue of individual respondents since 1961'.[66] Although official policy dictates that a national census will be held every decade, there has only been one held in the last 35 years, in 1998. The absence of enumerative support for ethnicity-based claims works to undermine their efficacy.

That the intransigence of existing borders for provincial units can lead to heightened political conflict where the distribution of such resources is intra-provincially inequitable is a problem that plagues all of the provinces. Hence, the demand of the minority Seraiki-speaking community of Southern Punjab, the *Muhajirs* in Sindh and the Pakhtoon in Balochistan has been for the division of existing

[64] See discussion of *Reko Diq* in Chapter 4, section VB.

[65] *Engro Fertilizers Limited v Islamic Republic of Pakistan and Federation of Pakistan* PLD [2012] Sindh 50.

[66] A Weiss, 'Much Ado about Counting: The Conflict over Holding a Census in Pakistan' (1999) 39 *Asian Survey* 679.

provinces to ensure both decision-making closer to the ground, as well as more equitable sharing of resources. While Zia briefly considered a plan that would divide the whole country into 21 administrative units, ensuring ethnic homogeneity in each, demands for division have generally been rebuffed. The fixity is also explainable in reference to the formal constitutional structure. The maintenance of Pakistan's provincial boundaries as they are from the making of the 1973 Constitution onwards presents a distinct contrast to the manner in which provincial units were consolidated as well as divided in India post-Independence. There, the imperative was to enable linguistic groups to be agglomerated within provincial boundaries. The constitutional formula for the recognition of new provincial units is also notably more relaxed there than in Pakistan. In India, a bare majority in the federal parliament plus the consent of the provinces concerned is sufficient to establish a new territorial and administrative entity. In contrast, the Constitution by way of Article 239(3) prescribes that a two-thirds majority plus a resolution of the affected provincial Assembly also passed by a two-thirds majority there must authorise such an innovation in political structure.

One final development to be noted in reference to the *Muhajir* and Baloch conflicts is that the Supreme Court in recent years has taken *suo moto* notice of the spiraling violence in Sindh and Balochistan and directed the federation to combat this violence in both cases. In the *Karachi Law and Order* case of 2011, the court paid special attention to the workings of the police. Citing a high officer from within the police forces, they quoted a figure of 30–40 per cent of police personnel being 'non-cooperative either for the reasons that they have secured their appointments on political considerations or they have associated themselves with different groups including political parties, having vested interests in the affairs of Karachi'.[67] The nature of such vested interests was described as including the promotion of ethnic or sectarian group interests or involvement and or abetment of extra-legal activities such as extortion, land grabbing, kidnapping for ransom, etc.

In the *Balochistan Law and Order* case, it is the federal government that is called upon to ensure immediate action under the Constitution to provide the security to the people of Balochistan.' The discovery

[67] *Watan Party v The Federation of Pakistan* PLD [2011] SC 997.

of 'mutilated dead bodies' as well as the need to investigate 'missing persons, target killings, abduction for ransom and sectarian killings' are tied to the fulfilment of constitutional obligations owed by both tiers of government to the people of Balochistan.[68] The provincial government is directed to pay compensation to those affected by such violence. However, what is missing is a direct indictment or criminalisation of the acts of military and intelligence agencies in the perpetuation of such violence.

VI. LOCAL GOVERNMENT

Whereas the original 1973 Constitution had included the promise of local government amongst the principles of state policy, the introduction of Article 140A under the chapter titled 'provincial powers' provided a guarantee for its realisation. Previously, this third tier of government had been most ardently invigorated during periods of military rule. As with Ayub and Zia, Musharraf had also installed an apparatus for local government under the Local Government Ordinances of 2001. Replicating the form of previous systems, elections were held on a non-party basis under the devolution plan. Because these military leaders intended this level of government to provide a vent for local grievances and to legitimate central governance, the system was in all cases created by the federal and not the provincial government. Musharraf's plan went further than previous efforts in terms of devolving effective powers over service provisioning, including in the area of education. Greater fiscal control was also accorded in this structure of local governments. With Musharraf's ouster from power and in the return to democratic rule, local government structures were also widely dismantled. Along with other reforms for devolution, the Eighteenth Amendment Act also provided a constitutional guarantee of local government in Article 140A: 'Each Province shall, by law, establish a local government system and devolve political, administrative and financial responsibility and authority to the elected representatives of the local governments'.

While in other cases the contest over demarcating constituencies for these elections led to delays, a public interest case pertaining to a

[68] *President, Balochistan High Court Bar Association v Federation of Pakistan* SCMR [2012] SC 1958.

disputed road-widening scheme in Lahore was amongst the catalysts in Punjab for the delivery of the promise of Article 140A. The *Imrana Tiwana* petition[69] alleged that the authorisation for the project, given by an unelected local development agency, was contrary to what the Constitution had provided. Issues such as land use, water and sewage management have long been governed in Lahore, along with other large metropolitan areas, by such executive bodies that have delegated powers by their respective provincial governments. They have come to be seen as official channels for unjust land appropriation, key players in the fuelling of speculative land markets[70] and generally, administrators of a brand of corruption that forestalls rather than facilitates people's access to basic governmental services.[71]

The bench at the Lahore High Court accepted the argument that the new constitutional structure implied by Article 140A established a fence around the effective powers that local governments now possessed. Further, that the development agencies, as delegates of provincial powers, had necessarily to cede certain aspects of control to the elected local government. A strong case for an alternate model of local government was culled both from the reformed constitutional guarantees as well as by invoking international examples. Specifically, it was noted that the guarantee of local self-government provided in the Indian and South African constitutions invested local governments with core responsibilities. In total, this specific reform of the Eighteenth Amendment was seen as a way for reimaging federalism not simply as one of horizontal power-sharing, but one of integrative and vertical power-sharing between these tiers of government.

On appeal at the Supreme Court,[72] the interlocutory order granted against further construction of the project in dispute was vacated and a far more sparse definition of local government re-inscribed. Acting

[69] *Ms Imrana Tiwana v Province of Punjab* PLD [2015] Lahore 522.

[70] See HB Rashid 'The Tall Building Complex' *Pakistan Today* (13 May 2013) <www.pakistantoday.com.pk/2013/05/13/comment/columns/the-tall-building-complex/>.

[71] See Suo Motu Case no 10 of 2009 SCMR [2010] SC 885 and Human Rights Cases no. 4668 of 2006, 1111 of 2007 and 15283-G of 2010 PLD [2010] SC 799 for instances of how such development agencies are implicated in such practice.

[72] *Lahore Development Authority v Ms Imrana Tiwana* SCMR [2015] SC 1739.

on the principle of minimalist intervention, the Supreme Court overturned the High Court's nullifications; the Supreme Court did not see it necessary to vest this tier of government with inalienable powers into the future.

Across the country, the laws enacted to mandate local body elections have suggested an abidance of previous forms of paternalistic management and a deep distrust of grass-roots democracy and the associated notions of subsidiarity for law-making. For instance, in all of the provincial Acts, there is authorisation for the provincial government to remove the heads of local governments. However, while the Supreme Court has shown an unwillingness to safeguard any specific form or powers for local governments, it has been adamant about ensuring that the one Article 140A guarantee results in the establishment of a local tier of government, including for Islamabad, the federal capital.[73]

FURTHER READING

I Ali, *The Punjab Under Imperialism, 1885–1947* (Princeton, Princeton University Press, 2014).

M Axmann, *Back to the Future: The Khanate of Kalat and the Genesis of Baluch Nationalism, 1915–1955* (Karachi, Oxford University Press, 2012).

SM Khan, 'Ethnic Federalism in Pakistan: Federal Design, Construction of Ethno-Linguistic Identity and Group Conflict' (2014) 30 *Harvard Journal on Racial and Ethnic Justice* 77.

FH Siddiqi, *The Politics of Ethnicity in Pakistan: The Baloch, Sindhi and Mohajir Ethnic Movements* (New York, Routledge, 2012).

O Verkaaik, *A People of Migrants: Ethnicity, State and Religion in Karachi* (Amsterdam, VU University Press, 1994).

[73] *Raja Rab Nawaz v Federation of Pakistan* SCMR [2014] SC 101.

7

Rights: Equality and Liberty

Fundamental Rights – Limitation Clauses – Preamble – Anti-Discrimination – Gender-based Discrimination – Political Dissent – Preventive Detention – Missing Persons/Enforced Disappearances

THE CHALLENGE IN writing about rights in the Pakistani context is to describe the specificity of their articulation without making exaggerated claims about their distribution. Such caution should not be confused for rights pessimism; it would be difficult to insist that rights on the books are equivalent to rights in practice anywhere. In Pakistan, though, there are reasons for additional caution—the nature of legal hybridity is such that significant legal domains are insulated from fundamental rights protection. Additionally, the law and order state forged in the years after Partition has steadily protected its prerogative to curtail liberty and other rights both through express limitations on constitutional protection as well as by regular recourse to extra-legal measures through both civilian and military governmental regimes.

A major and important feature of the rights guaranteed in the 1973 Constitution is that each right is matched with an expanse of fairly wide limitations. This chapter describes the common law principles forged for interpreting these limitations clauses. Following that, are a brief overview the rights accorded in the 1973 Constitution along with a description of some of the fractures of the political terrain that influenced an ambivalence into the expression of these rights.

Detailed study of the right against gender discrimination and the right to be detained under law illustrate this inheritance as do the multiple metamorphoses enacted by constitutional suspension as well as other milestones of political development in Pakistan. In reference to gender discrimination the domains of education and employment evidence a slow building response of redress and protection from the higher judiciary. Although limited in impact to women in relatively privileged positions, this regime of law presents a stark contrast to the operations of personal law and Islamic criminal law, which continue to yield discriminatory effects for women, as discussed extensively in Chapter 8.

The regime of preventive detention and its constitutional safeguards have been described here as it is amongst the sites where state power to curtail the personal liberty of citizens is least fettered. The allowance for preventive detention is a carry-over from colonial rule incorporated into every constitutional document framed in the post-colonial period; used initially to suppress regional grievances and broadly constrain opposition during both civilian and military rule, its more recent uses are mostly in aid of controlling terrorism. Inspired by the trans-national reframing of preventive detention regimes during the waging of the seemingly-interminable war on terror post-9/11, the outright effacement of rights to be detained in accordance with constitutional safeguards is reflected in the plight of missing persons in Pakistan.

I. RIGHTS AND REVIEW UNTIL 1973

Building upon a colonial history in which the judiciary had in some ways exercised its review capacities aggressively, the 1956 Constitution extended the powers of judicial review by formalising rights guarantees and allowing for the invalidation of governmental actions where these rights were contravened.[1] The structure of rights could readily be mapped onto those acquiring the status of universal human rights. However, these rights were also saddled with limitations clauses. A contrast here might be drawn between those jurisdictions where limitations

[1] Constitution of Pakistan 1956, Art 4. For the colonial history see Rohit De, 'Emasculating the Executive: The Federal Court and Civil Liberties in Late Colonial India: 1942–4' in T Halliday, L Karpik and MM Freeley, *Fates of Political Liberalism in the British Post-colony: The Politics of the Legal Complex* (Cambridge, Cambridge University Press, 2012).

have been imposed by courts when they reason consequentially about specific facts that are presented to them, thereby defining exemptions, and those where the right is limited from the outset.[2] Pakistan, as with India and a number of other jurisdictions, is amongst the latter.

In a context of continuing political tumult in which judges saw themselves as co-managers rather than watchdogs of the budding state, the courts exercised extreme caution in the brief period of this Constitution's existence, preferring to read rights-offending statutes so as to harmonise their provisions with the constitutional right at stake. They also chose the course of determining that not every listed right was universal or absolute.[3] Even laws of the colonial era, in which an unequal justice was doled out to those once classified as criminal, tribes were upheld in such a climate.[4] While steering clear of finding repugnancy and exercising invalidation, the courts nevertheless did start to elaborate principles by which the limitations clauses of rights statements could themselves be delimited.

Limitations are seemingly widest when not qualified by substantive criteria, and appear as 'subject to law' or 'in accordance with law'. They are narrowed when only 'reasonable restrictions' are allowed, and narrower still when the grounds for such restriction are expressly provided. The question of how to read these limitations clauses was dealt with quite early, while the 1956 Constitution was still operational.

In *Achharyya*[5] the court grappled specifically with the question of whether rights made 'subject to law' can be taken away by validly enacted law. Chief Justice Muhammad Munir declared unequivocally that they could not, and that to allow the same would be to perpetrate a 'fraud on the citizens'. Laws that imposed limitations upon the right would be subject to review. This case has also come to stand for the principle that rights can be unequally distributed amongst a diverse population but that the mode of classifying different classes and groups to mark this distribution itself has to meet a reasonability

[2] ME Adjami, 'African courts, international law, and comparative case law: Chimera or emerging human rights Jurisprudence?' (2002) 24 *Michigan Journal of International Law* 103.

[3] *Abdul Aziz v The Province of West Pakistan* PLD [1958] SC (Pak) 499.

[4] *Bazal Ahmad Ayyubi v The West Pakistan Province* PLD [1957] (WP) Lahore 388.

[5] *Jibendra Kishore Achharyya Chowdhury v The Province of East Pakistan* PLD [1957] SC 9.

standard. While specifying that classifications on irrelevant criteria, those that are capricious and arbitrary, will be disallowed,[6] the court accepts however that certain classifications are warranted.

In the year 1958, both the declaration of martial law as well as the Supreme Court's judgment in *Dosso*[7] resulted in the 1956 Constitution being abrogated. As a consequence, no fundamental right 'nor any provision of the abrogated constitution could now be a source or basis for any legal right'.[8] This was a prelude to the subsequent experience in which the 1962 Constitution sought initially to confine judicial review to entertaining writs on governmental action outside any enforcement of fundamental rights. However, again, that would change with the First Amendment to the 1962 Constitution, and in subsequent years further principles for review on the basis of fundamental rights would be defined.

The 1964 case of *Abula'la Maudoodi*[9] discusses some of the parameters of review that were introduced to assess what might constitute 'reasonable restriction' on rights. The Ayub Khan government had enacted the Political Parties Act of 1962 in an attempt to augur a managed transition to a controlled democracy. Through its various provisions, certain political parties were completely banned from functioning. Among them was the Jamaat-e-Islami, which sought a declaration that this was an unreasonable restriction of its fundamental right of association.

The Supreme Court in this case responded by specifying that a 'reasonable restriction cannot amount to a complete denial or total prohibition of the right for all times to come or for an indefinite period'. Use of the word 'restriction' makes the extent of the encroachment a relevant factor in determining the reasonableness thereof. However, the court was deferential to executive powers broadly and was thereby unwilling to accept that the vesting of unfettered discretion in a single administrator would matter for purposes of reasonability or

[6] Repeating the dictum of *Achharyya*, Chief Justice SA Rehman held that only irrational or arbitrary discrimination, such as would amount to 'legislative despotism', would offend the need for rational classification.

[7] *The State v Dosso* PLD [1958] SC 533.

[8] ABM Patwari, *Fundamental Rights and Personal Liberty in India, Pakistan and Bangladesh* (New Delhi, Deep and Deep, 1988) 9.

[9] *Saiyyid Abula'la Maudoodi v The Government of West Pakistan* PLD [1964] SC 673.

compromise the law-like quality of the restriction, where a right was made 'subject to law'. Instead, Justice Cornelius states:

> It is not difficult to conceive of situations where power must be vested in some authority to take immediate action to prevent acts fraught with imminent danger, even though such prevention encroaches upon the fundamental rights guaranteed to citizens by the Constitution of the country.

A case that has less universal approval within the Pakistani courts is *Shorish Kashmiri*.[10] In a line of important detention cases that include both *Dosso* and *Achharyya*, the bench defined the protection of law as broad and incorporative, not only of statuary law but also judicial principles. Law is 'comprehensive' and 'postulates a strict performance of all the functions and duties laid down by the law'. This was an early statement approving a due process standard for judicial review. However, altogether far more narrow views of what constitute law were already in the field as per *Maudoodi*, as noted above, and there would be an equal push in both directions within jurisprudence for some time.[11]

II. THE STRUCTURE OF FUNDAMENTAL RIGHTS IN THE 1973 CONSTITUTION

Ambivalence towards the enshrinement of fundamental rights affected the draft of the 1973 Constitution and this is apparent both in the limitations defined for these rights as well the structure and content of the Preamble. While much of the language of the Preamble carried over the content of the Objectives Resolution, a three-way ideological battle with unlikely alliances drawn across seemingly incommensurate positions also influenced drafting. As described elsewhere, the National Awami Party (NAP) situated itself further to the left of the ideological spectrum from where Bhutto drew his populist support. The NAP, in its alliance with the *Jamat-e-Ulema-e-Islam* (JUI) repeatedly toned down its demands, most remarkably so by ceding that secularism need not be amongst the guiding principles stated in the Preamble. Bhutto,

[10] *Government of West Pakistan v Begum Agha: Abdulkarim Shorish Kashmiri* PLD [1969] SC 14.

[11] *FB Ali v The State* PLD [1975] SC 506.

in the midst of his heightened rift with the NAP/JUI, and having marginalised much of his own left party cadre, was also thus willing to trade in specific mention of the programme of Islamic socialism and placate the centrist non-ideological base of his main allies in this parliament.[12]

Shortly after East Pakistan was lost and the project of Muslim nationalism seemingly damaged, the notion of secular power being in sovereign trust for Allah, reflecting thereby a unitariness of state power over society, was the overwhelming sentiment of the Preamble. In it, the first mention of rights is halfway down in an unnumbered clause. The specific clause provides a guarantee of fundamental rights inclusive of 'equality of status, of opportunity and before law, social, economic and political justice, and freedom of thought, expression, belief, faith, worship and association'. The statement also provides that they will be 'subject to law and morality'. Significantly, the enumerations of these rights, which are included in the Second Chapter of the Constitution, are even in the Preamble qualified by limitations and their possible circumscription.

Part II of the Constitution, following the Preamble and Introductory clauses, is entitled Fundamental Rights and Principles of Policy. Chapter I of Part II comprises Articles 8–28, and each of these Articles recognises a liberty, immunity or capacity as fundamental and protected for either all persons or for citizens of Pakistan. Chapter II, Articles 29–40, provides the Principles of Policy, the aspirational goals meant to guide legislators in the act of creating law and policy, considered non-justiciable in the strict sense.

Analogous to a provision of the 1956 Constitution, Article 8(1) reads 'Any law, or any custom or usage having the force of law, in so far as it is inconsistent with the rights conferred by this Chapter, shall, to the extent of such inconsistency, be void.' Article 8(2) further provides that the 'State shall not make any law which takes away or abridges the rights so conferred and any law made in contravention of this clause shall, to the extent of such contravention, be void.' It also defines wholesale exemptions where a law governs 'members of the Armed

[12] 'Bhutto's rule a bundle of contradictions' *The Times of India* (24 December 1972) <www.search.proquest.com.ezp.lib.unimelb.edu.au/docview/739882995?accountid=12372>; SR Ghauri, 'Dismay over Bhutto draft Constitution' *The Guardian* (London, 13 April 1972).

Forces, or of the police or of such other forces as are charged with the maintenance of public order, for the purpose of ensuring the proper discharge of their duties or the maintenance of discipline among them.' Additionally, laws contained within Schedule I to the Constitution are immunised against being held to the standard of rights abidance.[13]

Article 8 of the 1973 Constitution heralded at least the possibility of refounding a thorough review of laws to accord with fundamental rights when they were enacted. Furthermore, the prospect of such a review was bolstered by way of Articles 184 and 199, which provide the High and Supreme Courts with extensive powers to try cases related to fundamental rights. Under Article 199, the High Courts could offer traditional remedies associated with the prerogative writs and also the power to give an(y) order to any person for the enforcement of any of the fundamental rights upon the petition of an 'aggrieved person'. The Supreme Court was conferred an additional jurisdiction under Article 184(3) to take up any matter of 'public importance' pertaining to the enforcement of fundamental rights and grant a suitably-fashioned remedy. These are quite expansive powers but remained mostly unpracticed until an Indian-inspired programme of fostering public interest litigation started to impact superior courts' judges in Pakistan in the 1990s.[14] It was in this context that Article 9, which reads 'No person shall be deprived of life or liberty *save in accordance with law*' (emphasis added), has become a vehicle for the judicial conferral of specific entitlements, such as to a safe environment, education, access to utilities, all as subsidiary features of this right.

To accord with the rights of liberty are a set of rights and safeguards for fair arrest and trial, which are often read in conjunction with Article 9. Article 10 'Safeguards as to arrest and detention', is discussed in the greatest detail below in a case study of preventive detention practices from Partition onwards. Article 10A, introduced in 2010, the 'Right to fair trial' provides for due process guarantees in criminal trials; Article 12 provides protection against retrospective punishment; Article 13 provides protection against double punishment and self-incrimination. Finally, Article 14, which safeguards the 'Dignity of man' and 'subject to law, privacy of home' also provides in

[13] First Schedule: Laws exempted from the operation of Article 8(1) and (2).

[14] See text in Chapter 5, section III.

Article 14(2) a prohibition against torture 'for the purposes of extracting evidence'. This body of rights is protected against suspension during emergencies.[15]

A further array of traditional civil and political rights appear together in Articles 15–19 as freedom of movement, assembly, association, speech and the right to information. Each of these is conditioned by an enumeration of conditions for the imposition of reasonable restrictions. For instance, freedom of movement is subject to 'any reasonable restriction imposed by law and in the public interest'. For the right of association such reasonable restrictions may be 'in the interest of sovereignty or integrity of Pakistan, public order or morality'. The list of restrictive conditions applicable to the exercise of speech has grown to include, in addition to those listed above, 'the glory of Islam, friendly relations with foreign states, decency, contempt of court',[16] commission or incitement to an offence.

The hard distinction between civil and political on the one hand, and on the other, economic and social, is effaced somewhat by the inclusion of Articles 22 and 27, which bar discrimination in state or state-funded education and employment. The material redistributive aspect of this can be located in the possibilities opened up for quotas and other preferential treatment on the grounds of regional origin, sex etc. The complementary Principles of Policy address matters such as increasing the participation of women in national life (Article 34); protection of minorities (Article 36); the promotion of social justice, the eradication of social evils (Article 37) and the furtherance of the economic well-being of the people (Article 38). These principles have often been read in conjunction with Articles 22 and 27 and in public interest cases to introduce conditions for the realisation of rights.

Provisions within the fundamental rights chapter which bespeak the rejection of official secularism include the circumspect Article 20, 'Freedom to profess religion and manage religious institutions,' which provides every citizen the right to 'profess, practice and propagate

[15] See text in Chapter 4, section IB.

[16] Glory of Islam and contempt of court were added in the 1973 Constitution. Defamatory speech had been included in the list of such 'restrictive conditions' in both Constitution of Pakistan 1956 and Constitution of Pakistan 1962.

his religion'[17] and for religious communities to establish, maintain and manage their institutions. The right is not a broad 'freedom of religious conscience' provision. In line with the prevailing view amongst Islamic states in which a bar on apostasy was enforced, the international instrument's insistence that people be able to freely convert out of their religions was not considered appropriate for incorporation and thus this right is a lesser one than is advocated for in such instruments.[18] Additionally, and perhaps only of historical interest, is how far Article 11 bears the imprint of the interventions of the *Ulema* in the constituent Assembly debates from 1973. After much debate, the prohibition on slavery and forced labour was written into the Constitution in the declaratory language of 'slavery is non-existent and forbidden' so as not to attract the cover of Islamic legal precepts that regulate slave holding and manumission where it does exist.[19]

Property protections as per Articles 23 and 24 include both the private right to hold and acquire property as well as the right to be compensated in cases of state acquisition of private property. This latter provision was resisted by the NAP in particular, which would have preferred that property be capable of expropriation without guarantees of compensation.[20] Its own marginal position without the support of the JUI led to the toning down of this initial stance and thus a justiciable property right has existed alongside the now more expansive reading of a fundamental Islamic right to property as per a Federal Shariat Court reading of 1993.[21]

Altogether then, while the ambit of rights and perhaps the conceptual lineaments of their form were in many ways the bequest of more globalised movements, the manner of their elaboration within local environment has been a markedly local and political affair.

[17] 'His' appears in place of 'any' as it was stated in an otherwise identical Article 18 in the 1956 Constitution.

[18] Aaron Tyler, 'Administering a Sacred Trust: The Place of Religious Tolerance in the State of Pakistan' (2005–2006) 5 *UCLA Journal of Islamic and Near Eastern Law* 131.

[19] Pakistan National Assembly Debates, 1st Parliamentary Year, Second Session, 13 March 1973, vol II, No 19, 1176–94.

[20] 'Pakistan Constitution Drafting 1973' *The Times of India* (30 March 1973).

[21] *Qazalbash Waqf v Chief Land Commissioner* PLD [1990] SC 99.

III. GENDER EQUALITY AND EQUALITY LAW

In common parlance, Article 25 is often referred to as the 'non-discrimination' clause of the 1973 Constitution. The 1973 Constitution was the first to add a guarantee against discrimination on the basis of 'sex alone' to a right that had previously been a broad guarantee of legal equality for all citizens. Article 5 of the 1956 Constitution had guaranteed equality and equal protection of the law to all citizens and the 1962 Constitution had spread these protections over two articles.[22]

Prior to the proclamation of martial law in 1958, the Supreme Court received a petition under Article 5(1) challenging the separation of electorates and representatives on the basis of sex, innovated by the Punjab Government for district body elections. As a result, the number of representatives for women was sparse in relation to their overall electoral strength. The Supreme Court relied upon an incontrovertible history of denying suffrage on the basis of gender to suggest that this form of 'special treatment' for women was in fact reasonable. Because there was no 'fundamental right' of suffrage within the constitutional structure, the court held that the provinces were accorded a full range of manoeuvres for tinkering with different models of suffrage.[23]

Such a judgment was not unanticipated and for this reason women's groups had organised dissent when the 1956 Constitution was announced. In addition to the absence of specific sex equality protections, they were concerned about the absence of guarantees of 'equal pay for equal work' and somewhat ambivalent about the 'preferential' treatment accorded through the establishment of women's reserved seats for parliament.[24] The prior dissolution of the first Constituent Assembly meant that two proactive female voices that could have influenced constitutional drafting were gone and the second Assembly had no female representation. The very fact of this protest being waged was telling, nonetheless, of the broader forms of social ferment and reorganisation that had preceded it. Although far too complicated and multidirectional than can be charted here, the visible entry of women

[22] Constitution of Pakistan 1962, Art 2 and Art 6.

[23] *Chaudhry Ata Elahi v Mst Parveen Zohra* PLD [1958] SC 298.

[24] Sara Ansari, 'Winds of Change? The Role of Women Activists in Lahore Before and After Partition' in M Abid and Qalb-i-Abid (eds), *History, Politics and Society: The Punjab* (Lahore, Pakistan Study Centre, 2009) 93–106.

into the public political sphere had been aided by their active incorporation into nationalist movements in the lead up to independence.[25] However, the post-Partition period had also been one of reversal insofar as women's visibility, mobility and opportunity were concerned. The anxieties of masculinity that had been awakened in the heightened violence at the time of Partition were sought to be closed off by the state, including by way of the workings of the Recovery and Return Laws on both sides of the border.[26]

When the 1962 Constitution was announced, a specific sex equality right was again absent. There was no easily available mechanism for moving the law towards greater formal equality and even a 'progressive court' upheld the differential treatment of women and men in reference to provisions of the Muslim Family Law Ordinance (MFLO), itself a law passed through the lobbying of women's organisations for a more equitable interpretation of Shariat principles.[27] Additionally, in a case that was prelude to a great many others fought on this issue in the following decades, separate seats and quotas for male and female applicants to medical colleges were settled in favour of retaining these quotas. In this, the *Humera Satwat* case, even as women's 'righteous indignation' was acknowledged at policies that dictated that they could only compete for a small number of seats in medical colleges, the court deferred the matter to executive actors for consideration.[28]

The 1973 Constitution would supplement the non-discrimination right with Article 25(2), 'There shall be no discrimination on the basis of sex alone'. Additionally Article 25(3), 'Nothing in this Article shall prevent the State from enacting any special provision for the protection of women' seemed to herald the determination to bolster women's access to economic and political opportunity. In reality though, the sheer formalism of legal doctrine—one which had long accepted reasonable classifications with regard to the broader and less specific 'equal protection' right—provided slow and uneven redress for existing inequality.

[25] D Willmer, 'Women as Participants in the Pakistan Movement: Modernization and the Promise of a Moral State' (1996) 30 *Modern Asian Studies* 573.

[26] R Menon and K Bhasin, *Borders & Boundaries: Women in India's Partition* (New Brunswick, Rutgers University Press, 1998).

[27] *Syed Ali Nawaz Gardezi v Lt Col Muhammad Yusuf* PLD [1963] SC 51.

[28] *Humera Satwat Yusuf v The Government of the Punjab* PLD [1971] Lahore 641.

A slow evolution towards forging non-discrimination standards is apparent in the line of cases stemming from challenges to medical college admissions quotas and even more haphazardly in reference to a group of employment discrimination cases. These are described below.

A. Medical Colleges Cases

It would take almost an additional two decades before a situation analogous to the one in the 'righteous indignation' case was held to be discriminatory on the grounds of sex alone. Some of the delay in the realisation of the promise of this more concise protection was consequent upon the many suspensions of rights that occurred over this time, most extensively under Zia in the years 1977–1985.

An early case to arise upon the restoration of rights tested the legality of reservations specifically for women and asked the question of whether such reservations discriminate against men?[29] The court made light of the concern that such reservations for women deny men their right to be considered solely on merit and allowed these reservations on the ground that Article 25(3) affords policy makers the leeway to enact preferential rules for women. In fact, the court offered a list of areas in which they could foresee the possibility of such protective or preferential policies being adopted. Maternity policy, free education and provision for separate accommodation and entrances for women in public facilities were amongst the areas listed where such policy could be innovated. In language that is highly paternalistic and patronising, the court essentially provided that women as a class need protection until such a time that the habits of life that have thus far inculcated dependence can be changed.

It was only in 1987 that cases testing the validity of limits placed on women's access to open merit seats came up again to be adjudicated. One case[30] initiated at the Lahore High Court (LHC) was then reopened as an intra-court appeal and then for a further appeal at the Supreme Court. The specific questions posed were whether there could be gender-based quotas for open merit seats and whether or not the

[29] *Ehsanul Haque v Federation of Pakistan* PLD [1976] Lahore 501.
[30] *Mussarat Uzma Usmani v Government of Punjab* PLD [1987] Lahore 178.

general protection against discrimination contained in Article 25(2) was liable to be narrowed where more specific protections by way of the fundamental right of Article 22 are read alongside it. Article 22 establishes 'safeguards as to educational institutions in respect of religion, etc' and expounds that 'no citizen shall be denied admission to any educational institution receiving aid from public revenues on the grounds only of race, religion, caste or place of birth.'

In the initial judgment, the reservation of a majority of the supposedly open merits seats for men was held to be prima facie violative of Article 25. The court reflected that in a period of rights suspension that had preceded, a general reasonable classification test was used and such an assignment of seats could possibly have been validated with the use of other justificatory criteria, such as the greater need for male doctors. However, where the Article 25 right had been restored, they were unwilling to allow the import of other criteria to protect discriminatory practice. In fact, the court rejected the employment of a reasonable classification test where Article 25 could be invoked, other than in cases where such a classification would work to ensure equality for women or confer upon them some additional benefit. It also narrowed the application of Article 22 to very specific cases involving institutions that are neither wholly governmental nor wholly private but are funded partly by the government. More importantly, it did not see this as a special provision that can be used to read down or limit another constitutional guarantee.[31]

It was primarily on this basis that the second bench at the LHC differs, seeing the application of Article 22 as limiting the general protections of Article 25. Comparing across to India, where an analogous protection for admissions at educational institutions expressly includes gender as a prohibited ground for discrimination, the bench read the absence of such enumeration in Pakistan as signifying an absence of protection.[32]

In the Supreme Court appeal,[33] reported as *Shirin Munir*, Justice Shafiur Rahman et al declared that they must provide an 'authoritative pronouncement' in the circumstances. For equality advocates the result

[31] ibid.

[32] *Government of Punjab v Naila Begum* PLD [1987] Lahore 336.

[33] *Shirin Munir v Government of Punjab* PLD [1990] SC 295.

is a favourable precedent. Broadly, by suggesting the need for harmonious interpretation of varied constitutional provisions and rights guarantees, it suggests that even in the specific conditions to which Article 22 safeguards are directed, the absence of a clear specific sex protection cannot take away from, or limit the application of the general protections accorded by Article 25(2). Therefore, there are no immunisations, even by way of the express language and 'ring-fencing' of certain domains as per Article 22, against the broader equal protection, equal treatment and non-discrimination rights of Article 25. Rather, the two provisions read together imply that a 'reasonable classification' test needs to be employed in all circumstances. It further holds that there is no basis for the sex of applicants to be a reasonable classification to influence admission.

The impact of *Shirin Munir* continues and in the years 2014 and 2015, to a set of remarkably contrary circumstances, the dicta of that case has been applied. Two cases from the LHC[34] and the Balochistan High Court (BHC)[35] were fought against the application of a ceiling on the admissions of women to medical and dental colleges. In a much altered landscape of unprecedented women's educational achievement, the regulatory body of medical practioners in the country commissioned a study which revealed that, in an open merit system, women were securing up to 68% of all seats in the country's medical institutions. A variety of medical colleges reacted by imposing a 50% quota for men and women. In both High Courts, this system of parity was held to be contrary to the non-discrimination standard. The test advanced was that protection of Article 25 could only be denied where a clear public policy objective was at stake and the denial or restriction bore a rational nexus to such object.[36] The policy objective advanced by the practitioner board, that women's inability to continue in the profession for reasons of child birth and marriage, compromise the extent to which medical services can be made available across the country, was rejected. The contrary principle, that no limitation on women's educational opportunities can be brooked was clearly articulated by both benches. Limiting women's educational access or attainment was not to be made the means of ensuring other policy goals.

[34] *Syeda Sadia v Bahauddin Zakariya University* YLR [2011] Lahore 2867.

[35] *Talal Haleem v Principal Bolan Medical College, Quetta* PLD [2015] Quetta 97.

[36] ibid.

B. Employment

Judicial reasoning in employment inequality cases arising under Article 25 has been given added impetus for doing away with acts of overt discrimination by the existence of Article 27. Thus, where the absence of 'sex' as a barred ground for discrimination in the area of education as per Article 22 has had a somewhat confusing impact over the years, the presence of sex amongst the prohibited grounds of discrimination for 'service within the state' has lent itself to expanding protections.[37] In addition, the Principle of Policy providing that the state will endeavour to expand women's participation in all aspects of national life is also formally appended to the available mechanisms for correcting discrimination in the sphere of employment.[38]

Altogether, though, sex discrimination protections seem to extend only to situations of direct and systematic violation. There are very few employment equity cases that reach the higher courts at all. One should not assume, however, that such cases are being heard at a lower level of the court system in greater numbers. The reasons are many and implicate the lacunae in Pakistan's legal system as far-reaching and hugely detrimental, enabling discrimination on many registers to go unchecked. Pakistan lacks a statutory regime of human rights protection for the private sphere, so that the realms of private enterprise, private housing, are almost fully outside the purview of fundamental rights protection. An exception has sometimes been made of the private educational sphere for the reason that it is performing a 'governmental function' and therefore remedies will be sought when a petitioner alleges discrimination.[39] Additionally, there are no provisions within labour or industrial relations laws to safeguard against gender-based discriminatory practices by either employers or unions.

While it has increased somewhat, from around 10 per cent in 2000 to closer to 15 per cent to 2010, women are vastly under-represented in the country's formal labour markets. Additionally, even when performed in the formal sphere, women's labour is often treated as

[37] *Mst Sarwari Bibi v Arshad Ali Khan* YLR [2007] Lahore 702.

[38] *Mrs Naseem Firdous v Punjab Small Industries Corporation* PLD [1995] Lahore 584; *Nazar Elahi v Government of Punjab* CLC [2013] Lahore 1457.

[39] *University of Dacca v Zakir Hussain* PLD [1965] SC 90; *Aitchison College v Muhammad Zubair* PLD [2002] SC 326.

'informal', so that it is classed as temporary employment and does not enjoy any protections from within what are in any case piecemeal and patchy existing labour laws. These statistics also disguise women's labour that is performed within the household, not only towards the household but in small production processes and the crafts industry as well as reflecting the general under-reporting of employment statistics given the dimensions of the vast informal sector.[40] Protections against discrimination thereby are enjoyed in small pockets.

Cases that have arisen suggest that de facto violative practices such as advertising that 'males only' need apply will be subject to a thorough-going scrutiny.[41] In that regard, it is also noteworthy that Article 27(2) provides a possible exemption to the need to retain employment equity on the basis of what has been termed a 'bona fide occupational requirement' in other jurisdictions. It is yet untested as to what would form a bona fide exception on the basis of sex. The court has ruled that even traditionally male jobs such as *lumbradar*s (village headmen) cannot be denied to women.[42]

Another set of cases in which overt and explicit discrimination was challenged involved the practices of the national airline, Pakistan International Airlines (PIA). PIA had retained a long-standing policy that women members of the cabin crew needed to retire at the age of 35, even as male cabin stewards could continue in service until the age of 60. Early petitions were converted to out of court settlements and PIA[43] retained the policy for many years until a number of petitions were coupled and heard together at the Supreme Court.

Unsurprisingly, the court found PIA's practices to be discriminatory. Nonetheless, in this judgment the court managed to introduce some amount of ambiguity around the edges of its reasoning. For instance, Justice Sardar Muhammad Raza Khan reasoned, 'we are of the view that had the Air Hostesses been singularly placed altogether in a different group, the fixation of their retirement age at a different level from other groups of employees of PIA would not have been a discrimination, being intra sex and not inter sex'.[44] Such a statement

[40] C Candland, *Labor, Democratization, and Development in India and Pakistan* (Abingdon, Routledge, 2007).

[41] *Mrs Naseem Firdous v Punjab Small Industries Corporation* PLD [1995] Lahore 584.

[42] *Mst Sarwari Bibi v Arshad Ali Khan* YLR [2007] Lahore 702.

[43] *Chairman PIA Corporation v Sherin Dokhth* SCMR [1996] SC 1520.

[44] *Pakistan International Airlines Corporation v Samina Masood* PLD [2005] SC 831.

could suggest that a reassignment of nomenclature alone could have redressed the perceived discrimination. Further along, however, they also reiterate that the nature of the duties performed between female and male members was similar in all cases, and that this 'is not a distinction based on intelligible differentia but clearly is a distinction based on sex'.

A range of women's groups petitioned over many years to have the language of Article 25 changed to read 'sex' in place of sex alone so as to at least make space to try cases involving indirect and systemic discrimination. This was a significant change within the package of 18th Amendment reform and was passed without any dissent. However, to date no major reported case has been fought on the altered provision. Additionally also, a coalition of six women's groups and NGOs successfully fought to have a national law enacted in 2010 providing some redress against sexual harassment at the workplace. This law applies to private and public employers, provides a far-reaching definition of harassment, and establishes a national ombudsman entrusted with ensuring that the whole machinery is operating, as well as the power to enforce penalties upon accused parties.[45] An additional element of gender justice that has found recent expression within the Pakistani legal landscape is that of a mandated recognition of transsexuals. A number of judgments address the absence of recognition by the state faced by transsexuals, and the resulting denial of their access to state services.[46] These cases have proceeded under Article 9 and cite the pervasive social stigma and vulnerability that transsexuals face in Pakistan; no tests of discrimination are formally used.

IV. PREVENTIVE DETENTION

The need to pass specific laws mandating the practice of preventive detention by the colonial government occurred only after the writ of habeas corpus was made actionable for Indians in the subcontinent. An amendment to the Code of Criminal Procedure in 1898 expanded the

[45] The Protection against Harassment of Women at the Workplace Act, 2010.

[46] *Dr Mohammad Aslam Khaki v Senior Superintendent of Police (Operation) Rawalpindi* PLD [2013] SC 188.

use of this writ to all persons 'improperly or illegally detained in public or private detention'. It was in wilful derogation of speech, assembly and association that laws of preventative detention were fashioned, in many ways to stem the growth of nationalist politics. The Defence of India Act 1915 introduced preventive detention under conditions of emergency and then the infamous 1919 Anarchic and Revolutionary Crimes Act provided for their continued coverage beyond an emergency. After their repeal, the Defence of India Act 1939, once again in a period of emergency, reintroduced the legal authorisation for preventative detention.[47]

In a succession of cases that flowed from the exercise of such powers, the Privy Council in the UK upheld that the powers of detention by the executive authority were neither to be made subject to a test of reasonableness, nor were courts to intervene to check the discretionary authority of the executive where it was 'satisfied' that the person detained was a threat to the purposes being protected under the article. In recounting this colonial history, Imtiaz Omar notes that 'preventative detention had been a potent and effective mechanism to contain political dissent in the colonial state' and that, somewhat paradoxically, the 'constitutional systems of the post-colonial states have expressly legitimatized' and kept such powers.

The first law enacted to authorise preventive detention in independent Pakistan was the Public Safety Ordinance of 1949. The central government was authorised to act 'if satisfied' that the person detained was a threat in a manner prejudicial to public safety and public order. In 1952, after the lapse of the PSO, the Security of Pakistan Act was passed and although it was anticipated that it would be extinguished after three years, continues to operate. In addition, a number of provincial laws authorising preventative detention were passed. These laws, in their initial form, defined no method of seeking review. Nor did they prescribe any safeguards to ensure the communication of grounds to the detainee and, furthermore, specified no time limit for detention. The laws themselves were allegedly necessary to stem the grave disorder stemming from Partition and to facilitate the resettlement of migrants. Yet, the 1952 Act expanded the grounds under which people

[47] I Omer, *Emergency Powers and the Courts in India and Pakistan* (Netherlands, Brill, 2002).

could be detained to include any threat to 'defence, external affairs, the security of Pakistan, or in the maintenance of public order'.

Each of these statutes provided an administrative review board, but one comprised of executive actors. Altogether, there was a low threshold of protection for detainees, so that executive powers had been bolstered from what they were under colonial statutes.[48]

The 1956 Constitution altered the landscape by offering the right to be detained but subject to certain constitutional safeguards and in conformity with law. It introduced the right to be informed of the grounds of arrest, the right to counsel and to be produced 'before a magistrate within a period of twenty-four hours'. There was also a rather capacious exception to the foregoing in cases of persons 'arrested or detained under any law providing for preventive detention'. Simultaneously, the avenue of filing a habeas corpus petition even where the detention had been made by way of a law, was allowed. For reasons of haste and even of impartiality, this was a much preferred route for detainees, although not always unproblematic.[49] As noted earlier, the *Dosso* judgment rendered these avenues unavailable and review only picked up pace well after Ayub and the 1962 Constitution were in place.

In light of the *Maudoodi* case discussed earlier, the conditions of preventive detention were also subject to a more stringent review, one that did not concede the powers of decision-making altogether to detaining authorities. In the 1967 *Ghulam Jilani*[50] case the Supreme Court utilised an objective test for the reasonableness of the grounds offered by the detaining authority to justify detention. In upholding the decision that forms of direct action initiated by opposition parties and politicians provided sufficient grounds for detention, the Court specified that the detaining authority was burdened with showing that there had been an 'application of mind as to the necessity of such a person's detention' and that a similar conclusion would be drawn by a 'reasonable person'.[51]

[48] *Rafique Ahmad Sheikh v Crown* PLD [1951] Lahore 17.

[49] Earlier, s 491 of Criminal Procedure Code, 1898 had been the means by which a Habeas Corpus petition could be filed.

[50] *Malik Ghulam Jilani, Inayatullah and Nazir Ahmad Chaudhari v The Government of West Pakistan* PLD [1967] SC 373.

[51] See F Hussain, *Personal Liberty and Preventive Detention* (Peshawar, University Foundation Press, 1989).

The detention in *Jilani*, authorised by the Defence of Pakistan Ordinance 1965, was accepted as lawful. The court was unwilling to look at the indefinite nature of detention as in any way violative of broader liberty concerns. In regard to the contention that the actions that had attracted the detention orders were 'within the legitimate political sphere' in a context where assemblies were functioning and newspapers being published, the court suggested that taking out processions and fomenting discontent against the government immediately at the conclusion of a war was in fact to be 'playing with fire'. Where the government makes allusion to concerns of heightened and national 'importance', there seems to be a meeting of minds between the judiciary and the executive in this period.

This period was one in which various sites of political action were being heavily policed. The nature of state action particularly reflected the concern to quell regional unrest. The courts were willing to accept that persons proclaiming that any part of the population had a nationality 'besides that of Pakistan' were to be thus detained. Through the early 1960s, Abdul Ghaffar Khan was repeatedly taken into custody and 'every six months his detention was extended. At the end of 1962, Amnesty International named Ghaffar Khan 'Prisoner of the Year' and demanded his release.[52] It is said of Sindhi nationalist, GM Syed that he spent approximately 30 years of his life in jail, dying in custody in 1995. Amongst other notable leaders thus lawfully interned was Sheikh Mujibur Rehman from East Pakistan who, after first propounding the Six Point agenda for greater regional autonomy, was interned for more than 21 months, mostly within the territorial expanse of West Pakistan. However, perhaps more in that case than in the many others where the political ramifications of such detention were subdued, this act of detention led to a general strike in support of Mujib and the executive and his political opposition were unable to break the political support for his agenda even as they kept him out of the political ring at such a pivotal time.[53]

[52] *The State v Abdul Ghaffar Khan* PLD [1957] (WP) Lahore 142 (called Bacha Khan).

[53] See DP Singhal, *Pakistan* (Prentice Hall, 1972) 107. Late in Ayub's reign, the 'Jurisdiction of Courts (Removal of Doubts) Order of 1969' barred the courts from entertaining petitions against any martial law order or any act undertaken under such an order, even if by a junior functionary if he/she was delegated authority under any martial law or order.

Prior to the passage of the 1973 Constitution the detention regime was mostly at the service of the central government's 'search for national unity'. Such integration prioritised controlling or repressing dissent both at the centre and within the provinces. These goals 'were perceived primarily in bureaucratic rather than in political terms'.[54] The detention of leaders was invariably accompanied by mass detentions of people who were their affiliates and supporters. Very little of that has made its way into the official or even judicial record although police and military brutality in the course of such detention is well documented.

A. Preventive Detention under the 1973 Constitution

During debates for the passage of the 1973 Constitution, the possibility of removing constitutional protection for preventative detention under any circumstances was tabled. Bhutto's law minister and chief defender of the draft Constitution championed the clauses nonetheless. He offered the assurance that the review board, to be constituted now only of senior members of the judiciary, would act as adequate protection against arbitrariness.[55] The conditions for detention were made more restrictive, insofar as the detaining authority was required to communicate grounds 'as soon as possible and at the latest within one week' and that the length of initial detention could be no more than one month before review board authorisation would be necessitated. Furthermore, the total length of detention could not exceed eight out of 24 months from the moment of apprehension other than for those working for the 'enemy'. As with the 1956 Constitution, this latter category of persons were not provided with any of the constitutional safeguards as to notice of grounds, length of detention, and so forth.

Hours after the passage of the 1973 Constitution, fundamental rights were suspended in the country. The popularly elected government of Bhutto availed itself of the opportunity to engage in levels of political victimisation and suppression of dissent, aided now by the

[54] S Ansari, *From Subjects to Citizens* (Cambridge, Cambridge University Press, 2014) 214.

[55] Pakistan National Assembly Debates, 1st Parliamentary Year, Second Session, 13 March 1973, vol II, No 19, 1131–76.

heightened ideological search for unity that Bangladesh's breakaway had enabled. However, citing that a democratic transition had already occurred, many judges held detaining authorities responsible for maintaining fidelity in their orders to the full panoply of safeguards that had been constitutionally mandated.[56] In addition they cited the fact that Article 233 gave emergency authorisation for suspension of fundamental rights but did not authorise derogation from Article 10 protections.

The governmental response was to engineer a set of constitutional amendments aimed at broadening the powers of detention and then immunising the same against judicial oversight: the Third, Fourth and Fifth Amendments were fashioned, at least in part, to accomplish this goal. The Third Amendment reinstituted the three-month period of limitation for initial detention and expanded the time duration for the giving of grounds from 'as soon as may be or within one week' from the original text to 'within 15 days'. The upper limit of detention was also removed for additional classes of persons.[57] The Fourth and Fifth Amendments, by circumscribing the powers of High Courts to provide relief through orders, bails, interim orders about preventive detention, solidified the apprehensions of political opponents and the public alike about the forms of impunity sought by the government. The regime's parliamentary assurances to retain the safeguard of an impartial judiciary against undue and unlawful detention were being undermined through their own actions.[58]

Courts were not necessarily more deferential to executive action in the aftermath. High Courts in this period decreed that a writ of habeas corpus would not be barred simply because a reference to the review board had been filed or because the period of review had already exceeded one month or because it was sought to be extended.[59] On the substantial issue of protecting political speech and expression, the Lahore High Court was the most adventurous. In a case heard in the Lahore High Court in 1976, the court quashed a detention order

[56] *Mst Bakhtawar v The State* PCrLJ [1976] Lahore 393.

[57] Including for anyone 'who commits or attempt to commit any act which amounts to an anti-national activity as defined in a Federal Law or is a member of any association which has for its object, or which indulges him, any such anti-national activity'.

[58] See text in Chapter 5, section I.

[59] *M Ghafoor v Government of NWFP* PLD [1974] Peshawar 28.

against a political opponent of the Bhutto regime by establishing that calling into question the fair name of the ruling party or the Prime Minister was not sufficient grounds to show that if not detained, the person delivering the speech was likely to 'jeopardize public order'.[60] 'Mere criticism', even if strongly worded, could not be held to be 'prejudicial' to the maintenance of such public order.[61] Additionally, the Peshawar High Court in the *Nek Amal* judgment noted that what had been communicated to the detainee was that he had made a speech that was considered to be 'inflammatory and tended to incite violence among the landlords-tenants of Malakand Agency'. Chief Justice Safdar Shah felt this to be a 'conclusion' based on no further controvertible evidence, such as the place where the speech was given or the language employed.[62]

The conditioning of the courts to read constitutional protections more broadly than had been the case in the early years of transition and during the existence of martial law provided some limited room for manoeuvre vis-à-vis the functioning of courts during the long reign of Zia. While the *Nusrat Bhutto* case established the validity of martial rule on the basis of the doctrine of necessity and thereby also allowed for Zulfiqar Bhutto's detention orders to be validated, a string of subsequent cases show a greater deference to balancing the rights of personal liberty that were at stake in revocation of the rights and procedures established by Article 10 of the 1973 Constitution.

In a case where the detention of two former ministers within the Bhutto regime had been engineered by Martial Law Order No 12, the operative mechanism by which Zia sought to vacate the field of Article 10, broad-ranging discussions about the enforcement of rights during martial law were brought onto the record.[63] Nonetheless, against this, the courts had already indicated that they would retain powers to test martial law orders and regulations against the 'conditions of necessity' by which the larger scheme of martial rule had been validated.

[60] *Ghulam Ahmad v Punjab Province* PLD [1976] Lahore 773.

[61] ibid.

[62] *Nek Amal v Political Agent, Malakand PLD* [1975] Peshawar 67.

[63] *Mumtaz Ali Bhutto v Deputy Law Administration Sector I Karachi* PLD [1979] Karachi 307.

In that context then, the majority in this case upheld the primacy of 'liberty' even as they acknowledged that situations of emergency can strictly delimit individual liberty guarantees and that there will be permissive and even indemnified violations by authorities responsible for restoring situations of normalcy.[64]

While this case involved some notable personalities, the maintenance for the next seven years of a martial law under Zia entailed that the practice of detention was perhaps unchecked at the level of local martial law administrators. As was already apparent under this case and in others, the expansion of law to mean validly enacted Regulations and Orders under martial rule included punitive or preventive measures for those where they were found to be 'acting in any manner prejudicial to the purposes for which Martial law has been enacted'. The courts remained in an eternal cycle of also bringing into the field those principles and judicial determinations which could afford principled resistance to the expansionary capacities of an executive that was increasingly ruling with an iron fist. The Eighth Amendment of the Constitution did away with many of the restrictions imposed upon Article 10 by the Zia regime.

B. Heightened Scrutiny—Restoration of Democracy and Preventative Detention

A quick run-through of the law of preventive detention as it currently stands should provide some hope about judicial reasoning in Pakistan and the ways in which it has progressively freed itself in many ways from the national security paradigm of earlier decades. Simultaneously, however, there is plenty of reason for scepticism about the place and efficacy of law in general within Pakistan. This is most apparent in the phenomenon of missing persons, those held in extra-legal custody by security agencies in post-2001 Pakistan and the reframing of positive law broadly to accord arrest and detention greater exceptional status within the constitutional framework.

[64] *Nusrat Bhutto v Chief of Army Staff* PLD [1977] SC 657.

The Anti-Terrorist Act, 1997 was passed with the explicit mandate of curtailing the activities of 'sectarian' organisations, those 'pertaining to, devoted to, peculiar to, or one which promotes interest of a religious sect or sects, in a bigoted or prejudicial manner'. Until recently, it was the major law in the field of detaining and prosecuting suspected terrorists. Whilst the statute conferred no additional capacities for authorising detention, the pace of such detentions for those deemed to be affiliated with sectarian organisations was speeded up by virtue of the names of proscribed organisations and individuals being appended to lists for whom additional policing was thus mandated. The individuals whose names appear within Schedule III of the Anti-Terrorist Act are made then to furnish bonds and foreswear any 'terrorist' acts, the commission of which could land them in specially constituted anti-terror courts. The appearance of a person's name on such a list has ensured, it seems, the greater likelihood of their being preventively detained under either the Maintenance of Public Order Ordinance or the Security of Pakistan Act, and thus an increasing number of cases have arisen pertaining to such persons over the last decade and a half. Where the writ of habeas corpus has been heard, the evidence of 'mere membership' in such organisations has been held to be insufficient as grounds for their detention.[65]

Courts will almost always entertain a habeas writ in the case of preventive detention[66] and have assumed absolute pre-eminence over 'judicial, quasi-judicial and executive functionaries of the Provincial and Federal Governments under Article 199 of the Constitution'.[67] The procedural preconditions for lawful detention include a disclosure of grounds to the detainee, which must occur within a reasonable period of time so as to comply with the constitutional condition under Article 10(4) that it should be 'as soon as may be'.[68] Although allowance is made to vary the length of time in consideration of the anticipated duration of detention, absolute non-communication is found to render

[65] *Abdul Rauf v Chief Commissioner, Islamabad* PLD [2006] Lahore 111; *Iffat Razi v Government of Punjab* PLD [2002] Lahore 194.

[66] *Qazi Hussain Ahmad v Secretary to Government of NWFP YLR* [2003] Peshawar 330.

[67] *Masal Khan v District Magistrate, Peshawar* PLD [1997] Peshawar 148.

[68] *Dr Niaz Ahmad v DCO* PLD [2014] Lahore 516.

both the remedy of representation between a review board nugatory as well as the order, upon a habeas petition, unlawful.[69]

The clause by clause perusal of the original detention order has repeatedly established the principle that the detention will be held to be unlawful if even one ground is bad in law.[70] Detentions based upon the past conduct or habitual criminality[71] of a detainee have similarly been declared to lack reasonableness. In addition, the courts have demanded that grounds be neither vague nor indefinite and that the harm sought to be avoided must be shown to have an immediate likelihood of happening if the person were not detained.

Furthermore, the courts have excavated the objects to which statutes such as the MPO and SPA are aimed by elaborating the conditions of what poses an actual threat to public order. It has been given that in order to find such a threat, 'it must be shown that the act or activity is likely to effect the public-at-large.'[72] The mere creation of a law and order problem does not in any way create a sufficient threshold condition to enable preventative detention to take place.

By engaging in a balancing test between rights and collective, state-defined purposes, the courts have allowed the former to make inroads on what has traditionally within Pakistan remained the unassailed right of the executive to decide. Furthermore, by identifying other rights as somewhat impugned in the facts of certain cases, they have also expanded the protective ambit of these rights protections. For example, even in the case of militancy and those shown to be disseminating material under the auspices of a banned organisation, the right of freedom of speech, as granted in Article 19, was felt to be broad enough to provide cover to this activity. In reference to material that was simply expressing disapprobation of governmental policy, Justice Muhammad Akhtar Shabbir of the Lahore High Court opined: 'I am unable to understand as to how distribution of these pamphlets in the general public was termed as terrorism or sectarianism'.[73]

[69] *Mir Javaid Al v Government of Sindh* MLD [1988] Karachi 879; *Muhammad Siddiq Khan v District Magistrate* PLD [1992] Lahore 140.

[70] *Shamas Din v Deputy Martial Law Administrator Lahore* PLD [1979] Lahore 74.

[71] *Masal Khan v District Magistrate, Peshawar* PLD [1997] Peshawar 148.

[72] *Mrs Arshad Ali Khan v Government of the Punjab* SCMR [1994] SC 1532.

[73] *Mulazim Hussain Shah v Province of Punjab PLD* [2006] Lahore 108.

In coming to an account of the missing persons phenomenon in Pakistan, it is important to note that judicial vigilance in seeking credible grounds for the preventive detention of terror suspects cannot wholly explain the state's recourse to such measures. The most notable person to be thus freed, at least thrice in the course of a few years, is Hafez Saeed. Saeed is one-time known leader of the *Lashkar-I-Tayyaba*, a banned organisation that was once fostered by elements of the Pakistani state to aid its goal of sustaining the anti-Indian Kashmiri Jihad. In these petitions to challenge his detention by the state, the security agencies who had directed his arrest seem unwilling to share evidence to establish that his freedom is a threat to public security. There is a long-standing suspicion that the state shields those who are 'strategic assets' and punishes those who are no longer so, making a distinction between 'good' and 'bad' militants.

C. Missing Persons—The International War on Terror in Pakistan

As noted by the Missing Persons Commission,[74] the problem of people being picked up, allegedly by the security agencies of the army, started to manifest itself early in 2003. The rate at which people thereafter were being apprehended increased manifold and when, in 2007, the Chief Justice of the Supreme Court was made to take 'long leave' by the President General Pervez Musharraf, it was roundly acknowledged that one of the nerves he had touched was by taking up cases investigating these disappearances.[75]

[74] The Commission of Inquiry on Enforced Disappearances (CIED) has been appointed by the Supreme Court to investigate cases of missing persons in the country and trace missing persons with the assistance of law enforcement agencies. The Commission was formed in 2010 and on 1 January 2011, 138 cases of missing persons were transferred to the Commission. It continues to be in operation.

[75] In his address to the nation while imposing emergency, Musharraf stated that the courts 'are working at cross purposes with the executive and legislature in the fight against terrorism and extremism, thereby weakening the government and the nation's resolve and diluting the efficacy of its actions to control this menace'. 'Gen Musharraf's second coup' *Dawn news* (4 November 2007) <www.dawn.com/news/274263/gen-musharraf-s-second-coup-charge-sheet-against-judiciary-media-promoting-negativism-country-s-integrity-at-stake-legislatures-intact>.

The Pakistani strategy of enforced disappearance was influenced no doubt by the creation of a globalised preventative detention regime for which Guantanamo Bay and the deployment of the 'enemy combatant' classification has been essential. This multi-tier regime included extraordinary renditions through which additional detentions were parcelled out to offshore facilities, including Pakistan. Both Guantanamo and the extraordinary renditions programme provided leeway for the US to detain and hold persons that 'otherwise would have been subject to traditional geographic constraints and their associated legal regimes'[76] had they been located within the geographic bounds of the United States.[77] Pakistan's mimickry of this was aided by the parcellisation of FATA as outside of constitutional protection, but the programme of enforced disappearance is broader than affecting only the population within FATA's territorial boundaries.

Early petitions to the court, especially those filed under the auspice of the Human Rights Commission of Pakistan, were, in conjunction with investigative reports undertaken by mostly foreign media sources, revelatory for the Pakistani public at large about what was happening. What was almost immediately apparent, but perhaps not as openly discussed, was that the global war on terror had provided an opening not only for counter-insurgency campaigns directed at actual or would-be Islamist militants, but that older insurgencies, particularly of the Baloch, were going to be dealt with in the same manner. Thus, of the 99 verified missing represented in an early HRCP challenge to the government, 66 were Baloch.[78]

At the second hearing of this case, it was reported that a small number amongst the missing had been recovered. This recovery was very much the result of a haranguing that the court gave to agents of Pakistan's executive, in a manner that was never before imagined, little less administered. Starting in 2006, and, again after the Chief Justice's restoration in 2009, a large number of petitions were filed and heard. In these, provincial governments, the Ministry of Interior, heads of

[76] G Sitaraman, *The Counterinsurgent's Constitution: Law in the Age of Small Wars* (Oxford, Oxford University Press 2012) 60.

[77] A report by the Open Society Justice Initiative (OSJI) it has come to light that Pakistan, along with 54 more countries, cooperated with the United States and the CIA in its extraordinary renditions program.

[78] Civil Miscellaneous Application no. 4420/2009 in Constitutional Petition 05/07.

Pakistan's intelligence agencies were all summoned by the court to account for disappearances.

In consideration of the person who has gone missing, the testimonies of the few released reveal far deeper rights violations than should have to be suffered by anyone. For instance, one person who was released was so emaciated and weak at the time that he could not be recognised by family members and died within weeks. He weighed just 35 kilograms. A fairly credible picture of torture, solitary confinement and the disorientation that accompanies not knowing the cause of detention, your whereabouts or the likelihood of being released is what emerges from what these people have relayed about their conditions of detention.

In 2014, the last of the major 'missing persons' case to date was heard at the Supreme Court. In it, the tone in which the intelligence agencies are addressed is noteworthy, with their 'word' being taken as its 'weight in gold', so that even Chaudhry had been chastened and the inquisitorial nature of the enquiry somewhat reversed.[79] However, there remains a persistent directive for the discovery and restoring to liberty of missing persons. Notably, the Supreme Court has relied to a greater extent on international law and convention to argue that the practices of forcible disappearance constitute a 'crime against humanity' by the state.[80]

Two successive civilian governments have responded to provide greater legal cover to the actions of the army and security agencies. The law regarding detention has changed in light of the Actions (in Aid of Civil Power) Regulation, 2011 and the Protection of Pakistan Act, 2014 (PPA). The Actions (in Aid of Civil Power) Regulation—which is applicable to Federally and Provincially Administered Tribal Areas—confers powers of internment on military authorities during the time that a counter-insurgency campaign is being waged. It has had retroactive application to the conduct of a major anti-militant army campaign in the region of Swat, a part of PATA. Broadly, it authorises the seizure of property as well as providing the powers to punish 'miscreants' in the course of such campaigns, including by death. Its more precise purpose in reference to internment is to mandate apprehensions on the basis of the commission or the suspicion of crimes

[79] *Mst Rohaifa v Federation of Pakistan* PLD [2014] SC 174.
[80] Human Rights Case no 29388-K of 2013, PLD [2014] SC 305.

that include non-obedience of civilian of military officials. There are few safeguards attached to these internments, which can last as long as a counter-insurgency campaign is underway. As with the global war on terror, there is no precise indication of what the point of terminus of such a campaign would be. A review board of governmental and army officers is the mandated forum for authorising detention beyond an initial period that can last for up to four months. It is reported that there are approximately 1,500 persons currently in such detention centres throughout the areas under the powers of the Action in Aid Regulations. In one recent case, the court called for further particulars about persons deemed to be 'undeclared detainees' under the law but in a show of 'judicial restraint' conceded that it could only direct that the executive branch desist from detaining persons from parts of Pakistan where there was no such legal coverage.[81] This was itself a recognition of the fact that intelligence agencies have interned people who are neither residents of the tribal areas nor present there at the time that they were apprehended.

In the PPA section 6 allows for preventative detention for a maximum of 90 days if the government has reasonable grounds to believe that the person is acting in a manner prejudicial to the integrity, security, defence of Pakistan or public order. However the Act itself makes these detentions subject to Article 10 of the Constitution. While the PPA has not been widely used, the existence of the Actions in Aid Regulations has provided the necessary cover for apprehensions of alleged militants from across the country.

The variance is great in terms of the numbers that are circulated about who and how many are held by the state and how many may have perished under conditions of detention and torture. For example, Mama Qadeer, father of a young Baloch nationalist whose mutilated corpse was returned to the family after having been missing for two years, cites 21,000 missing persons from across the country.[82] A former

[81] ibid.

[82] 'When we conducted the long march towards Islamabad, we had a list of 18,000 individuals which we presented to the UN and EU. Since then there have been 3,000 other persons who have been missing from the province. Overall there are 21,000 missing persons and 6,000 dead bodies have been found from various parts of Balochistan', he claimed. Kunwar Kuldune Shahid 'Silencing the Lone Voice on Balochistan's Missing Persons' *The Diplomat* (6 April 2015) <www.thediplomat.com/2015/04/silencing-the-lone-voice-on-balochistans-missing-persons/>.

member of the Federal Task Force on Missing Persons, Faisal Siddique, counters that there is 'little evidence for such exaggerated figures'.[83] As with many other historical episodes of such 'disappearances' happening within the body politic, it may not be possible to establish certainty about what has been happening within Pakistan over the last 15 years or so, for many years to come.

FURTHER READING

KA Ali, *Communism in Pakistan: Politics and Class Activism 1947–1972* (London, IB Tauris, 2015).
SS Ali and J Rehman, *Indigenous Peoples and Ethnic Minorities of Pakistan: Constitutional and Legal Perspectives* (Richmond, Curzon, 2001).
N Hussain, M Samiya, and S Rubina, *Engendering the Nation-state* (Lahore, Simorgh Women's Resource and Publication Centre, 1997).
SA Shah, *International Law and Drone Strikes in Pakistan: The Legal and Socio-Political Aspects* (New York, Routledge, 2015).

[83] Faisal Siddiqi 'Missing Persons' *Dawn news* (13 June 2015) <www.dawn.com/news/1187811>.

8

Islam

Shariat – Islamisation – Federal Shariat Courts – Council of Islamic Ideology – Sectarianism – Political Islam – Blasphemy Laws – Hudood Ordinances – Objectives Resolution

AN OPENING NOTE in Chapter 1 directed the reader away from the common and increasingly popular view that Islam has been the primary steering force in determining the course of Pakistani constitutionalism. In Chapter 2, the immediate history of post-Partition state consolidation included a description of the early contestation over the Islamic character of the Pakistani state. Alongside what was mostly a platitudinous official recognition of Islam in these early years, the rising influence of Islamic spokespersons in the polity was also briefly charted. This influence was on the increase even as the state sought to implant the seeds of a rationalist reformation of Islamic thought and practice during Ayub's modernist experiment (1958–1969). Some representative religious voices worked to reinforce and expand the recognition of Islam as state religion in the text of the 1973 Constitution and employed the state apparatus to make official determinations on principles of faith shortly thereafter. However, the contest between merely establishing an official religion and an abidance of Islamic principles of law as imperative commands was only settled in favour of the latter with Zia-ul-Haq's assumption of power in 1977.

Zia's alterations were undertaken as executive Acts and thereby did not reflect prior popular authorisation. Constitutional changes included the incorporation of the Objectives Resolution into the main body of the Constitution and the establishment of a parallel Shariat court system. Additionally, bodies of Islamic law were promulgated to enjoin the Muslim populace in living according to Quran and Sunnah, as understood by a narrow ring of Zia's advisors. In tandem with broader features impacting the social and political sphere, this structure has produced a syncretic legality, one that has had disproportionate and rights-constricting impact upon women and religious minorities.

A final section of this chapter describes the exertions of the Musharraf regime (1999–2008) in seeking to amend and reform Islamic law in Pakistan. This process highlighted the layered ways in which the formalisation of Islamic law and increasing piety of the social sphere have established a broad social and political constituency that is receptive to reformation only when undertaken within the bounds of Islamic law and normativity. The reform of Islamic legal provisions continues to be a divisive issue, one that often and regularly spills over into violence.

I. ISLAM AND STATE

Zia's radical changes cannot be accounted for without recognition of anteceding events that created a terrain of receptivity for his innovations. In addition to alienating the *Ulema*, which was aggrieved for having been shunted away from power, Ayub's authoritarian management energised additional groups that were consolidating political programmes and resistant strategies in an Islamic idiom. These oppositional movements gained further ground during Bhutto's reign before being appropriated into the structures of government with Zia's rise to power.

While Ayub Khan's programme of national development was ostensibly one of staunch secularism he did seek the services of liberal and reformist Islamic scholars to try and enact a broader social reformation. Prominently, the modernising theologian, Dr Fazl-ur-Rahman was appointed the first head of the Islamic Research Council, an institution established by the 1962 Constitution. Ayub had previously passed the Muslim Family Laws Ordinance (MFLO) amidst great hue and cry amongst members of the *Ulema*. The MFLO contained provisions for the registration of marriages, the limitation and regularisation of polygamy and other features that were decried for being 'un-Islamic' by scholars of Islam. Even in the face of such protest Ayub directly patronised the development of Rahman's rationalist interpretation of Islamic law. In his more radical departures from traditionalist thought,

Rahman questioned the veracity of some traditional sources of Islamic law and counselled that not every law and prohibition within the text of the Quran was meant to have universal application. The radical nature of Rahman's work incited great opposition and in the face of popular protests against him he was forced to flee the country.[1]

Through the same period, the incorporation of a liberalised Islam into the legal structure had an unlikely proponent in the Supreme Court Chief Justice AR Cornelius (1960–1968). Cornelius attributed the acceptance and popular support for laws authority in Europe to its early articulation in religious or natural rights propositions through the intermediation of judges.[2] In spite of having authored a notable dissent to the majority judgment in *Dosso*, Cornelius was closely aligned with Ayub through his reign and subsequently served as law minister in the Cabinet of Yahya Khan (1969–1971).

As a counter to the liberal Islam that was patronised by Ayub, political Islamists were gaining popular currency through the anti-authoritarian stand taken by Maudoodi and the Jamaat-e-Islami as well as the Jamiat Ulema-e-Islami (JUI). These parties joined forces with an array of non-religious parties to support the candidacy of Fatima Jinnah in the 1965 presidential elections as a counter to the rule of Ayub. This decision caused fractures within the Jamaat, with a faction breaking away because they viewed such an alliance as counter to a clear Islamic prohibition on the elevation of a woman to the position of head of state.[3] In spite of a growing constituency amongst professional and lower class urban voters, the Jamaat gained few seats in the 1970 elections in either Eastern or Western wings of the country. The JUI, however, became a coalition partner of the secular left NAP in the NWFP Assembly.

After the loss of Bangladesh and through the course of Bhutto's rule, Islamist parties and members of the *Ulema* acted as a pressure group against what were viewed as Bhutto's personal impieties as well

[1] See F Rahman, 'Currents of Religious Thought in Pakistan' (1986) 7 *Islamic Studies* 1. See also MQ Zaman, 'Islamic Modernism and the Shari'a in Pakistan' (2014) 8 *Yale Law School Occasional Papers* 1.

[2] CB Lombardi, 'Can Islamizing A Legal System Ever Help Promote Liberal Democracy?: A View from Pakistan' (2010) 7 *University of St Thomas Law Journal* 649.

[3] See SVR Nasr, *Mawdudi and the Making of Islamic Revivalism* (New York, Oxford University Press, 1995).

as a denunciatory force against his agenda of Islamic socialism. Over 100 members of the established *Ulema* signed a petition that cited the un-Islamic basis of Bhutto's drive to implant some vestiges of socialism in the country. To a greater extent than the *Ulema* though, Islamic parties have been credited with success 'in instituting many Islamist assumptions in popular political culture and framing key debates in an Islamist frame of reference', eventually contributing in some ways to the 'collapse of Zulfiqar Ali Bhutto's experiment with socialism' (1971–1977).[4]

Bhutto's socialism was prefixed with the appellation of 'Islamic', both as authenticity claim against his religious detractors as well as in an anti-imperialist gesture of pan-Islamist solidarity, which was gaining ground in the post-colonial world. It was devoid of any Islamic derivation per se, but this cloak of legitimation facilitated the maintenance of the Objectives Resolution among the preambular statements of the 1973 Constitution; it also allowed for the inclusion of further provisions, such as the prescription that the head of state should be a Muslim. In addition, the Council of Islamic Ideology (CII) was created by way of Article 28 to advise the government, or relevant governmental ministries, on prospective changes to laws for religious conformity as well as to accept references from the government on the repugnancy of laws to the injunctions of Islam. Article 228 prescribes that membership of the CII shall comprise various schools of religious thought as well as religious laypersons who have expertise in other domains of policy. No paramountcy was accorded to the recommendations of the CII and consequently the Islamic nature of laws was to be adjudged ultimately by Parliament, as had been the case with the 1956 Constitution.

Bhutto was, however, open to appeasing religious sentiment where it threatened his rule and it was shortly after the promulgation of the 1973 Constitution that the NWFP Assembly, under the Chief Ministership of Mufti Mahmood of the JUI, began a regional programme of Islamisation. In this process some certainty was sought about whether Ahmadis were non-Muslims. Amongst the justifications offered for calling upon the state to enter into the terrain of theological disputation

[4] JL Esposito, JO Voll and O Bakar, *Asian Islam in the 21*st *Century* (Oxford, Oxford University Press, 2008) 32.

was that as the recently passed Constitution 'required the head of state to be a Muslim, it was incumbent so as to prevent a non-Muslim from becoming the head of state'.[5] Against the 1954 Munir Report's claims that no consensual definition of who constituted a Muslim could be established,[6] the NWFP Assembly, shortly preceded by the Azad Kashmir Assembly, passed a resolution calling upon the central government to label Ahmadis non-Muslims. A Saudi Arabian-based *Ulema* council showed support for this resolution. Members of the anti-Ahmadiyya movement used a face-off between students and some members of the Ahmadi community in their spiritual base at Rabwa in Punjab to push this agenda. Bhutto himself appointed a judicial commission to enquire into the 'Rabwa incident', the report for which remains classified. Simultaneous to the writing of this report, the government succumbed to pressure to hold a special session of parliament to look into the Qadiani question broadly.[7]

The result was the Second Amendment to the Constitution, which specifically delegated Ahmadis the status of a non-Muslim religious minority. The Act specified that Ahmadis were thus relegated because persons of this faith did not

> believe in the absolute and unqualified finality of Muhammad (Peace be Upon Him), the last of the Prophets or claims to be a Prophet in any sense of the word or of any description whatsoever, after MUHAMMAD (Peace be Upon Him), or recognises such a claimant as a Prophet or religious reformer, is not a Muslim for the purposes of the Constitution or law.

Given the provision's constitutional status, it has been the backdrop for a range of administrative and legal measures to further constrain a range of rights that the Ahmadis can assert in Pakistan, many of which were later introduced by Zia.

While the Second Amendment surely reflected a consensus amongst Sunni and even Shia *Ulema* on the bounds of allowable innovation to Islamic doctrine, it did not itself introduce any particular prohibitions on the Ahmadi community in Pakistan. The founding of a movement to uphold and protect the finality of the Prophet in the early years after Partition, having been left out of the political consensus of the state for

[5] AU Qasmi, *The Ahmadis and the Politics of Religious Exclusion in Pakistan* (London, Anthem Press, 2014) 173.

[6] See text in Chapter 2, section III.

[7] Qadiani is considered a pejorative term by Ahmadis.

so long, would, after the passage of the Second Amendment under its belt, have far greater opportunities to alter law and governmental policy during the reign of Zia-ul-Haq.

II. ZIA AND ISLAMISATION

A confluence of factors sped up the pace of Islamisation undertaken by Zia-ul-Haq after his assumption of power in 1977. Integral to these efforts was Pakistan's opportune location as a bulwark against further Communist expansion following the Soviet invasion of Afghanistan. *Jihad* against the Communist 'infidels' was a project that found many support bases within Pakistan and these were further supported through a substantial injection of US resources. The 'state necessity' doctrine granted the dictator almost limitless discretion to alter laws and the Constitution, and Zia was quick to use this to harken to a social order that transcended his original promises to simply restore law and order to the tumultuous political terrain in which his coup was staged.

Prior to an accounting of the specific mechanics of Islamisation under Zia, it is important to understand that in the merger of state and Islam a chief obstacle is encountered in naming or designating a body capable of articulating Islamic Law or *Shariat.* The accepted primary and central sources of Islamic law are the Quran and Sunnah. Amongst these two the Quran is the supreme authority but, as has often been noted, the divine book is not a legal manual as such. Rather, the extension of sources to Sunnah incorporates the 'normative example of the Prophet', his words and deeds in compilations of Hadith undertaken by the Prophet's contemporaries or near-contemporaries. *Shariat,* or Islamic Law is thus the product of the exertions of many generations of scholars and jurists working within the Islamic tradition to derive law from these sources. Historically, such exegetical exercises have led to the development of a plurality of legal schools of thought across the Muslim world.[8] In the subcontinent, *Hanafi* jurisprudence was

[8] See, generally, MH Kamali, *Principles of Islamic Jurisprudence* (Cambridge, Islamic Texts Society, 2003); WB Hallaq, *A History of Islamic Legal Theories* (New York, Cambridge University Press, 1997); see also A Rahim, 'A Historical Sketch of Mohammedan Jurisprudence. III. The "Jurists", the Modern Writers, and the British Indian Courts' (1907) 7 *Columbia Law Review* 255.

given official recognition from the time that codification became an established practice under the Mughal ruler Aurangzeb. Nonetheless, where Islamic law is enforced without the state's mediation, a plurality of interpretive traditions guide *muftis* or judges in the ways that various sources of law are to be reconciled. The need to formally rationalise these into singular rules and hierarchies whittles down the range of otherwise available interpretations on Islamic law.

As Martin Lau notes, two types of Islamisation might be entailed when altering a legal system or structure: 'One is full and systemic, so that a complete replacement of an existing apparatus is undertaken'.[9] For that no examples can be cited. In the case of Pakistan, policies to Islamise a legal system are based on the introduction of 'institutional and legal mechanisms which allow for a gradual and controlled introduction of Islamic law.'[10] The mechanisms that Zia chose were the creation of a parallel judicial structure, the incorporation of the Objectives Resolution as a substantive part of the constitutional structure in 1985 and a range of Islamic laws beginning in 1978. These were in addition to the ways in which an Islamic political sphere was sought to be created through mechanics detailed earlier.[11]

A. Shariat Courts

The Shariat Court and the Shariat Appellate Bench of the Supreme Court were amongst the innovations introduced by Zia as part of the *Nizam E Mustapha* [Movement for the establishment of Mustafa's (Muhammad) law], oriented to the creation of what he termed a 'truly Islamic' society in Pakistan. This parallel judicial structure was amended several times. In fact, although the Federal Shariat Court (FSC) was introduced by insertion of Article 203B, it took 12 different presidential orders to finally settle issues of jurisdiction and composition. It is important to note that the Islamic court system was established in tandem with the promulgation of the Hudood Ordinances, and they

[9] M Lau, *The Role of Islam in the Legal System of Pakistan* (Leiden, Martinus Nijhoff, 2001).

[10] ibid 294.

[11] See Chapter 3.

were the court of appeal from district courts in cases involving the offences that they created.

In 1978 Zia directed that Shariat benches be established at all the High Courts of the provinces to 'hear Shariat petititons' and appeals on newly introduced Islamic penal provisions. These were then replaced by the single Federal Shariat Court in 1980. Although subject to some alteration, the general ambit of the FSC's functioning comprised the following: original jurisdiction 'to examine and decide the question, whether or not any law is repugnant to the injunctions of Islam';[12] revisional jurisdiction 'to call for and examine the powers of any criminal courts that are related to the enforcement of Hudood punishments'.[13] Finally, it has revisional jurisdiction to revise its own findings on the issue of repugnancy. For those who accepted some incorporation of Islamic laws into the corpus of Pakistani laws, the court's composition struck an acceptable compromise: it was to be composed of three members of the *Ulema* and five members of the superior judiciary. Appeals from the FSC would be heard at the Shariat Appeals Bench of the Supreme Court where again, judges and members of the *Ulema* would be appointed for each case. In addition, Article 203C particularly indemnified 'the Constitution' as well as other subject areas from the Court's jurisdiction. In spite of such immunisations, for those fearful of whole scale Islamisation, the nature of the Shariat court's powers of judicial review was so significant that it was thought to have 'no parallel in judicial history'.[14]

The conduct of Zia's Islamisation programme entailed that fidelity to the practices of Islamic deliberation and a thorough perusal of sources gave way to the promotion of determinate ends as necessarily comporting with Islamic truth. Issues of derivation and lineage, however, were central to the Federal Shariat Court itself in the first case it adjudicated. In *Hazoor Baksh*, the court undertook a particularly rigorous examination, through a close reading of Islamic sources, of the prescribed punishment of stoning to death for adultery contained in

[12] MS Shahidullah, *Comparative Criminal Justice Systems: Global and Local Perspectives* (Sudbury, Jones and Bartlett Publishers, 2012) 501.

[13] ibid.

[14] MH Cheema, 'Beyond Beliefs: Deconstructing the Dominant Narratives of the Islamization of Pakistan's Laws' (2012) 60 *American Journal of Comparative Law* 875.

the Hudood Ordinances. It found that the Hadith 'cannot lay down a positive law contrary or repugnant to the Holy Qur'an, nor can it alter, amend or modify Holy Qur'an'. Thus, only those 'Ahadith' are relevant which either explain an existing Quranic law or reveal a principle which is absolutely in keeping with the spirit of the Holy Qur'an.[15] The court thus disregarded the recorded practice of the Prophet and his companions of awarding this punishment prior to the revelation of a Quranic verse that 'prescribes 100 stripes for an adulterer, whether married or unmarried'. They thus declared the Hudood Ordinance prescribed punishment of stoning to death as being un-Islamic.

This verdict caused extreme furor amongst Islamists and embarrassment for General Zia, who disbanded this FSC. A reconstituted bench upheld the legitimacy of *Rajm* (stoning to death) and against the methodological propositions advanced in the earlier case, countered that Hadith and Sunnah can be held to be of equal guidance in the promulgation and enforcement of laws.[16] The FSC has been steadfast in demanding death as the only punishment for other offences, including of blasphemy, described further below.

The further record of the FSC can be measured in the alterations wrought throughout the judicial system. One chronicler of this history measures the increasing incorporation of Islamic sources even within the jurisprudence that is generated in the secular court system. Much of this follows upon an activist FSC's attempt to garner more and more legitimacy for itself as it competitively expanded its powers of review progressively over the decades following its formation.[17] What aided this in part was the incorporation of the Objectives Resolution as Article 2A of the Constitution. As part of the Revival of the Constitution of 1973 Order of 1985 (RCO), it was lifted from being merely a preambular statement to becoming a justiciable part of the constitutional text.

B. Objectives Resolution

In the field of constitutional interpretation the status of the Objectives Resolution had been deliberated well before 1985. One of the

[15] *Hazoor Bakhsh v Federation of Pakistan* PLD [1981] FSC 145.

[16] *Federation of Pakistan v Hazoor Bakhsh* PLD [1983] FSC 255.

[17] Cheema, 'Beyond Beliefs: Deconstructing the Dominant Narratives'.

most astounding uses of the Objectives Resolution was in the *Asma Jilani*[18] case of 1973, which reversed the findings of *Dosso*[19] from 1958. In *Jilani*, the court rejected the notion of revolutionary legality and the lingo of Hans Kelsen's structuration of a 'doubly-positivistic' outlook on law in which the legitimacy of an existing law derived neither from its moral content nor from its social acceptance. Rather the pure positivism was embodied in the fact that the hierarchy of norms, the legal system, was grounded by an abstract ethical postulate, the Grundnorm.[20]

In *Jilani* a substantive content was imparted to the Grundnorm by identification of the Objectives Resolution as the highest norm in the land. Pure positivism was determined to be unsuitable for a state founded in the name of religion. It was further implied that members of this state and its society would enjoin themselves into the state only on the basis of positive adherence to the content of 'living a life in accordance with the Quran and Sunnah'.

Bolstered by the *Asma Jilani* case, courts sought jurisdiction in domains where they may otherwise have exercised caution. In judging certain legal enactments of the Yahya regime, the Lahore High Court in the *Zia-ur-Rehman* case went so far as to describe the Objectives Resolution as a supra-constitutional instrument. Justice Zullah made the observation that not only 'our founding fathers but also the people at different times of our short history have assented' to it.[21] He seemed to be unaware of, or ready to efface, the actual wrangle of its initial passage in the first Constituent Assembly in which all East Pakistanis and minority members of the Assembly had voted against it. At appeal in the Supreme Court, Justice Hamoodur Rehman narrowed the possible uses of the Objectives Resolution: 'even though it is a document which has been generally accepted and has never been repealed or renounced, [it] will not have the same status of authority as the Constitution itself until it is incorporated within it or made part of it'.[22]

[18] *Asma Jilani v Government of Punjab* PLD [1972] SC 139.

[19] *State v Dosso* PLD [1958] SC 533.

[20] See H Kelsen, *Pure Theory of Law* (New Jersey, The Lawbook Exchange Ltd, 2002).

[21] *Zia-ur-Rehman v The State* PLD [1972] Lahore 382.

[22] *State v Zia-ur-Rehman* PLD [1973] SC 49.

When, through the RCO of 1985, Article 2A was added to the constitutional text, it was not unexpected for petitioners to push for a revision of laws, and in some cases of constitutional provisions, on the basis of what was being propounded as being a paramountcy clause. Many of these cases came to the superior courts after Zia had, as one of his last acts prior to his unexpected death, passed the Enforcement of Shariah Ordinance of 1988. This law enabled the higher courts to decide whether 'any law relating to Muslim personal law, any fiscal law, or any law relating to the levy of taxes and fees or banking or insurance practice and procedure or any provision of such law is repugnant to the Shariah'.[23] The High Courts in some instances had an activist Islamist judiciary willing to brook the confusions unleashed by the prospective invalidation of a range of laws and governmental actions on the principle of non-conformity with Islamic law.[24]

Importantly, the Sindh High Court made the determination in the *Bank of Oman* case[25] that the incorporation of Article 2A was of far reaching impact and that 'Any provision of the Constitution or law, found repugnant to them, may be declared by superior Court, as void'. It found the only limitation on the court's review powers was respect for the 'special and separate jurisdiction of the Federal Shariat Court'. In a slightly later case, again from the Sindh High Court, the Objectives Resolution in its incorporated form was held, by virtue of being a later amendment, to have paramountcy against the rest of the Constitution, so that articles that predate it must be 'harmonised' with it. Thus, Article 8(3), which accorded special status to a range of laws by indemnifying them against judicial review on the grounds of fundamental rights, was read down to enable such a harmonisation of the *MFLO*, one of the laws offered protection by its inclusion in the First Schedule to the Constitution. Impliedly the court held that all laws were subject to review on the grounds of their conformity to 'the injunctions of Islam'.

[23] Enforcement of Shariah Act 1991, s 8.

[24] See *Irshad H Khan v Parveen Ijaz* PLD [1987] Karachi 466: Justice Tanzilur-Rehman articulates a repugnancy test on the basis of Article 2A for Constitution and law.

[25] *Bank of Oman Ltd v East Trading Co Ltd* [1987] Karachi 404.

In 1992, the Supreme Court addressed the invocations of the Objectives Resolution as Grundnorm and higher law as an 'old controversy' that has been revived by its incorporation in a 'much more pointed and vigorous form' into the main text of the Constitution.[26] Addressing judgments from the High Courts in which the Resolution had been vested with 'control of the Constitution', it resolutely held that this was an erroneous interpretation. Recounting a much more accurate and fractious view of the Resolution's initial passage, the Resolution was presented as having been at the outset no more than a mere declaration of intent by the framers of the Constitution about the nature of the Constitution to come. Referring to the language of the Resolution as 'vague, subtle and flexible', such as in proscribing the making of laws that transgress 'the limits set by Allah', Justice Nasim Hasan Shah, as author of the majority decision, declared that it is for the people's 'chosen representatives' to frame laws that are in consonance with such principles. Thus, in strict legal terms, this case marked a drawing of bounds against the expansion of judicial review powers on the basis of seeking repugnancy of existing laws against the 'Quran and Sunnah' in the regular courts. Courts were thereafter not to seek to review constitutional provisions nor ordinary laws to accord with the principles of the Objectives Resolution.

This was not an injunction that carried weight with the FSC. The record of the FSC's invalidation of statutes has grown to be quite high: 55 federal and 212 provincial laws have been invalidated by the FSC over a period of 30 years.[27] In some important areas, such as in defining the *qisas* and *diyat* provisions of the criminal law, these invalidations have led to legislative action. In other cases, such as in the invalidation of land reform statutes passed by the legislative Assembly during the Bhutto years, the impact has been indirect. Unable to undo the redistributions undertaken on the basis of these legislative acts, the principle of inviolable protection for private property rights in Islam, as outlined in the *Qazalbash Waqf*[28] case, has nonetheless marked a clear red line for policy makers. Another notable feature of this case was a narrowing of the conditions in which a public good argument can trump

[26] *Hakim Khan v Government of Pakistan* PLD [1992] SC 595.

[27] See 'Jurisdiction of the Court' Federal Shariat Court of Pakistan (2012) <http://federalshariatcourt.gov.pk/Jurs.html>

[28] *Qazalbash Waqf v Chief Land Commissioner* PLD [1990] SC 99.

Islamically-sanctioned rights, such as the property rights elaborated by the Shariat Bench of the Supreme Court in *Qazalbash Waqf*.

C. Islamic Laws

The range of Islamic laws brought into being by Zia included the creation of new criminal laws as well as alterations to procedural laws. Two areas of law that have had disproportionate impact on women and minorities in the state are the Hudood Ordinances and an array of amendments to the Pakistan Penal Code (PPC) under the heading of Offences Related to Religion. The content of these laws has been subject to contestation not only on the grounds of societal impact but also in terms of the correctness of their derivation. Whether the Islamic credentials of these laws are of direct derivation or of broad inspiration, *Ulema* and Islamist political parties have rallied to keep these laws unaltered and on the books.

i. Hudood Laws and Women

The Hudood Ordinances introduced Islamic criminal provisions and punishments for sexual offenses, theft, highway robbery, and consumption of alcohol in 1979.[29] Such laws were meant to reflect an ostensible consensus that there are some negative prohibitions which are accompanied by Quranically-sanctioned punishments. These punishments include stoning to death, amputation of limbs and public flogging.

Of the four Hudood Ordinances, those dealing with *Zina*, illicit sexual relations, have been the most controversial. Punishment is prescribed for both consensual and non-consensual sexual relations between men and women outside of marriage and can include flogging or stoning to death dependent upon the marital status of the accused. *Zina-bil-jabr* (zina with force) replaced the existing penal code offence of rape. The act of having sex 'against the will of the victim' or with fraudulently elicited consent is punishable with death. In both cases,

[29] See M Cheema and A Mustafa, 'From the Hudood Ordinances to the Protection of Women Act: Islamic Critiques of the Hudood Laws of Pakistan' (2009) 8 *UCLA Journal of Islamic and Near Eastern Law* 1.

the maximum punishment can only be awarded if the eye-witness testimony of four adult male witnesses of upstanding character is available or if a confession is made by the accused.

Where lesser evidence than is Quranically prescribed is available, a realm of discretion opens up for lawmakers. This realm of discretion enables the construction of lesser offences and punishments, collectively referred to as *tazir*. In this discretionary sphere, lawmakers are to be guided by the Hadith and the compendium of Islamic legal scholarship for defining offences, punishment and standards of evidence.

In terms of actually prosecuted cases the overwhelming majority of *zina* and *zina-bil-jabr* cases have been tried on the basis of testimony, forensic and circumstantial evidence. In other words, the absence of four male witnesses has not implied that cases of *zina* or *zina-bil-jabr* cannot be prosecuted. However, if that addresses one popular misconception about the law concerning sexual offences in Pakistan, the reasons for its notoriety are far greater and are reflected in a history of grave injustice being perpetrated against the women of Pakistan on the basis of the Zina Ordinance's specific workings.

Women's organisations were established soon after the passage of the Hudood laws, including the Women's Action Forum in 1982, to counter what was felt to be an assault upon the rights of all Pakistani women in the name of Islam. A year later a major protest rally following upon the adoption of the *Qanoon E Shahadat* (Law of Evidence) was met by a heavy-handed police response. Zia and his cronies chose to characterise the women who opposed these measures as enemies of Islam rather than simply as proponents of a brand of secularism that established a line between religion and state.

Right from the moment of implementation, anxieties about the Zina Ordinance proved to be well founded. Most tragically, it lent itself to the criminalisation of women complainants of *zina-bil-jabr* by enabling the conversion of a rape complaint into the criminal charge of such a victim for the act of *zina*.[30] The prerogative of defining the criminal provision that would be attached to the offence was exercised by the police officer handling the complaint. What often happened was that the police would charge the women with *zina* even as the male accused was being charged with *zina-bil-jabr*. A vast number of women were

[30] ibid.

thus taken into custody stemming from their complaints of rape to await trial for this non-bailable offence.[31]

The second stage at which women could be criminalised following a complaint of rape was within the courtroom. In addition to specifying that the value of a woman's testimony in property matters would be counted as half of a man's, the 1984 *Qanoon-E-Shahadat* also had an impact on the conduct of criminal trials. Article 17 provided that women's testimony in reference to Hudood or special law cases was to be determined 'according to law' and this provided an opening for courts to negate the value of women's testimony altogether given that the stipulated standard of evidence for *hadd* punishments was the testimony of male witnesses. In other words, the distinction between *hadd* and *tazir* was effaced in reference to the evidentiary standard. In addition, the *Qanoon-E-Shahadat* provided under Article 151(4) 'when a man is prosecuted for rape or an attempt to ravish, it may be shown that the prosecutrix was of generally immoral character'. The possibility of impeaching women's character on the grounds of immorality was both a deterrent to the filing of rape complaints as well as a means by which courts could more readily convert rape allegations into *zina* charges.

Two most notorious cases reflecting the extreme vulnerability of women under the law were tried in the first five years after the *Zina* Ordinance became law. Both these cases involved young women who had been impregnated by their alleged assailants. In *Jehan Mina*, a young woman charged that her uncle and cousin had raped her but neither was convicted of the crime. On the other hand, her 'unexplained pregnancy' was held to be sufficient proof that she, an unwed woman, had engaged in an act of *Zina*.[32] The second case involved an 18-year-old near-blind woman who, for failure to identify her assailants given her ocular infirmity, was convicted of *zina* owing to her pregnancy at the trial court level. Her punishment was to be corporal punishment, 30 lashes and a fine. This case garnered great public protest and the Federal Shariat Court took *suo moto* notice and reversed the conviction.

[31] See MS Shahidullah, *Comparative Criminal Justice Systems: Global and Local Perspectives* (Burlington, Jones & Bartlett Publishers, 2012). By 1988 in Punjab province alone there were 6,000 women in prison. Further, 'from 1980 to 1987 the Federal Shari'at Court alone heard 3,399 appeals of zina involving female prisoners': at 505.

[32] *Mst Jehan Mina v The State* PLD [1983] FSC 183.

In *Safia Bibi*, the FSC was able to narrow the openings by which women had been convicted of *zina*.[33] Although the court did not indict the actual mechanics of converting an allegation of rape into a charge of *zina*, they did establish that the burden of proving consent lay squarely on the shoulders of the prosecution whenever a woman was charged with *zina*. An inability to prove rape did not automatically imply satisfaction of the burden to prove commission of *zina*.[34] They provided an elaboration of Islamic jurisprudence to illustrate that circumstantial evidence, including 'unexplained pregnancy', was not itself sufficient to uphold any inference of consent on the part of a woman. When, in 2006 the Women's Protection Act sought to reform the Hudood laws, the conversion of a rape allegation into a charge of *zina* was fully closed off.

It is important to understand that the charge of *zina* was and continues to be framed against women in a range of additional circumstances. Often women's exercise of free choice in decisions pertaining to marriage is the 'provocation' for the filing of such charges. The consequence of cohabitation without the sanctification of marriage is, of course, the possible application of the charge of *zina* upon such an accused. In such circumstances, the courts were enjoined repeatedly in the 1990s in the enterprise of defining valid marriage.

The outstanding question of whether or not a Muslim woman is entitled to contract a marriage without the consent of her *wali* (guardian), even past the age of majority, was fully settled through the *Saima Waheed case*.[35] The Lahore High Court, whilst sounding a note of caution about women flouting social mores, did nonetheless find positive precedent for declaring that there is no Islamic injunction to necessitate the consent of the woman's *wali* at the time of marriage.

Subsequently, courts invoked Article 9 of the Constitution, which guarantees life and liberty in accordance with law, alongside Article 35, a Principle of Policy for the 'protection of family', to enable women to freely enter and exit the contract of marriage. Following *Shehla Zia*, in which the right to life was read as incorporative of capacities beyond 'mere vegetative life', the right was rendered more capacious for being

[33] *Mst Safia Bibi v The State* PLD [1985] FSC 120.

[34] MH Cheema, 'Cases and Controversies: Pregnancy as Proof of Guilt under Pakistan's Hudood Laws' (2006) 32 *Brooklyn Journal of International Law* 121.

[35] *Abdul Waheed v Asma Jehangir* PLD [1997] Lahore 301.

in protection of a 'validly married couple's' freedom from official and familial harassment.[36]

Another parallel set of cases involved courts looking into the extent to which state involvement is mandated in the enquiry into the validity of the marriage or its dissolution. Rendered often in response to Article 199 petitions seeking to quash criminal proceedings stemming from biased policing, some of these landmark cases have made recourse to the language of international human rights instruments. Pakistan's status as a signatory to the Convention on the Elimination of all Forms of Discrimination against Women was used to counter the assertion that Islamic social order or personal laws run contrary to 'universal mores'. Thus, vestiges of feudal relations or cultural predispositions are indicted for running contrary to what Islam and human rights can conjointly deliver to Pakistan's women.[37]

However, in spite of these cases, which restore women's capacity to make marital decisions, the overlapping regimes of Islamic and other laws provide significant openings for violence to be doled out, particularly to female transgressors of what is, in geographic pockets at least, a prevailing social order. The much-publicised occurrence of honour killings arises often in cases such as have been described above with the family, ex-husband or some other party seeking to mete out vigilante justice to a female transgressor by putting her to death.[38] This is often accompanied by some customary legitimation of this punishment and a prior hearing in a forum such as a *jirga* or *panchayat*, which have no status in the Pakistani legal system per se.

If these cases make it to court, there is ample opportunity for judges to exercise leniency in the conviction and punishment of offenders. The existence of *Qisas* and *Diyat* laws, as well as the mitigation of offences on the basis of a grave and sudden provocation defence both provide legal grounds for offenders to escape maximal punishment for the murder of women, and less often men, in crimes of honour.

[36] *Sajida Bibi v In charge Chouki No 2 Police Station Sadar Sahiwal* PLD [1997] Lahore 666.

[37] See *Humaira Mehmood v The State* PLD [1999] Lahore 494. See also KC Yefet, 'What's the Constitution Got to do with it? Regulating Marriage in Pakistan' (2009) 16 *Duke Journal of Gender Law & Policy* 347.

[38] See 'Pakistan: Honour Killings of Women and Girls' (Amnesty International, 1999).

The *Qisas* and *Diyat* laws prescribe 'an eye for an eye' type punishments or enable the exchange of 'blood money' for the voiding of punishment in offences of murder and bodily hurt. These laws emerged as consequence of a highly-charged FSC directing the government to correct inherited penal provisions to bring them in line with Islamic injunctions. In *Federation of Pakistan v Gul Hassan Khan* 1989, existing provisions of the Pakistan Penal Code and the Code of Criminal Procedure Act were found 'repugnant to Islam'. The consequence was an alteration of the criminal law to create categories of murder and bodily harm in reference to degrees of intention and culpability that accorded with principles of Islamic law. Additionally, these offences were mostly considered compoundable, so that the heirs of a victim exercised the right to demand retributive death (*Qisas*) or could choose to waive the crime in favour of monetary compensation (*Diyat*).

This constellation of laws has lent itself to being used in perpetuating honour crimes without penal consequence to the perpetrators. A typical scenario is that it is a member of the woman's family who has perpetrated the crime, usually with the collusion of other members of the family. Amongst these family members are the 'heirs' of the deceased and they can secure the perpetrator's release from the punishment that accord with a conviction, without the state even intervening to ensure that compensation is paid. Although courts retain the discretion in some of these murder offences to sentence the perpetrator in spite of the heir's pardon, it has only rarely been the case that the state exercises this right.[39] This absence of oversight by the courts is even more surprising given that the 2004 Criminal Law Amendment Act altered the relevant law to state that in cases where an act is 'committed in the name or on the pretext of honour' imprisonment for not less than ten years shall be mandatory.[40]

Important for understanding the conduct of cases arising in reference to Islamic provisions of law is that judicial determinations flow

[39] 'Slow March to the Gallows—Death Penalty in Pakistan' (Human Rights Commission of Pakistan, 2007) <www.fidh.org/IMG/pdf/Pakistan464angconjointpdm.pdf>.

[40] Pakistan Penal Code, s 311. Note, however, that this does not close off the possibility of compoundability. Rather, only where the family waives the right to *Qisas*, the court can decide that a crime of honour is to be awarded the greater punishment.

from a merger of common law and Islamic legal reasoning. The common law defence of grave and sudden provocation has been and continues to be available for the accused, particularly in cases where a female kin has upset the sensibilities of her male relations. Judicial acquiescence in its use suggests that the protection that is accorded to women in choice of marriage may more accurately be characterised as protection for the institution of marriage rather than of women's choice. When the liberty or life of a male accused is at stake, ample instances can be cited where the apprehension of a woman's infidelity or a family's loss of certainty about the chastity of female relations is given weight as a precipitating factor for the taking of life.[41]

What is interesting about the Hudood Ordinances or other Islamic laws is that there is no specific immunity accorded to them against review on the basis of fundamental rights. In other words, there is a positive possibility of voidability granted by Article 8 of the Constitution, which reads 'any law, any custom or usage having the force of law, insofar as it is inconsistent with the rights conferred by this chapter, shall to the extent of such inconsistency, be void'. These laws are not formally exempted from rights review.[42] Given that such openings were available, why then were the Hudood laws maintained on the books in spite of their being explicitly and thus egregiously in violation of certain rights, such as freedom of religion and against gender and other forms of discrimination?

One can only surmise at an answer. One such necessarily partial answer has to acknowledge the divided jurisdiction that the parallel judicial system established. The FSC system ensured that 'questions of law' pertaining to the application of Hudood laws would travel upwards to this court and from it to the Shariat Appellate Bench of the Supreme Court. While the intention at the outset was met for some time, and the secular court system exercised little oversight over the administration of an Islamic law regime, the secular court system itself wrested back some of its powers of review through a variety of

41 See Cheema, 'Cases and Controversies'.

42 The First Schedule to the Constitution lists laws to be exempt from rights review. Additionally, until it was removed through the Eighteenth Amendment Act, the Seventh Schedule of the Constitution provided a list of laws that could only be altered through the constitutional amendment formula.

mechanisms. Writs were entertained where they challenged the 'Hudood laws on procedural grounds', such as the improper refusal of bail or alleged that 'a police investigation had been conducted inadequately'. However, this claim over jurisdiction enjoined the courts to temper their findings through invocations themselves of Islamic law and principle.

As the hardship of women under the Hudood laws came to be more closely documented, even quasi-governmental organisations such as the National Commission on the Status of Women made recommendations for their repeal. Also, the challenge of speaking in the language of Islamic law and jurisprudence was also taken up by women's rights organisations, so that alternate interpretations of the verses from which the Hudood laws were derived were offered as counter to the interpretation that informed the form of these laws. For instance, it was argued that the evidentiary standard for proving *zina* was established so as to safeguard women's reputations and had nothing at all to do with the offence of rape; rape itself was thereby reclassified as amongst the crimes that cause social disorder and are liable to be punished more harshly in accord with such a classification.

ii. Islamic Law and Minorities

While much of the non-Muslim population left immediately in the months around Partition, a continued trickle thereafter would reduce this population to less than 5 per cent of the overall population before a decade had elapsed from Pakistan's founding. The figure is currently estimated to be a mere 3 per cent. These non-Muslim minorities include Christians, Hindus, Parsis, Ahmadis and others. Adherents of the main sects of Islam, Shia and Sunni, are estimated to constitute 25 per cent and 75 per cent respectively.[43]

Although the minimalist incorporation of Islam into the constitutional structure prior to Zia has been recounted in the early chapters of this book, it is important to note that the *Ulema* had remained engaged in issues of public importance throughout the years after Partition. With Zia's drive to Islamicise, the *Ulema* were offered the possibility

[43] 'Rampant Killings of Shia by Extremists' (Human Rights Watch, 2014) <www.hrw.org/news/2014/06/29/pakistan-rampant-killings-shia-extremists>.

of increasing their relevance where previously they had been excluded from the corridors of power. Zia's reign also marked a turning for Islamist parties such as the Jamaat; whereas previously Maudoodi had steadfastly opposed military rule, he was successfully enticed into providing support for Zia.

Additionally and importantly, the movement, *Tahafaz-e-Khatam-e-Nabuwat* [Protection of the Finality of the Prophet] had episodically brought members of the Sunni *Ulema* into organisational coherence; under Zia its prominent members were directly patronised by the state. For the *Khatam-E-Nabuwwat*, the reinforcement of the Prophet's status as God's final dispenser of religious truth established a central pillar of Muslim faith. The Ahmadi community has been its most consistent target for demonstrating unbelief. Additionally though, the theological exertions it has undertaken have defined the conditions of apostasy, a charge historically made against the Shia by a line of Sunni theologians. Members of the movement have been central to expanding the laws of blasphemy in the country, and in propagating the view that death is the only allowable punishment for the crimes of blasphemy and apostasy.

Alterations to the law of blasphemy to protect the Prophet's companions from defamation were at least partially framed with the intention of prosecuting Shia clerics accused of vilifying these personages. A primary theological schism between Sunni and Shia turns on the relative value each assigns to the place of the Prophet's son-in-law, Ali Ibn Talib. For Sunnis he is one of the four rightly-guided Caliphs who ruled early Islamic society after the Prophet's death. The Shia believe him to be the divinely-ordained successor to the Prophet, who was denied a timely succession. The reverential status they accord him is contrary to Sunni orthodoxy. In the hearings around the Ahmadi question in 1974 a prominent Shia cleric explained the status accorded to Ali as one of *Wallaiyat* [Guardianship of the Faith] and thereby provided categorical denial of any equivalence of status between Ali and the Prophet.[44] Nonetheless, for those members of the *Ulema* who have sought to accuse the Shia of non-belief and apostasy, this certainly did not settle the matter.

[44] T Kamran, 'The Pre-History of Religious Exclusionism in Contemporary Pakistan: Khatam-e-Nubuwwat 1889–1953' (2015) 49 *Modern Asian Studies* 1840.

For many Shia, Zia's Islamisation was from the start an attempt at Sunnification of the state and polity. The project of containing the Iranian revolution and its ideological enterprise was one that drew Pakistan closer to traditional Sunni powers, including Saudi Arabia. The Saudis pumped money directly into the country to support Sunni seminaries and *madressahs*. Nonetheless, the Iranian revolution had bolstered the resources of the Shia community to the extent that a much more militant posture was undertaken to ensure their exemption from the application of certain Islamisation laws such as through the *Zakat and Ushr Ordinance* of 1980.[45] Against Zia's initial insistence that the Sunni Hanafi Fiqh would guide all official policy, the Shiite community displayed its capacities for resistance and the regime relented in allowing them to be guided by their own *Fiqh* (jurisprudential school) in these matters.[46]

Jamal Malick[47] points out the particular contradiction of the Zia era whereby, in attempting to marginalise secularist voices within the Council of Islamic Ideology, he appointed a larger number of *Ulema* from amongst the diverse schools of *fiqh* as well as representing some broader cleavages within the major Sunni schools. A period of internal fracturing and a spate of public resignations in reaction to the preponderant orientation in policy initiatives towards a Wahabi Sunni ideology ensued. Zia, whose impatience for legal reform waited for neither nuanced reasoning nor consensus-based deliberation, managed the Council with increasing condescension. It is extensively reported that a Wahabi cleric from Saudi Arabia unofficially headed the CII in the days that it was preparing a draft Hudood Bill. An advocate who heads up the *Khatam-e-Nabuwat* wing in organised Bar politics was both instrumental to pushing through the anti-Ahmadi laws and in drafting the blasphemy laws.

[45] See MQ Zaman, 'Islamic Modernism and the Shari'a in Pakistan' (2014) 8 *Yale Law School Occasional Papers* 1.

[46] Constitution of Pakistan 1973 (as amended), Art 233. See also SVR Nasr, 'The Rise of Sunni Militancy in Pakistan: The Changing Role of Islamism and the Ulama in Society and Politics' (2000) 34 *Modern Asian Studies* 139, 160.

[47] J Malik, *Colonization of Islam; Dissolution of traditional Institutions in Pakistan* (Lahore, Vanguard Books, 1996) 45–46.

iii. Ahmadis and the Law

Following upon the Second Amendment to the Constitution in 1974 the same parties that had agitated for a declaration of Ahmadis as non-Muslims sought further legal aid in curtailing the activities that Ahmadis could engage in. To this end, they sought and were granted judicial injunctions against Ahmadis who referred to their places of worship as Masjids and their call to prayer as *Azaan*. Such intervention was sought on the basis that Ahmadis, as infidels, had no legitimate claim on these sacred rites and symbols of Islam. In 1978 the matter was adjudicated upon at the Lahore High Court against the guarantee of fundamental rights.[48] Article 20, which provides 'every citizen shall have the right to profess, practice and propagate his religion' and also that religious communities have the right 'to establish maintain and manage its religious institutions' is the constitutional guarantee of freedom of religion.

In *Abdur Rehman Mubashir*,[49] the lower court's grant of injunction is firstly decried for offering a civil remedy that accords only with the protection of property rights. Further, Justice A Hussain found no reason to label these acts by Ahmadis as constitutive of a public nuisance even if 'Muslims may not like the Ahmadis to call their place of worship by the name which Muslims' places of worship' are called or 'feel flurried by seeing them offering their prayers in imitation of the Muslims'. Lastly, even in a perusal of what could be established as Muslim common law, there was no principle that the two-member bench in this case could find as 'proof of the proposition' that non-Muslims cannot construct their places of worship 'in any manner resembling mosque or call it by the name of Masjid or say Azan in it or perform his prayer in it in the same manner as is ordained for the Muslims'. Accepting, however, that the Article 20 right could be reduced by laws aimed at the maintenance of public order and morality, the judges cited the absence of any such law under which they could offer the remedies being sought.

It was precisely such a law that was subsequently passed by Zia-ul-Haq and the Majlis-e-shoora. The Anti-Islamic Activities of Quadiani Group, Lahori Group and Ahmadis (Prohibition and

[48] *Abdur Rehman Mubashir v Ameer Ali Shah* PLD [1978] Lahore 113.

[49] ibid.

Punishment) Ordinance, XX of 1984 created two wholly new offences within the PPC. These provided that Ahmadis could not misuse the epithets, descriptions and titles, etc, reserved for certain holy personages nor misrepresent themselves as Muslims or propagate their religion. The first, section 298B, was directed at the kinds of acts that were sought to be controlled in *Mubashir*: the calling of places of worship as *Masjids* and the call to prayer *Azaan*. Section 298C further barred any Ahmadi from posing as a Muslim, calling their faith Islam or propagating their faith. This prohibition is complete and includes words' 'either spoken or written' and visual representations. Additionally, any act that 'in any manner whatsoever outrages the religious feelings of Muslims' shall be punished. Both provisions provide for imprisonment for up to three years and a fine.

Such criminal prohibitions empowered district administration in the management and policing of the Ahmadi community throughout the country. The most aggressive forms of such policing tended to be in Punjab. When the Ahmadiyya community sought to celebrate its centenary of founding in the city of Rabwah in the district of Jhang in 1989, the local district administrator placed a ban on such celebrations. The Lahore High Court deemed itself unable, even on the basis of extraordinary constitutional jurisdiction, to interfere with the law and order concerns of the district administration.[50] The planned public celebration, which included banners proclaiming '100 years of truth' indicated to the court that this was not an event oriented to professing and practicing the religion but was rather oriented to 'propagation of the religion' and would thereby outrage the feelings of Muslims.

The severance of propagation from the trio of rights that Article 20(1) guarantees was seemingly justified by the prohibition in section 298B of the PPC. A discussion of the allowable limitations on rights was deferred to the Supreme Court, where the case that would result in the *Zaheerudin* judgment was pending at the time. In *Zaheeruddin v The State*,[51] in addition to a challenge posed to another prohibitive order on centenary celebrations, the conviction of an Ahmadi person wearing a badge printed with the *Kalima Tayyaba* [purity] had also risen to appeal.

50 *Khurshid Ahmad v Government of Punjab* PLD [1992] Lahore 1.
51 *Zaheeruddin v The State* SCMR [1993] SC 1718.

As discussed in Chapter 7, the limitation clauses attached to fundamental rights provisions in the 1973 Constitution have generated significant principles for courts to engage with when undertaking rights review. Justice Shafiur Rehman, as the lone dissenting voice, relied upon the limited meaning attached to the expression 'subject to law' from previous precedent to deem that several of the particular prohibitions in section 298C were contrary to the protections of Article 20 and thereby unconstitutional. Additionally, the vagueness of the term 'posing as a Muslim' rendered it meaningless and for this reason the wearing of a badge emblazoned with the *Kalima* did not constitute such a crime. The majority opinion, in contrast, omitted a discussion of domestic precedent and reconciled the vast restrictions imposed on the Ahmadiyya community with principles from other jurisdictions enabling restrictions on religious expression. Perhaps the most perplexing exercise undertaken by Qadeer Chaudhry et al is to analogise the symbols and epithets of Muslim practice with intellectual property. It is an interpretation that strains credulity insofar as the Muslim *Ummah* is neither a corporate entity nor one that has traditionally spoken in a unitary voice. Nonetheless, exclusive use is assigned to it and any attempt to use these terms presumed to injure the feelings of community members. The court perused the whole history of the Ahmadia movement, characterising its origins in the period of colonial rule as a 'serious and organized attack on its [Islam's] ideological frontiers'.

Another stark difference between the dissent and majority judgment turned on the expanse of revisional powers thought to be unleashed by Article 2A. Shafiur Rehman followed *Hakim Khan* and determined that the Objectives Resolution does not provide a means of whittling down rights. The majority elided any discussion of precedent to find that Article 2A and thereby Islamic law and principles can provide the requisite measure of 'positive law' by which fundamental rights may be limited. Tellingly though, no particular Islamic or Shariat principles were elaborated as illustration.

This case established a solid precedent that the restrictions on Ahmadi practice were reasonable.[52] As with other minorities in

[52] *Ata Ulla v The State* PLD [2000] Lahore 364; further provided the principle that even architectural features from a *Masjid* could not be used to adorn the places of worship of Ahmadis.

Pakistan, it is not only through the formal system of justice that they have been subjected to situations of peril and precarity. Following the passage of Ordinance XX in 1982, the fourth Caliph or successor of Mirza Ghulam Ahmad moved to London and with him the administrative and spiritual base of the community was refounded there; the community in Pakistan has become a regular target of hate crimes and speech.

III. BLASPHEMY

The colonial state provided a guarantee of non-discrimination between religious communities existing in India. Section 295 of the Indian Penal Code of 1860 contained a single offence under the heading 'Blasphemy and Hypocrisy'; the sacred symbols and rites associated with religious traditions were given protection against the acts, words, etc of those seeking to defile or defame a rival community. The state itself took on the role of protector for acts of religious devotion in its attempt to mitigate conflict between groups and implant a vestige of secular management therein. Importantly though, the law was intended to protect religious minorities and Muslims in particular within the broader Hindu majority state.

During the years 1982–1986 this blasphemy law was supplemented with three further offences. Section 295B penalises a person who 'defiles, damages or desecrates a copy of the Holy Qur'an' or uses it or any extract in a 'derogatory manner or for any unlawful purpose'. This offence is punishable with life imprisonment. Section 295C provides that

> whosoever by either spoken or written, or by visible representation or by any imputation, innuendo, or insinuation, directly or indirectly, defiles the sacred name of the Holy Prophet Muhammad (peace be upon him) shall be punished with death, or imprisonment for life, and shall also be liable to fine.

The final provision is section 298C, which defines an act to defile the sacred name of other holy personages including the wives, family members, caliphs or companions of the Holy Prophet as a crime punishable by up to three years' imprisonment. Importantly, all of these offences are directed at protecting Islam and Muslim religious sentiment.

Since 1986, more than 1,300 people have been charged for blasphemy offences. Of those there have been close to 500 convictions. More than 60 people have been killed in acts of violence incited by allegations of blasphemy. Over half of the charges laid on the basis of these provisions have been against religious minority groups. The significance of that can only be understood by repeating that minorities account for less than 3 per cent of the country's population.[53]

The coded offence of blasphemy, much like the Hudood laws described earlier, provides evidence that the incorporation of Islamic legal norms can overflow formal legal orders and create pockets of informality within the legal system. Tellingly, whereas the original colonial blasphemy offence established a *mens rea* or intent element to establish culpability, these later additions do not include such a requirement. This has led to pronouncements of guilt on the basis of alarmingly low evidential standards. As a strict liability offence, the possibility that the mere repetition of offending words, even in a courtroom, could provoke an application of the blasphemy charge further lowers the burden of proving the offence. Thus, convictions have been granted in cases without the act of alleged blasphemy being spoken or displayed. Additionally, the absence of an explicit intention requirement has resulted in the conviction of mentally incapacitated people as well as juveniles.[54]

In 1990 the FSC declared that death, and not life imprisonment, was the only allowable punishment for a section 295C violation.[55] In combination with the ready availability of clerical orders or fatwas pronouncing alleged offenders as *Wajib-ul-Qatl* (liable to be killed.) private retributive acts against alleged offenders have been steeply on the rise. Although defenders of the laws claim that the formalisation of the offence has resulted in a reduction of vigilantism, such a claim is contrary to the evidence.[56]

[53] S Alvi, 'Campaigning to Reform Pakistan's Deadly Blasphemy Law' *Al-Jazeera* (28 April 2015) <www.aljazeera.com/indepth/features/2015/03/campaigning-reform-pakistan-deadly-blasphemy-law-150310053331313.html>.

[54] Z Hayat and O Siddique, 'Unholy Speech and Holy Laws: Blasphemy Laws in Pakistan—Controversial Origins, Design Defects and Free Speech Implications' (2008) 17 *Minnesota Journal of International Law* 303.

[55] *Muhammad Ismail Qureshi v Pakistan* PLD [1991] FSC 10.

[56] ibid.

Importantly, these laws have lent themselves to being used against people or groups embroiled in property or other personal disputes. That mere allegations, particularly when made against members of religious minority groups, can result in a wholesale and genocidal destruction or clearance of areas is related at times to acute competition over resources amongst communities. The poverty and precarity of the Christian community in Pakistan has ensured its persistent vulnerability to such attacks.[57]

Human rights groups and academics have dedicated significant effort to highlighting problems in the framing and operation of these laws. This attention has certainly also been the outcome of the global publicity garnered for such Islamic prohibitions dating from the unrest that followed the publication of Salman Rushdie's, *The Satanic Verses*. That it was the Ayatollah Khomeini who issued a fatwa calling for Rushdie's assassination, the latter a citizen of the UK, is indicative of the ways in which an Islamic normative order is presumed by many of its adherents to trump temporal authority. This was also a precursor event to mark the turn by which Shia religious authority within Pakistan would also come to defend the ambit of the blasphemy laws; this unanimity has helped to cement the impression of these laws as divinely sanctioned.[58]

IV. MUSHARRAF REFORM AND AFTER

In the period immediately following his 1999 coup, Musharraf had vaguely outlined a programme of reforms similar to those of the modernising secularist General Ataturk in Turkey. Forced to acknowledge limitations to his rule in accordance with the verdict of the *Zafar Ali Shah* case and as certain political exigencies were more palpably felt, Musharraf's drive towards an official secularisation also diminished. With 9/11 as the pivotal intervening event, the government that was

[57] Q Julius, 'The experience of minorities under Pakistan's blasphemy laws' (2016) 27 *Islam and Christian-Muslim Relations* 95.

[58] F Khan, 'Shia Clerics Warn Government against Tampering with Blasphemy Laws' *The Express* Tribune (17 December 2010) <www.tribune.com.pk/story/91118/shia-clerics-warn-govt-against-tampering-with-blasphemy-laws/>.

reconstituted after the 2002 elections did endeavour to make certain reforms that would lend legitimacy to its position as an ally in the global 'war on terror' or fight against 'radical Islam'.

Those alterations of policy that aligned with the US agenda in their initial articulation included the promotion of secular education and a modernising reform of *Madressah* curricula, which were nonetheless mediated in their delivery by political bartering and an incomplete commitment to financing such a transition. The fragmentary support that Musharraf had been able to build for the managed democracy he instituted in 2002 included the predominant religious parties in the country, including the Jamaat-e-Islami and the Jama Ulema-e-Islam. Many political commentators pointed to the continuation of the 'mullah-military' alliance in Pakistani politics. Although ideologically coherent and aligned under Zia, the alliance was provisional and shaky under Musharraf, ensuring that major trade-offs would be made for Musharraf's reforms to be realised in any form.

In the 2002 elections an umbrella coalition of Islamist parties under the banner of Mutahida Majlis-e-Amal (MMA) won a convincing victory in the strategically important North West Frontier Province and secured sufficient seats nationwide to become the official opposition in the National Assembly. For many in Pakistan this signaled a slide towards 'talibanisation', even though the MMA was steadfastly silent on army actions being undertaken by the military against militant outfits within FATA and KP. Nonetheless, the MMA did endeavour to expand the application of a stringent interpretation of Shariat within the province by passage of the 2005 Hisba Bill in the NWFP Assembly. This law proposed the creation of an ombudsman's office to fulfil the ends of '*Amir bil maroof*' and '*nahiunalmuntakir*'—or to 'forbid bad and prescribe good' in the broader social sphere. Such an office was to be supported by a council of advisors as well as to be given authority to establish a police force with the specific mandate of enforcing certain vestiges of public morality. The closest analogue for the institution that was anticipated is the *Mutaween* of Saudi Arabia.

A reference was posed to the Supreme Court by the President to exercise its advisory jurisdiction in making a determination about the constitutionality of the Hisba Bill. The Court found that the Bill offended a range of fundamental rights and delegated too much penal and quasi-judicial power in a manner not foreseen by the

Constitution.[59] It also found repugnancy against the 'injunctions of Quran and Sunnah' on at least two counts. The first was tethered to Article 227 of the Constitution, which provides that laws brought into conformity with Quran and Sunnah must, where they pertain to personal law, be in accord with the interpretations of Muslim sects. The establishment of offences related to religious comportment and observance not respectful of differences between sects were thus ultra vires the Islamic provisions of the Constitution.[60] The second manner of finding repugnancy was in noting that 'there is no provision of the Sharia, which mandates for the imposition of penalties for vague offences'.[61] They go on to state that the Sharia itself has defined 'offences' and accompanying punishments.

After the Hisba reference was heard, and more than 20 years after their initial promulgation, General Musharraf took on board the goal of setting right some of the rights violative practices of the Hudood laws. He did this first and foremost by disappointing those who had taken his credentials as a secularist at face value and who had anticipated wholesale reform in that direction. This same constituency had already suffered earlier disappointment at the hands of their female Prime Minister, Benazir Bhutto, in her two previous periods of rule. More autonomously powerful than Benazir, whose powers were subject to the military itself, Musharraf was also straight-jacketed by strategic concerns to keep certain Islamic militant networks in a state of appeasement. Nonetheless, it was a turn to militancy amongst members of the public that suggested the need for certain reformation within the country, a package and set of aspirations aptly named 'Enlightened Moderation'.[62]

Broadly framed as a means of allowing Muslim nations such as Pakistan to catch up with the western world in terms of scientific education and a broadly-defined rationalism, the programme also affirmed salient differences between Islamic and non-Islamic societies. The

[59] See *Reference No 2 of 2005 by the President of Pakistan* PLD [2005] SC 873, para 60.

[60] See J Redding, 'Consititutionalizing Islam: Theory and Pakistan' (2004) 44 *Virginia Journal of International Law* 759, 810.

[61] See *Ata Ulla v The State* PLD [2000] Lahore 364, para 54.

[62] See R Jackson, *Mawlana Mawdudi and Political Islam: Authority and the Islamic State* (London, Routledge, 2010).

reformism thus needed the sanction and consent of religious scholars, who could provide authoritative judgement about the need to change these laws. The Council of Islamic Ideology was enlisted towards such an end and a renowned Quranic scholar who had previously held many distinguished posts in western European universities, Dr Khalid Masud, was appointed the chairman of the Council in 2004. In 2006 the Council filed its report about the need for the thoroughgoing amendment of these laws. A private member's bill called the Women's Protection Bill was introduced in Parliament. The combined opposition of the MMA threatened resignation if the laws were passed. In an act of appeasement, and against the advice of the CII, the government appointed an *Ulema* Council to be responsible for making recommended alterations to the Bill to Parliament. Eventually what was passed was a revised Bill which provided procedural safeguards to women complainants of *Zina-bil-Jabr* but which reincorporated the offence of 'fornication' into the existing penal code. The *Hadd* punishments and their accompanying standards of evidence were not altered.

What was telling as the backdrop for such alterations is that there were an array of organised debates staged for the media between Islamic groups and amongst them and members of 'civil society' in the lead-up to the passage of this Bill, aimed clearly at ameliorating any public dissent at the alteration of 'divine laws'. That people's intimacy with the sources of Islamic law and with various juristic schools of thought was, seemingly, taken for granted was perceptible through such an engagement, affirming the truth of scholarly insights into the nature of Muslim public spheres and the religious pedagogical role that has increasingly, in a transnational way, imparted the modes of reasoning and criticism that were once monopolised by the *Ulema* alone, to a broader literate public.[63]

However, along with the creation of a Muslim public sphere, what has also come into greater relief in these many years is that a history of pronouncing *takfir* or unbelief by the *Ulema* has also permeated the social sphere. In combination with the official support lent to militant networks through the 1980s and 1990s, an escalation of violence against religious minorities has been unabated and continues through

[63] S Aziz, 'Making a Sovereign State: Javed Ghamidi and "Enlightened Moderation"' (2011) 45 *Modern Asian Studies* 597.

to the present. The spike in violence between Shia and Sunni in the 1990s was the backdrop for the promulgation of anti-terror laws discussed elsewhere in this book. This sectarian violence has taken on a different caste after 2001 where existing militant formations entered into alliance with Al-Qaeda and Taliban affiliated groups so that the targeting of Shia, Ahmadi and Christian sites of worship and gathering have occurred with alarming regularity. Additionally, practitioners of syncretic and indigenous forms of Islam, predicated often on a veneration of Sufi saints, have also frequently been targeted by such violence.

After Musharraf, Islamist political parties have seized opportunities to bargain for appointments to the CII in exchange for support to insecure governing coalitions. The PPP government in 2009 thus appointed the stridently anti-reform Maulana Sherani as Chairman to appease the JUI. Thereafter, the CII delivered a set of questionable and socially-regressive decrees on Islamic law in the following years. Alongside this, the issue of minority targeting, specifically through the operations and invocation of the blasphemy law, have generated significant public calls for reform of the blasphemy laws.

Although several governments have lent rhetorical support to altering these laws, the only concrete step taken was a Bill tabled by a leading member of the People's Party government in 2009. In the following year, before the Bill was debated, the Governor of Punjab, Salman Taseer was gunned down for having publically critiqued these laws. The author of the Bill, Sherry Rehman, was charged but not convicted of blasphemy for seeking these alterations. This set of events merely capped a succession of incidents in which lawyers defending blasphemy accused, teachers and university professors engaging their students in historical learning about Islam and others have fallen victim to this law and its invocation.

A line of immanent critique from within Islamic jurisprudential parameters has lately been deployed to counter the idea that the blasphemy laws in their current form are true to the guidance of Islam. Cited are authoritative sources that counsel against charging non-Muslims for blasphemy, that allow for pardon on the basis of sincere apology and which question the compulsory award of death as punishment. However, the circulation of such critique has been limited and confined mostly to arenas in which such reformism is welcome. On the other hand, a range of Islamist leaders and spokespersons have repeatedly taken out public processions and exerted pressure upon the government to refrain from acting to change these laws. The current impossibility of altering the anti-Ahmadiyya laws is even more extreme.

In this context, one can only hope that a few recent judgments issuing from the Supreme Court indicate some possibilities of incremental alteration to the operation of these laws.

For instance, in 2014 Chief Justice Tassaduq Hussain Gillani took *suo moto* notice of extreme acts of violence being perpetrated against non-Muslim and Muslim minorities in the country. Citing instances of church bombings, forcible conversions of Hindu women and the targeted violence against members of the Shia community, Gillani elaborated the constitutional safeguards for minorities. Contrary to past precedent, Chief Justice Gillani suggested that Article 20 provides a comprehensive right to freedom of religious conscience upon which the more particular rights to 'practice, profess and propagate' religion are hinged. Furthermore, Article 20 is only subject to the general restrictions of law, public order and morality' and that these cannot be 'reducible to the Islamic meanings of these terms'.[64]

In this case, Chief Justice Gillani accepted that a strict demotion of religion to the realm of private life cannot be accomplished and that even in the most secular-seeming states, this divide is not absolute. Citing the at times inequitable distribution of social goods flowing from the assignment of Islam a special place in the life of the nation, the Court still counselled for state action on the need to stem religious intolerance and for specific measures to safeguard the full panoply of rights stemming from freedom of conscience for all citizens, including the right to propagate religious views. In many ways, this case marks a turning in the Supreme Court's jurisprudence on religious matters. It could potentially serve as a strong precedent from which to start dismantling restrictive laws such as those upheld in *Zaheeruddin*.

The recent conviction of Mumtaz Qadri, the guard who killed Governor Salman Taseer, was upheld on appeal at the Supreme Court.[65] Rejecting the defence of 'grave and sudden provocation', the court also affirmed Qadri's death sentence. More importantly, Justice

[64] PLD [2014] SC 699, para 15: *suo motu* Actions Regarding Suicide Bomb Attack of 22.9.2013 on the Church in Peshawar and regarding threats being given to Kalash tribe and Ismailies in Chitral.

[65] *Mumtaz Qadri v The State* PLD [2016] SC 17.

Khosa countered the assertion that an act of criticising the blasphemy law is itself blasphemous. By detailing the historical origins of the laws, the judgment indicates that the fallibility of human reason may be potentially conveyed in the form that they have taken.

FURTHER READING

N Khan, *Muslim Becoming: Aspiration and Skepticism in Pakistan* (Durham NC, Duke University Press, 2012).

M Lau, *The Role of Islam in the Legal System of Pakistan* (Leiden, Martinus Nijhoff, 2001).

J Malik, *Colonization of Islam: Dissolution of Traditional Institutions in Pakistan* (Lahore, Vanguard Books, 1996).

AU Qasmi, *The Ahmadis and the Politics of Religious Exclusion in Pakistan* (London, Anthem Press, 2014).

MQ Zaman, *The Ulama in Contemporary Islam: Custodians of Change* (Princeton, Princeton University Press, 2007).

Conclusion

THIS BOOK IS intended only to present a provisional map of some of the pressing issues that arise for a Pakistani public within the operations of a public law and constitutionalism. What is apparent in this synoptic account is that many of the claims that may be made for the rule of constitutionalism, those that are reflective of ideal understandings, in which a ready public proclaiming 'we the people' harnessed their will to a normative order, will fail to account for both text and intentionality in Pakistan's various constitutional orders. Although the language of success and failure has in parts been used, the book has not intended to provide a measure of whether or not constitutionalism has been effective. Inclusion and exclusion are written into and influence the shape of constitutional 'cover' in Pakistan; much of this is due to the inheritances of an imperial order in which plural spaces, some defined by indirect rule, were intrinsic to the maintenance of control. The successes that are cited are those where some space has been cleaved against the aggrandising claims of a state and a larger state system where the exception is often the rule.

Index

actions in aid of civil powers *see under* executive government
Afghanistan 7, 13, 220
Ahmad, Mirza Ghulam 41, 240
Ahmadiyya movement 41–2, 218–20, 235, 237–40
Ajmal Mian, Chief Justice 68
Ali Ibn Talib 235
Ali Shah, Chief Justice Sajjad 68
Aligarh movement 11
All Pakistan Shia Convention 43
armed forces *see under* executive government
Ashraf, Raja Pervaiz 115
Asian Development Bank 115
Awami League/Party 51, 70
Ayub Khan, President 34, 46–51
  administrative centralisation 49
  authoritarianism 47, 49, 102
  ban on parties 70
  displaced from power 50–1
  disqualifications 77
  and Islam 215
  local government 180
  modernisation programme *see under* Islam and the state
  takeover of power 46–7
  see also Constitution, 1962
Aziz, Shaukat 115

Babar, Zaheeruddin 2
Balochistan 6–7, 14, 24
  ethnic conflict 168, 169–70, 172, 173, 179–80
  preventive detention 210, 212
  quota system 174–5
  resource transfers 176–8
Balochistan States Union (BSU) 37–8
Bangladesh independence 51–3, 204, 217
  see also East Pakistan
Bareilvis 17–18
Basic Principles Committee 36
basic structure doctrine *see under* judiciary
Bengal 14–15, 22
  Bangladesh independence 52–3
  India, war (1965), effect 50
  military/bureaucratic underrepresentation 49
  multi-faith/secular state support 40–1
  remoteness 35
Bhutto, Benazir 56, 132, 140
  Islamic reforms 244
  and judicial independence 145–6
  no confidence vote 64
  use of emergency powers 166
Bhutto family 75
Bhutto, Zulfiqar Ali 51, 52
  and 1973 Constitution 53
  cooption of courts 55
  and ethnic conflict 170–1
  execution 121
  and fundamental rights 187–8
  and judiciary 127
  and military intervention 94
  murder trial 131–2
  as President 109–11
  and preventive detention 203–5
  as Prime Minister 54, 67, 71, 108, 109–10
  rigging allegations 88
Bills *see* parliamentary structure, legislative procedure
blasphemy laws *see under* Islam and the state
Boundary Commission 22–3
British Raj
  apex institutions 9
  colonial difference 10
  customary laws 9
  direct rule 8–10
  inclusion of Indians 9
  nationalism *see* nationalism
  rationalisation/systematisation of law 9
  Rebellion (1857) 8, 10
  uniform system 8
  see also East India Company

Cabinet of ministers 64
centralisation of power
  army's role 30
  civil service bureaucracy 30–1
  Constituent Assembly 31–3, 34
  Governor-General's role 29, 31–4

law-and-order state 29
One Unit Scheme 38–9, 70
and parliamentary system 28–9
Prime Minister's office 29
state necessity doctrine 33–4
Chaudhry, Chief Justice Iftikhar 113, 114, 122, 147
and basic structure 142–4
judicial appointments 147–8
review 136–8
suspension/restoration of 122, 138–42
Chaudhry, President Fazal Elahi 103
Chief Martial Law Administrator (CMLA) 129–31
civil powers, actions in aid of *see under* executive government
civil/military relations *see* executive government, militarised executive
colonial difference *see under* British Raj
committees (parliamentary), structure/role 65
Communist Party, ban 69
Company rule *see* East India Company
constituencies *see under* electoral system
Constitution, 1956
abrogation 46
fundamental rights 44
presidential powers 44–5
Quran and Sunnah guidance 46
regional powers 45
state languages 45
unicameral legislative assembly 43–4
Constitution, 1962
abrogation 51
centralisation 49
conservative recommendations 47–8
court jurisdictions 48, 49–50
Islamic Republic, renaming 48–9
pyramidical structure of assemblies 48
see also Ayub Khan, President
Constitution, 1973
abeyance period 55–6
basic structure doctrine 55, 105, 108, 114
bicameral legislature 53
Eighth Amendment 56, 64, 67
emergency provision 54
federation structure 53
fundamental rights 53, 54
see also rights and equality, fundamental rights
President 53, 56
Prime Minister 53
proportional representation 53
and representative government 59
return to 1973 structure 67
revisions (1985 onwards) 60
Second and Fourth Amendment 62
Thirteenth Amendment 56
Cornelius, Chief Justice AR 217
Council of Common Interests (CCI) 154
Council of Islamic Ideology (CII) 218, 236

Delhi Sultanate 2
Deobandis 17–18
detention *see* preventive detention
disappearances *see* preventive detention, missing persons
disqualifications 76–82
age criteria 77
complaint mechanism 76
conflicts of interest 78
detailed criteria 77–8
educational qualification 79–80
Islamic requirements 78–9
and personalisation of politics 82
reference to Election Commission 78
regime expansion 80–2
state employees 78
see also electoral system

East India Company
all-India Legislative Council 5
Anglo-Hindu/Anglo-Mohammadan law 6
and British Parliament 4–5
law reform commissions 5–6
local rulers' designation 6
Presidencies/*mofussil* 4
regional expansion 6–8
see also British Raj
East Pakistan
economic biases in West 45
military/bureaucratic underrepresentation 49
multi-faith/secular state support 40–1
preventive detention 202
see also Bangladesh independence
Election Commission 78, 82–8 *passim*, 91
electoral system
candidate expenditure limits 83
constituencies, demarcation of boundaries 86–7
digitisation of data 84–5
elections 82–3
electoral rolls 84–6

local government elections 91
party expenditure 83
registration of voters 84, 85
rigging, pre-poll/post-poll 87–8
rules and regulations 83
voters 84–5
see also disqualifications; representative government
Elizabeth I, Queen 4
emergency powers *see under* executive government; federalist structures
enforced disappearances *see* preventive detention, missing persons
equality *see* rights and equality
ethnic conflict *see under* federalist structures
executive government 93–4
actions in aid of civil powers 93
armed forces
appointments prerogative 95–6
federal government control 95
intervention legality 96–7
Joint Chief of Staff 95
key issues 95
police functions 97
'subject to law' limitation 96
see also militarised executive *below*
Cabinet of ministers 64, 109–10
civil powers, actions in aid of 93
courts
as referees (President v Prime Minister) 106–9
taming the executive 113–18
democratic executive powers/prerogative powers, review of 115–18
bureaucratic appointments 117–18
collective right to resources 116
international instruments/treaties 116–17
transparency violation 115–16
democratic impulse 94
emergency powers 97–100
constitutional emergencies 97–8
extra-legal emergencies 97
further powers 99–100
military courts 100
National Assembly powers 98
proportionality criteria 99
revocation 98–9
see also under federalist structures
executive ordinances *see* Presidential ordinances *below*
high treason charge 95, 114–15
militarised executive 93–4, 100–6
army promotions/foreign affairs/defence, political danger zones 111, 112–13
courts' role 102
educational quotas 101
industrial/economic enterprises 101
multi-scalar militarisation 101–2
praetorianism 100–1
see also armed forces *above*
military adventurism, high treason charge 95, 114–15
political power coalescence 94
praetorianism 100–1
Presidential ordinances
circumstances necessitating 120
debates on 118
permissive environment for 120
tax impositions 118–19
validity periods 119–20
Presidential powers 102–6
court cases 105–6
dissolution of National Assembly 103–4
formal powers 103–4
limitations on 104–5
and Prime Minister's role 105
state necessity doctrine 104
Prime Ministerial executive 109–13
army promotions/foreign affairs/defence, political danger zones 111, 112–13
bureaucratic-military complex, reforms 110–11
floor crossing barred 111–12
Islamisation furtherance 112
unitary power 109–10
executive ordinances *see* executive government, Presidential ordinances

Federal Shariat Courts (FSC) *see under* Islam and the state
federalist structures 63, 64
Bill ratification 153
Chief Minister/Provincial Ministers 153
coordination mechanisms 154
18th Amendment, jurisdiction after 161–4
industrial relations/employment standards 162–3
prior accountability/anti-corruption legislation 161
provincial legislative powers 161

emergency powers 165–7
dissolution powers of President 165
recent situations 167
tested by judicial review 165–6
see also under executive government
ethnic conflict
census information 178
and federal formula 167
federal responses 179–80
in Federation 168–72
fiscal transfer regime 175–6
and formal federalism 172–80
proportionality principle 172–3
provincial borders 178–9
quota regime 173–5
resource transfers 176–9
exceptions 154–7
executive powers in the federation, distributions 164–5
fiscal transfer regime 175–6
Governors 153
judicial review exceptions 155
key issues 151–2
legislative powers 157–60
courts' role 158–9
interpretative principles 160
repugnancy voidance 159–60
subject matter, federal/concurrent list system 158
territorial limitations 157–8
local government 180–2
majoritarianism 152
National Finance Commission Award 175–6
political structure 152–4
provincial legislative powers 161
Supreme Court exceptions 155–6
tribal areas 37, 61, 154–7
unicameral assemblies 152–3
see also Balochistan; Muhajir
Federally Administered Tribal Areas (FATA) 37, 61, 154–7
fiscal transfer regime *see under* federalist structures
Frontier Province 23–4
fundamental rights *see* rights and equality, fundamental rights

Gandhi, Mohandas 16, 20, 122
gender equality *see under* rights and equality
Gillani, Prime Minister Syed Yousaf Raza 81, 140
Guantanamo Bay 210

habeas corpus *see under* preventive detention
Haq, Anwar-ul-, Chief Justice 128–9
Hastings, Warren 5
high treason charge *see under* executive government
Hudood Ordinances *see under* Islam and the state
human rights
blasphemy laws 242
and judiciary 133, 136–7
human rights, *see also* rights and equality
Hussain, Maulvi Mushtaq 129

India, war (1965) 50
Indian National Congress (INC) 11
Indian Penal Code 9
Iqbal, Mohammad 43
Islam and the state
Ahmadiyya movement 41–2, 218–20, 235
legal restrictions 237–40
Ayub Khan's modernisation programme 215, 216–17
Bhutto's Islamic socialism 217–20
blasphemy laws
coded offences, 1982–1986 240–1
colonial law 240
criticism of law as blasphemy 248
death as punishment 241–2
evidential standards 241
as human rights issue 242
post-Musharraf critique 246–7
and Shia authority 242
Shia protection from 235
vulnerability of Christian community 242
Council of Islamic Ideology (CII) 218, 236, 245, 246
enlightened moderation 244–5
Federal Shariat Courts (FSC) 221–3
head of state requirement 219
Hudood Ordinances 221, 223
punishments 227
see also women and Hudood Ordinances *below*
key issues 215–16
Musharraf reform programme 242–6
enlightened moderation 244–5
Madressah curricula reforms 243
ombudsman's office proposal 243–4
organised debates 245
post-Musharraf 246–8
sectarian violence 245–6
suo moto notice of violence 247
war on terror, post 9/11 242–3

non-Muslim minorities 234
Objectives Resolution (1949) 40–1, 187, 223–7
political Islam 217
private/public divide 39
quasi-constitutional documents 40–1
Quran and Sunnah's status 41, 220
sectarianism 41–3, 73–4, 245–6
Shariat courts 221–3
Shia/Sunni divide 42–3, 234
women and Hudood Ordinances 227–34, 245
common law and Islamic legal reasoning 233
honour killings 231–2
illicit sexual relations (*Zina*) 227–8
marriage consent/decisions 230–1
rape complainants, criminalisation 228–30
review/repeal, fundamental rights case 233–4
women's organisations 228
see also Hudood Ordinances *above*
Zia and Islamisation 215–16, 220–40
Afghanistan context 220
body for articulation of Law 220–1
deliberation practices 222–3
Hudood Ordinances 221, 223
Islamic ideology and morality, and parties 71–2
Islamic laws 227–40
Objectives Resolution 223–7
Shia protection from blasphemy 235
Sunnification issues 236
types of Islamisation 221
Ulema's role 234–5
women *see* women and Hudood Ordinances *above*
Islamabad
capital 49
federal territory 157

Jalal, Ayesha 29
Jamaat-e-Islami 40, 42, 75, 187, 217
Jinnah, Mohammad Ali 1, 16–17, 20–2, 27, 32
authoritarianism 29
Islam's role 39
mergers across boundaries 35–6
judiciary
administrative merger (One Unit System) 123
advisory jurisdiction 125
and anti-terror measures 134–5
appeals process 124–5
appointment process disputes 122, 145–9
appointment/tenure/removal 123–4
basic structure doctrine 142–5
fidelity to constitutional text 143–4
Indian origin 142
non-affirmal in Pakistan 143
reversal of approach 144–5
Bhutto murder trial 131–2
Chaudhry, Iftikhar
review 136–8
suspension/restoration of 122, 138–42
Chief Martial Law Administrator (CMLA) 129–31
declaratory/non-binding judgments 125
early constitutions 123–4
executive control 124, 127
fundamental rights enforcement 125, 133–4
human rights monitoring/cell 133, 136–7
and independence debate 122–3
judicial activism 137
judicial independence 145–9
jurisdiction definition 124, 125–6
key issues 121–2
lawyers' movement 138–42
mego-politics intersection 142
Memogate incident 140–1
oath-taking refusal 138–9
and political parties 139–40
public perception 139
military loyalty 128–31
1990s 133–6
oath issue 130–1, 147
post-independence 122–4
public importance matters 125
public interest litigation 125, 133, 137
restrictions on 127
state necessity doctrine 129, 131
suo moto powers 136–7
superior judiciary 124, 130, 138, 148
Supreme and High Courts 124
transparency doctrine 137
tribal areas jurisdiction 135–6
women's appointment 148–9
writs against public functionaries 125
Junejo, Muhammad Khan 107

Kalat 7, 14, 23–4, 37
declaration of independence 46

Karachi
  ethnic conflict 168
  voter demographics 85
Kargil Valley military operation 112–13
Kashmir 24, 30, 156–7
Kelsen, Hans 47
Kennedy, Charles 173
Khan, Abdul Ghaffar 18, 23, 170, 202
Khan, Abdul Jabbar 23
Khan, Ghulam Ishaq, President 56, 107–8
Khan, Liaquat Ali 31–2, 41
Khan, Maulvi Tamizzuddin 32–3
Khan, Yahya 51, 52, 54, 55, 124, 217
Khilafat movement 16
Khomeini, Ayatollah 242
Khudai Khidmatgars 18
Khyber Pakhtunkhwa 6–7, 154–5, 161

Lahore, local government 181–2
Lahore Resolution 19
Lau, Martin 221
lawyers' movement *see under* judiciary
Leghari, President Farooq 68, 98, 106, 146
legislative procedure *see under* parliamentary structure
local government *see under* federalist structures

Mahmood, Masood 132, 218
Majlis-E-Shoora (assembly) 63
Malick, Jamal 236
Masud, Dr Khalid 245
Maudoodi, Abul-ala- 40, 42, 217
Memogate incident *see under* judiciary, lawyers' movement
Mian, Chief Justice Ajimal 130
militancy
  militant wings of mainstream parties 74, 76
  sectarian violence or terror-related (party) bans 73–4
  worker/union militancy 69
  see also representative government
militarised executive *see under* executive government
Mirza, Iskander, President 46
missing persons *see under* preventive detention
Mughal rule 2–3
Muhajir
  community 176
  refugee status 37
Muhajir Quami Mahaz (MQM) 171–2
Mujibur Rehman, Sheikh 51
Muhammad, Malik Ghulam 32, 47
Munir Report 42
Musharraf, General Parvez 56, 104–6, 109, 113
  anti-Islamic militancy 59–60
  and basic structure 142
  computerisation of electoral rolls 84
  disqualifications 77–80
  and ethnic conflict 172
  high treason charge 114–15
  and judiciary 122
  legal context of taking power 97
  local government 180
  and militant elements 76
  missing persons cases 209
  and public order 72–3
  reform programme *see under* Islam and the state
  suspension/restoration of Chaudhry 138–42
  and women's seats 61–2
Muslim League
  authoritarianism 29
  constitutional arguments 19–22
  dominance 69, 85
  formation 16–17
  government dismissed 72
  and Muslim pluralism 18
  and partition 22–3, 24
  regional disaffection 36
Muslim nationalism 1, 12–13, 20, 39, 188
Muttahida Qaumi Mahaz (MQM) party 85

nascent statehood 1
  pre-colonial India 2–3
  see also British Raj; East India Company; nationalism; partition
National Assembly *see under* parliamentary structure
National Awami Party (NAP) 71, 169
National Commission on the Status of Women 234
National Economic Council (NEC) 154
National Finance Award 36
nationalism
  post-1857 10–14
    Hindu dominance 12
    middle-class disaffection 10–11
    modes of government 12–14
    Muslim group consciousness 11–12
    Muslim League 16–17
    Muslim nationalism 1, 12–13, 20, 39, 188
  20th cent 14–17

during WWI 15–16
during WWII 20
group representation 15
Muslim League 16–17
Muslim pluralism 17–18
partition protests 14–15

Nazimuddin, Khwaja 31–2
non-Muslim minorities 234
parliamentary seats 62
North West Frontier Province (NWFP) 13–14, 151, 169
Northern Areas 53, 156–7, 173

Objectives Resolution (1949) 40–1, 187, 223–7
Omar, Imtiaz 200
One Unit Scheme 38–9, 70
dissolution 151, 168–9
opposition leader 63

Pakistan National Alliance (PNA) 96, 170
Pakistan Tehrik-e-Insaf (PTI) party 75, 88
parliamentary committees, structure/ role 65
parliamentary structure 61–8
Bills *see* legislative procedure
Cabinet of ministers 64
committees, structure/role 65
federal government 63, 64
legislative procedure 65–6
between houses 65, 66
money Bills 65
suspension of both houses 66
National Assembly
convening after general election 67
government Bills 66
non-Muslim minority seats 62
primacy 63
single-member territorial constituencies 61
women's seats 61–2
no confidence vote 64
opposition leader 63
President 66–8
assent to Bills 68
ceremonial role 66–7
Prime Minister 63
election 67
representation formulas 61–3
Senate
Chairman 64
composition 62–3
dissolutions 63
parties *see* political parties
partition
border uncertainties 22–3
British withdrawal 22
communal hatred 21–2
constitutional arguments 18–22
territorial acquisition 23–4
Patel, Doreb 131
People's Party 56, 70, 81, 169
PML-N party 88, 113
political parties
business-owning, trading and professional elites 75
election expenditure 83
Islamic ideology and morality 71–2
legitimacy 68–9
militant wings of mainstream parties 74, 76
proliferation/anxieties 69
and public order 72
right of association, reasonable restrictions 70–1, 72
sectarian violence or terror-related bans 73–4
worker/union militancy 69
see also parliamentary structure
politicians, legitimacy 68–9
praetorianism *see under* executive government
pre-colonial India 2–3
prerogative powers *see* executive government, democratic executive powers/prerogative powers
President *see under* parliamentary structure
Presidential ordinances/powers *see under* executive government
preventive detention 199–213
balancing test 208
colonial government practice 199–200
constitutional safeguards, post-1956 201–3
habeas corpus 199, 201, 204, 207
maximum period for 212
missing persons 206, 209–13
as crime against humanity 211
legal cover for security agencies 211–12
maximum period for 212
numbers held 212–13
petitions/investigative reports 210–11
renditions programme 210
review board 212
rights violations 211
Missing Persons Commission 209
national unity goal (pre-1973) 203

objective reasonableness test 201–2
post-1973 203–6
constitutional amendments 204
fundamental rights, suspension/ safeguards 203–4
martial law 206
political speech/expression, protection 204–5
restrictive conditions 203
post-independence 200–1
procedural preconditions 207–8
public security 208, 209
regional unrest 202–3
restoration of democracy 206–9
sectarian organisations 207
terrorism, war against 208, 209–13
unlawful grounds 208
Prime Minister *see under* parliamentary structure
Prime Ministerial executive *see under* executive government
Punjab
borders/boundaries 151, 178
British Raj 12–13
conquest 6–8
constitutional arguments 20

Qadeer, Mama 212
Qadri, Mumtaz 247–8
Quit India Movement 20

Radcliffe, Cyril 22–3, 24
Rahman, Dr Fazl-ur- 216–17
Raj *see* British Raj
regionalism 35–9
disaffection 36
establishment clique at centre 38
Federally Administered Tribal Areas (FATA) 37, 61
fiscal control 35–6
mergers across boundaries 35–6
mineral/energy resources 37–8
Muhajir (refugee) status 37
parochial interests 35
Urdu language supremacy 36–7
West/East identity tensions 38–9
Rehman, Justice Hamoodur 71
Rehman, Sheikh Mujibur 202
Rehman, Sherry 246
renditions programme *see under* preventive detention, missing persons
representative government
disqualifications *see* disqualifications
electoral system *see* electoral system
human development issues, neglect 90–1
major events 59–60
militancy *see* militancy
military takeovers, impacts 60, 89–90
National Assembly/Senate *see under* parliamentary structure
parliament *see* parliamentary structure
parties *see* political parties
political contests, changes 60
political protests, legitimate 91
rigging *see under* electoral system
rigging *see under* electoral system
rights and equality
enforced disappearances *see* preventive detention, missing persons
fundamental rights 44, 53, 54, 187–91
anti-discrimination 190
aspirational goals 188
inconsistent laws' voidance 188
liberty, rights of 189–90
life or liberty, deprivation of 189
preamble/background 187–8
preventive detention 203–4
property protections 191
public importance/interest cases 189
reasonable restrictions 190
religious freedom 190–1
review of enacted laws 189
security forces' exemptions 188–9
torture, prohibition 190
gender equality 192–9
absence of right (1962) 193
dissent/protest 192–3
employment cases 197–9
medical colleges cases 194–6
non-discrimination clause 192–3
separation of electorates/ representatives 192
see also women
judicial review, pre-1973 184–7
due process standard 187
formalising of guarantees 184
limitation clauses 184–5
reasonable restrictions 186–7
subject to law 185–6, 187
key issues 183–4
limitation clauses 184–5
missing persons *see under* preventive detention
political dissent 200, 203
preamble/background 187–8

preventive detention 203–4
preventive detention *see* preventive detention
see also human rights
Rowland, Sir Archibald 35
Rushdie, Salman 242
Russia, and the Great Game 7

Saeed, Hafez 209
sectarianism *see under* Islam and the state
Senate *see under* parliamentary structure
Shah, Chief Justice Sajjad Ali 145–7
Shah, Sabir 166
Shariat courts *see under* Islam and the state
Sharif family 75
Sharif, Nawaz 56, 68, 72, 85, 99, 105, 111–13
Kargil Valley military operation 112–13
Supreme Court dispute 147
Shia/Sunni divide *see under* Islam and the state
Sindh
borders/boundaries 151
British Raj 13
conquest 6–7
ethnic conflict 168, 169, 172, 173, 178
state building 27–8
see also Bangladesh independence; centralisation of power; Constitutions 1956/1962/1973; regionalism
Sunni/Shia divide 42–3
Syed, GM 170, 202

Tarar, President Rafique 98, 105
Taseer, Governor Salman 246
Toor, Sadia 38
treason charge *see* executive government, high treason charge

Urdu language
shared status 45
supremacy 36–7

voting practices *see* electoral system

West Bengal *see* Bengal
West Pakistan 35, 38, 45
Bangladesh independence 52–3
women
judiciary appointment 148–9
National Assembly seats 61–2
see also Islam and the state, women and Hudood Ordinances; rights and equality, gender equality
Women's Action Forum 228
Workers Party (election) petition 82–5, 90–1

Yahya Khan, General 51–2
Supreme Court verdict on 54–5

Zardari, President Asif Ali 80, 140
Zia-ul-Haq, General 55–6, 102–4
consultative and appointed assembly 63
courts as referees (President v Prime Minister) 106–9
disqualifications 77–8
and ethnic conflict 170–1, 179
and Islamisation *see under* Islam and the state
and judiciary 121, 128–31, 145
legal context of taking power 96
local government 180
non-Muslim minority seats 62
President's role, revisions to 67
preventive detention 205–6
promotion of Islam 59
and provincial legislative powers 158
rights' suspension 194